Family and Social Policy in Japan
Anthropological Approaches

Social policies reflect and construct important ideas in societies about the relationship between the state and the individual. *Family and Social Policy in Japan* examines this relationship in a number of hitherto unexplored areas in Japanese society including policies relating to fertility, peri-natal care, child care, child abuse, sexuality, care for the aged and death. The conclusion is that great change has taken place in all these areas through the 1990s as a consequence of Japan's changing economy, demography and the development of civil society. The case studies, based on intensive anthropological fieldwork, not only demonstrate how and why family and social policies have evolved in the world's second largest economy, but in the process provide a challenge to many of the assumptions of western policymakers. The empirical material contained in this volume will be of interest to anthropologists and to students and practitioners.

Roger Goodman is lecturer in the social anthropology of Japan at the Nissan Institute of Japanese Studies and the Institute of Social and Cultural Anthropology, University of Oxford. His publications include *Children of the Japanese State: The Changing Role of Child Protection Institutions in Contemporary Japan* (2000) and (with Gordon White and Huck-Ju Kwon) *The East Asian Welfare Model: Welfare Orientalism and the State* (1998).

CONTEMPORARY JAPANESE SOCIETY

Editor:
Yoshio Sugimoto, La Trobe University

Advisory Editors:
Harumi Befu, Stanford University
Roger Goodman, Oxford University
Michio Muramatsu, Kyoto University
Wolfgang Seifert, Universität Heidelberg
Chizuko Ueno, University of Tokyo

Contemporary Japanese Society provides a comprehensive portrayal
of modern Japan through the analysis of key aspects of Japanese society
and culture, ranging from work and gender politics to science and
technology. The series offers a balanced yet interpretive approach. Books
are designed for a wide range of readers including undergraduate
beginners in Japanese studies, to scholars and professionals.

Yoshio Sugimoto *An Introduction to Japanese Society,* second edition
    0 521 82193 2 hardback 0 521 52925 5 paperback
D. P. Martinez (ed.) *The Worlds of Japanese Popular Culture*
    0 521 63128 9 hardback 0 521 63729 5 paperback
Kaori Okano and Motonori Tsuchiya *Education in Contemporary Japan:*
    Inequality and Diversity
    0 521 62252 2 hardback 0 521 62686 2 paperback
Morris Low, Shigeru Nakayama and Hitoshi Yoshioka *Science,*
    Technology and Society in Contemporary Japan
    0 521 65282 0 hardback 0 521 65425 4 paperback

Forthcoming title
Vera Mackie *Feminism in Modern Japan: Citizenship, Embodiment and*
    Sexuality
    0 521 82018 9 hardback 0 521 52719 8 paperback

*For Sam, Joe and Abbie, the only children
whose lives are directly affected by my interests
in Japanese education and socialisation.*

RJG

Family and Social Policy in Japan
Anthropological Approaches

Edited by
Roger Goodman
University of Oxford

CAMBRIDGE
UNIVERSITY PRESS

CAMBRIDGE UNIVERSITY PRESS
Cambridge, New York, Melbourne, Madrid, Cape Town, Singapore,
São Paulo, Delhi, Dubai, Tokyo, Mexico City

Cambridge University Press
The Edinburgh Building, Cambridge CB2 8RU, UK

Published in the United States of America by Cambridge University Press, New York

www.cambridge.org
Information on this title: www.cambridge.org/9780521016353

First published 2002

A catalogue record for this publication is available from the British Library

ISBN 978-0-521-81571-0 Hardback
ISBN 978-0-521-01635-3 Paperback

Contents

Illustrations

Photographs

Figures

Tables

Acknowledgements

The papers in this volume were first presented at the 12th Meeting of the Japan Anthropology Workshop, which was held at the National Museum of Ethnology in Osaka in March 1999. The Japan Anthropology Workshop (more affectionately known as JAWS) was set up in 1984 to bring together a disparate group of anthropologists working on Japan; to raise the profile of the study of Japan in the field of anthropology; and to introduce the discipline of anthropology to scholars of Japan more generally. The Workshop has grown enormously from modest beginnings and by the time of the conference had almost 250 members, of whom over half attended what was its first meeting in Japan. In order to maintain the workshop atmosphere of the meeting, a total of seven self-contained panels were arranged, each with its own theme, one of which was an anthropological analysis of social policy in contemporary Japanese society.

I am delighted to have the chance to thank the very large number of people and institutions who supported the conference in Osaka in 1999 and who directly or indirectly have helped to bring this volume into being. In particular, I would like to thank my conference co-organiser, Professor Nakamaki Hirochika of the National Museum of Ethnography, who first had the idea of holding a JAWS Conference in Osaka and then did more than anyone else to make it a possibility. I would also like to thank the Director of the Museum, Professor Ishige Naomichi, and its founding director, Professor Umesao Tadao, for their unstinting and invaluable support of the Conference throughout. As well as generous financial support from the National Museum of Ethnology itself, the Conference received substantial funding from the Wenner Gren Foundation, Nisshō Iwai Foundation, ITOH Scholarship Foundation and the Kashima Foundation, which I am glad to be able to acknowledge here.

The all-day session on the anthropology of social policy in Japan was greatly enlivened by the presentations of three individuals whose contributions it has not been possible to include here. Seung-mi Han presented an excellent paper on the making of a foreigners' assembly in Kanagawa prefecture and two discussants, Ishida Hiroshi, a sociologist, and Ito Peng, a social policy specialist, gave a series of thoughtful and provocative comments on the significance of each paper from the viewpoint of their own disciplines which not only enlivened the debate that followed each presentation but which have clearly influenced the way each paper has been re-written subsequently.

The process of turning conference presentations into published manuscript has been unusually smooth due to the help of many people. Professor Yoshio Sugimoto was supportive of the idea of including the papers in the CUP Series on Contemporary Japanese Society. Two anonymous readers provided a series of extremely constructive – if at times mildly contradictory – comments and suggestions on which each author drew while rewriting their chapters. Successive editors at CUP, Phillipa McGuinness and Marigold Acland, have shown real interest in, as well as professional commitment to, the project. Others who I am keen to thank for their help in turning the manuscript into published form include Jane Baker, Paul Watt and Valina Rainer.

As editor, though, I would especially like to take this opportunity of thanking all the contributors to the volume who have borne this project from start to finish with such good humour.

Roger Goodman

Contributors

Eyal Ben-Ari is professor in the Department of Sociology and Anthropology at the Hebrew University of Jerusalem. His most recent research is on the Japanese military and the Japanese expatriate community in Singapore. Some of his recent publications include *Japanese Childcare: An Interpretive Study of Culture and Organization* (Kegan Paul International, 1997) and *Body Projects in Japanese Childcare: Culture, Organization and Emotions in a Preschool* (Curzon, 1997).

Victoria Lyon Bestor divides her time between serving as Executive Director of the North American Coordinating Council on Japanese Library Resources and her research and writing. She is currently researching a book titled *The Rockefeller Legacy in Japan*, is co-editor with Theodore C. Bestor and Patricia Steinhoff of *Doing Fieldwork in Japan*, forthcoming from University of Hawaii Press, and with Theodore C. Bestor of *Cuisine, Consumption, and Culture: Food in Contemporary Japan* for University of California Press. She is also the author of numerous articles and papers on the evolution of Japan's civil sector, the subject of her chapter in this book.

Roger Goodman is lecturer in the Social Anthropology of Japan at the University of Oxford, specialising in the study of Japanese education and social welfare. He is the author of *Japan's 'International Youth': The Emergence of a New Class of Schoolchildren* (Oxford University Press, 1990) and *Children of the Japanese State: The Changing Role of Child Protection Institutions in Contemporary Japan* (Oxford University Press, 2000).

Setsuko Lee graduated from the Chiba University School of Nursing and holds a doctorate in public health from the University of Tokyo. Currently she is an associate professor in the Nursing Department of Tokyo Women's Medical College, an associate of the Department of Community Health, School of International Health, Faculty of Medicine, University of Tokyo, and the director of the Japanese International Public

Health Association (Nihon Kokuseki Hokeniryō Gakkai). Her publications include the edited volume *Maternal and Child Health Care for Foreigners in Japan* (1998, Igakushoin) and *Demographic Statistics of Foreigners in Japan: North and South Korea, 2001* (2001, Mindan 21 Seiki Iinkai).

Vera Mackie is Foundation Professor of Japanese Studies at Curtin University of Technology in Western Australia and has recently held a visiting professorship in the Institute for Gender Studies at Ochanomizu University. Her publications *include Creating Socialist Women in Japan: Gender, Labour and Activism, 1900–1937* (CUP 1997), *Feminisms in Modern Japan* (CUP, in press), *Human Rights and Gender Politics: Asia-Pacific Perspectives* (co-edited with Anne Marie Hilsdon, Martha Macintyre and Maila Stivens, Routledge 2000) and *Relationships: Japan and Australia 1850s–1970s* (co-edited with Paul Jones, University of Melbourne History Monographs, 2001).

Glenda S. Roberts is a professor at the Graduate School of Asia-Pacific Studies at Waseda University in Tokyo, where she specializes in gender, work, and migration issues. Among her publications are *Staying on the Line: Blue-Collar Women in Contemporary Japan* (University of Hawaii Press, 1994), and, co-edited with Mike Douglass, *Japan and Global Migration* (Routledge, 2000).

Carolyn S. Stevens is senior lecturer in Japanese Studies at the Melbourne Institute of Asian Languages and Societies, The University of Melbourne, Australia. Her publications include *On the Margins of Japanese Society: Volunteers and the Welfare of the Urban Underclass* (Routledge, 1997) and various articles on marginality, social welfare and voluntarism. Her other research interests include Japanese popular music and fandom.

Leng Leng Thang is assistant professor in the Department of Japanese Studies, National University of Singapore. She has research interests on aging, intergenerational programming, gender and family. She is the author of *Generations in Touch: Linking the Old and Young in a Tokyo Neighborhood* (Cornell University Press, 2001).

Yohko Tsuji is a Japanese anthropologist trained in the United States. She is currently a Visiting Scholar at the Department of Anthropology at Cornell University. Her research primarily covers Japan and the United States and focuses on the family, aging, death, and social change.

A note to the reader

All Japanese names are given in the Japanese fashion with the family names first unless the author has lived a long time in the West and prefers to follow the Western fashion.

Macrons have been used to mark long vowels in Japanese, except in the case of well-known places, such as Osaka, Kyoto and Tokyo, and certain names where the individual prefers to romanise them using a different system, such as Yohko Tsuji. All monetary values are expressed in yen when discussing financial issues in Japan since translations into pounds or dollars are rendered almost meaningless by the rapidly changing exchange rates between the countries. For the purposes of comparison, however, in early 2000 £1 was around ¥165 and US$1 was around ¥105.

1   Anthropology, policy and the study of Japan

Roger Goodman

While most people probably associate the study of social policy with disciplines such as economics, politics and sociology, it is in fact an area with which anthropology has been involved, if not always happily, for almost a hundred years. Cambridge University in 1906 used the term 'practical anthropology' in describing a programme it ran for training colonial administrators and, in 1929, Bronislaw Malinowski (1929: 36) called for a 'practical anthropology' which would be 'an anthropology of the changing Native' and 'would obviously be of the highest importance to the practical man in the colonies.' While, according to Ferguson (1996: 156), Malinowski used this claim mainly as a means of raising research funding, in general, anthropologists maintained what can only be described as an uneasy cooperation with colonial authorities in many parts of the world.

Anthropology and policy: a long yet uneasy relationship

Although the effect on policy of the work of the anthropologists varied greatly from region to region (see the papers in Asad 1973), most subsequent commentators, such as Said (1978) and Foucault (1972), have not perceived the role of anthropologists in the colonial context favourably. Ben-Ari (1999: 387) summarises succinctly this view of the relationship when he writes that: 'Even if there was no direct correspondence between anthropological theories and systems of colonial government, anthropology did, it could be argued, participate in producing the assumptions upon which colonialism was based'. On the other hand, as Goody (1995), Kuper (1997, Chapter 4) and various of the authors in van Bremen and Shimizu (1999) point out, many pre-war and war-time anthropologists (in the UK, Holland and Japan) were actively involved in anti-colonial activities and were sometimes vocal advocates for the rights of the peoples they were studying.

In the immediate post-war period, however, the relationship between administrative authorities and anthropologists, especially in the United States, became officially much closer. This in part came about through the development of policy for the new regimes that were being established in the nations that had lost the war: Japan and Germany. Ruth Benedict's (1946) classic, *The Chrysanthemum and the Sword*, for example, was originally an anthropological analysis of Japanese society that was commissioned by the US government as background to how the country might be most efficiently occupied and democratised (see Hendry 1996). The main energies of those in applied anthropology, though, were in the third world where they worked alongside development agencies. Here, as indeed in Germany and Japan, the anthropologists set out to deal with issues of cultural interpretation and the generation of a more positive relationship between the 'undeveloped' and the 'developers.'

As in the pre-war period, so in the post-war era, the work of applied (as they largely became known) anthropologists often became mired in controversy. While they tried to stick to the principles of ethnographic description without becoming involved either in what they described or in the implementation of policy, this turned out to be far from an easy position to maintain and, on several widely publicised occasions, applied anthropologists found themselves dragged into a political fracas. In one case, the well-known Vicos project in Peru undertaken from Cornell University in the 1950s, the anthropologists actually ended up in the role of 'patron' on a large estate and helped to implement a reform plan that meant devolution of power to the producers (see Holmberg 1960). British functionalist anthropologists also, as Grillo (1985) points out, bought into this American-led obsession with modernisation and convergence theory (with its many similarities to Victorian evolutionism) and increasingly worked on colonial modernisation projects, particularly in Africa. The study of Japan was not immune to these trends as could be seen in the 1960s Princeton series entitled 'The Modernization of Japan,' even if some of the chapters in some of these volumes, such as Ronald Dore's work on Tokugawa education (1965), actually did much to undermine the view of Feudal Japan having been a 'backward' society.

As a consequence, in the following decades, and particularly by the new brand of neo-Marxist anthropologists of the 1970s, applied anthropologists were severely attacked for reinforcing (or at least not critiquing) the political and social inequalities that already existed between the more and the less developed nations (see Robertson 1984). In the infamous Project Camelot case, anthropologists were actually accused of undertaking research which was used to gauge the level of anti-Communist feeling in Chile in the 1970s and similar accusations were thrown at anthropologists who worked on Thai and Cambodian societies during the Vietnam war, at which point the status of applied anthropology hit an all-time low.

Such 'scandals,' combined with a continuing, perhaps growing, distance between the academic world and the practical one, led to the virtual cessation of relations between the academic and applied anthropologists: few applied anthropologists were invited to lecture in universities, and few academic anthropologists worked on applied projects. In general, the practising anthropologists were considered marginal to the anthropology taught in universities and the academic anthropologists too high in their ivory towers to be of any use in a practical situation. The enormous gulf between the two extremes could perhaps best be seen by comparing articles in the journals that represented some of their most influential work in the 1970s: *Human Organization* (put out by the Society of Applied Anthropology in the United States), on the one hand, and the new Marxist-inspired journal, *Critique of Anthropology*, on the other.

In Britain, at least, the gap between applied and academic anthropologists did not begin to close until the early 1980s when, under Margaret Thatcher, university posts were frozen – and a whole generation of anthropologists were driven to work in the non-academic world – and, simultaneously, universities were required to demonstrate their relevance to the outside world. GAPP, the Group for Anthropology in Policy and Practice, was formed in 1981 to bridge the gulf between anthropologists inside and outside academia, as well as to act as a network to help anthropologists use their skills in policy and practice and to train students in the additional skills they needed to make them attractive to employers.

If I can be forgiven a personal note, which perhaps in part explains my interest in the topics covered in this volume, I was a participant on a week-long GAPP residential workshop that was held in 1985. Another participant was Jean La Fontaine, who had recently taken early retirement from being Professor of Anthropology at the London School of Economics. La Fontaine (1988; 1990) was soon commissioned to undertake research into issues of child protection and child abuse, which in the mid-1980s were the source of a major moral panic in the UK, and in the early 1990s, she was asked by the Secretary of State for Health to undertake an investigation into the evidence for the existence of ritualised satanic child abuse. La Fontaine (1998) concluded, in part by drawing on parallels with witchcraft in the classic literature of anthropology, that there was no evidence for satanic abuse, rather that society found the whole concept and practice of child abuse so abhorrent that it could only deal with it by labelling it 'satanic'. La Fontaine's conclusion, while it was not, from an anthropological perspective, particularly radical, was widely greeted as a major contribution to the debate about child sexual abuse. It is curious, therefore, as Peter Riviere (1985) has suggested in his discussion of the Warnock Committee's work on reproductive technologies, how minor a role anthropologists have played in domestic policy and ethical debates in the UK (and it seems also the USA) when the insights that they have gleaned from studying other societies can often help to clarify what otherwise appear to be incomprehensible social phenomena or insoluble problems in their own. It is even more curious in the light of the fact that, due to budget cuts that have made overseas fieldwork more difficult, in many western countries over the past 20 years more anthropologists have turned their attention to studying sections of their own society (see Jackson 1987).

The public status of anthropologists in Japan has been rather more impressive. Anthropologists and ethnologists have enjoyed considerable political influence in Japanese society since Yanagida Kunio's ethnographic search for the 'indigenous features' of Japanese life attempted to establish a moral foundation for Japanese society in the Meiji period (see Kawada 1993). In the colonial period also, anthropologists played a much more important role in the development of colonial policy than their counterparts in Europe (Shimizu 1999). Today also, anthropologists are often invited, under the catch-all title of *hyōronka* (social critics), to join government committees which lead to policy initiatives. The names of Hamaguchi Eshun, Nakane Chie, Umesao Tadao and Umehara Takeshi are all well known in Japanese society not only for their academic work but also for the roles they have played on various government commissions, such as that played by Umehara Takeshi in the debate in Japan about brain death (see Mulvey 1996; Feldman 2000: 85, 101 and 105).

What anthropology can bring to the policy arena

The papers in this volume are based on the belief that anthropology can bring a perception on policy issues that differentiates it from other disciplines. One of the great strengths of anthropology, for example, lies in its ability to unpack the taken-for-granted assumptions that lie behind the production of policy. Most people think that they know what is meant by basic social categories such as 'child,' 'parent,' 'teacher,' or basic social institutions such as 'school,' 'hospital,' 'welfare home,' or basic social experiences such as 'birth,' 'marriage' and 'death.' Yet the moment that we attempt to translate any of these terms into another language (particularly a language as different from English as Japanese), we realise that these terms are social constructions, with meanings that are to a high degree culturally and historically contingent. To take just one example, the word *'sensei'* carries in a contemporary Japanese context a very different meaning to the word 'teacher' in a British one. *'Sensei'* in a Japanese school is still 'one who goes before' and who is charged with shaping the moral world of the children in his or her care and ensuring that they have learnt the facts that will give them the best chance of examination success; a 'teacher' in a British school is one who, in combination with parents, helps children develop their own strengths (see Cummings 1999, for more on the significance of the social and historical context of educational terms).

While the unpacking of otherwise-unquestioned assumptions might not immediately help the construction of social policy – indeed it might prove to be a hindrance – it will certainly do much to illuminate it since a great deal of the power of social policy emanates from the fact that many of the terms used are so essentialised. As McKechnie and Kohn (1999:1) point out, for example, it is difficult to argue against bland policy statements that call for 'better care,' since the word 'caring' is 'at least on the surface, fairly unambiguously associated with things positive.' The chapters in their edited volume demonstrate that the meaning of the word 'care' is actually highly contested and is highly resistant to clarification because of, as McKechnie and Kohn put it, the 'taken-for-granted, practical and yet highly emotionally charged nature of the caring practice.' Part of the power of anthropology, therefore, lies in its potential for showing other ways of doing and thinking that demonstrate the basically arbitrary way in which different societies organise their social, political, economic, religious and other institutions and systems.

To say that certain concepts need to be put in their correct cultural and historical context in order to be understood is not, however, the same thing as saying that they are untranslatable. This is an important point to stress because the view that some Japanese concepts are so unique that people from other societies cannot understand them is the basis of the *Nihonjinron* literature that has been associated by some with the growth of national chauvinism in Japan, particularly during the height of the economic bubble of the 1980s (see Dale 1986). While the construction and dissemination of *Nihonjinron* beliefs have sometimes been erroneously associated with the discipline of social anthropology (see, for example, Mouer and Sugimoto 1986), anthropologists have generally always been of the belief that not only can concepts be 'culturally translated,' but once a subjective meaning has been ascertained, such terms and ideas can be compared across radically different societies.

Most of the comparisons in the papers in this volume, however, are implicit rather than explicit. It is important to point out, therefore, that there is a burgeoning literature looking at Japanese social policy comparatively. At the broadest level, this has involved attempts to situate Japanese social policy in a global context. These attempts have included Esping-Andersen's (1990) system of 'decommodification' scores (which measure the extent to which services are obtained by 'right' and citizens can live without relying on the market) by which Japan is grouped with countries such as Italy, France and Germany; Korpi and Palme's (1994, cited in

Hill 1996) division between 'encompassing,' 'basic security,' 'targeted' and 'corporatist' systems, in which Japan falls into the last – sometimes also called 'Bismarckian' – category, which is based on social insurance programmes basically aimed towards the economically most active; Siaroff's (1994) analysis in terms of the input of 'female' care in the welfare system, which characterises Japan as one of the 'late female mobilisation welfare states' along with countries such as Greece, Ireland, Italy, Portugal and Spain; Therborn's (1986) analysis of welfare policies in terms of employment policies, which groups Japan with Norway and Sweden as countries where the policy of full employment has been a central plank of the welfare system; and Jones' (1993) analysis in terms of concerns about producing equality, in which she describes Japan, along with Taiwan and Korea and some of the other 'Little Dragons,' as constituting a discrete set of 'Confucian welfare states.' (For a succinct summary of all of these and other macro-comparative approaches, see Hill 1996.)

The problem with all of these approaches, as Gordon White, Huck-Ju Kwon and I (Goodman, White and Kwon 1998) have pointed out elsewhere in our comparative analysis of East Asian welfare states, is that they do not take into account the historical dimension of welfare state development. No welfare state is ever static and its current manifestation often reflects on-going political battles over the best way to provide welfare. This has certainly been the case for Japan, which developed very different welfare rhetoric in each of the last four decades. In some ways, more useful analysis is presented by detailed comparison of either individual welfare states (such as Gould's 1993 comparison of Japan with Sweden and the US, or Izuhara's, forthcoming, with just the UK) or of specific policies, such as policies for the aged (see, for example, Hashimoto 1996; Long, ed. 2000) or education (for an overview of which, see Beauchamp and Rubinger 1989).

The anthropology of policy has historically concentrated on the study of the production of policy, in particular colonial policy (Hann and Dunn 1996). In the case of Japan, the experience of colonialism, of course, was short-lived – limited to seven years of American occupation immediately after the Second World War. There is, however, as many historians have pointed out, a sense in which colonialism in Japan has, since the 1870s, been internally rather than externally imposed by the development of a strong state. To a considerable degree, therefore, the anthropology of policy in Japan has become the anthropology of the Japanese state and how the state imposes its policies on sections of its population (see Garon 1997; McVeigh 1998).

It would be a mistake, however – and perhaps particularly so in the case of Japan, which has one of the world's most educated populations –

to suggest that the state can impose its social policy on a passive populace. Indeed, to a large extent, state policy is determined by the demands of the population – demands that are often conveyed through intermediary institutions such as the mass media. It is the role of these intermediary institutions which explains how it is that a society can suddenly become fixated on a certain issue when that issue is in fact long-standing in nature and only one among many.

As the sociologists Spector and Kitsuse (1977: 12) have pointed out, social problems do not just emerge from a vacuum but are the result of 'the activities of specific and identifiable individuals (not "society") who are engaged in defining conditions in particular terms with specific (recorded) purposes in mind.' The process starts when a group or groups 'assert the existence of some condition, define it as offensive, harmful or otherwise undesirable, publicise these assertions, stimulate controversy, and create a public or political issue over the matter (1977: 142).' Social panics, to use the terminology of Stanley Cohen (1971), in recent years, seem to have followed an unusually predictable two-year sequence in Japan and have mostly been connected with the perceived 'problem of youth.' Starting from the mid-1980s, the sequence of panics has gone roughly as follows: *kateinai bōryoku* (violence by children against their parents); *kōnai bōryoku* (violence by children against teachers); *ijime* (bullying by children of other children); *tōkōkyohi* (school refusal syndrome); and, most recently, as described in my own paper later in this volume, the issue of *jidō gyakutai* (abuse of children by adults). In each case, the phenomenon has been 'discovered' and defined, normally by professionals who have been motivated to a certain extent by self-interest – although few would go as far as Ivan Illich (1977) did in the 1970s in suggesting that self-interest is almost the only reason professionals bring such issues to public notice. In some cases, groups of victims who have suddenly obtained access to the media, often because they are of a class background with sufficient economic and political power, have also been involved in defining the issue. Once the phenomenon has been discovered and defined, it can be 'measured,' and such measurements have appeared to show that it is rapidly on the increase. Pressure is then put on the state to develop a policy to deal with the issue and to provide financial backing. The policy is implemented, and the problem is 'measurably' brought under control until media interest begins to wane and a new problem 'emerges.' The current social panic about child abuse in Japan is a good example of this pattern. First officially defined, for reasons explained in my paper, by the Ministry of Health and Welfare only in 1990, the exponential growth in the figures (from 1,100 reported cases in 1991 to almost 25,000 in 2001) has led to pressure that has forced the state to develop policy and to invest money for 'dealing' with the issue.

Further, in the case of all moral panics in Japan involving the country's youth over the past two decades, it has been interesting to see the similarity of the explanations for their 'sudden' appearance. These centre on the breakdown of: the extended family, public morality, respect for seniors, the education system and the concept of community in general. As we shall see, the explanations that were given for the emergence of child abuse in Japan, for example, tied in with broad-ranging debates that were going on in Japan at the end of the twentieth century, including discussions of individual rights and the changing family structure. Fujimoto (1994: 35) provided a good example of some of these arguments:

Child abuse has never been a big social problem on a national level in Japan ... However with an infiltration of European and American life style in social, economic and cultural levels, the social problem such as child abuse which occurred in Europe and America affected Japan seriously.

As Cohen (1971) pointed out in his ethnography of the moral panics about mods and rockers in 1960s Britain, the analysis of such problems tells us as much about society's wider anxieties as it does about the individuals directly involved.

Much of the anthropology of policy involves the examination of official documents and the terms and the language in which policy is presented. As Foucault (1972, 1977) has argued since the 1970s, the power of the state has often lain in its ability to use apparently objective language – what he called 'political technology' – to hide the basic social assumptions of what it is really trying to change. The power of such policy is difficult to attack when it purports only to be presenting what is 'natural' and 'rational' and even more so when the language it uses is 'scientific,' technical and often, to the layperson, confusing. As Shore and Wright (1997: 7) point out, policies should be seen as Maussian 'total social phenomena' which are 'inherently and unequivocally *anthropological* phenomena (which) can be read by anthropologists in a number of ways: as cultural texts, as classificatory devices with various meanings, as narratives that serve to justify or condemn the present, or as rhetorical devices and discursive formations that function to empower some people and to silence others' (emphasis in the original).

The power of policy documents is perhaps nowhere more clearly expressed than in their use of statistics and it is here perhaps that anthropology can make its greatest contribution to the unpacking of social policy. Statistics are often called upon to legitimate and justify policy decisions – such as the system Eyal Ben-Ari describes in his chapter in this volume by which a child's development is defined as 'normal' or 'abnormal.' Yet it is seldom acknowledged that such statistics are, to some extent, reflections of the preconceptions of those who collect, collate and use them.

Statistics seem to be particular widely used in official documents in Japan, perhaps because of the high general level of numeracy in the population and the general respect for 'facts' over interpretation that is emphasised in the school system. Indeed, it is unusual to be able to think of a statistic in Japan that might exist but that has not been collected, and when such a situation does occur – for example, there are virtually no statistics on what happens to young people who have been in children's homes after they leave the care of the state, and very few official statistics on people from most of Japan's minority groups – then this is normally for significant political reasons. A further example can be seen in the large number of research projects that were undertaken in the late 1970s and early 1980s on the perceived plight of Japan's *kikokushijo* population (children who had returned from living overseas). Virtually none of these projects examined whether such children actually had problems in returning to the Japanese education system: they simply took it for granted that they did, set out to measure the extent of those problems and to propose ways in which they might be tackled (see Goodman 1993). As Stephen Jay Gould (1984), in his wonderful debunking of the statistical method, *The Mismeasure of Man*, points out, it cannot be assumed that factors which correlate are necessarily caused by each other. Interestingly, therefore, the one large-scale project (Takahagi et al. 1982) that did use a control test of children who had not been overseas and that suggested that the 'problems' of *kikokushijo* were not noticeably worse than those of other Japanese children was either ignored completely in official docu-ments (despite the fact that it was funded by the Ministry of Education) or else criticised by other researchers for not making any constructive suggestions on how to alleviate those problems that *kikokushijo* were shown to have (Goodman 1993: 166–7). For an anthropologist, therefore, the study of official statistics in any society is also the study of the people who collect those statistics, the questions they use to collect them, the labels they put on the tables to present them, and the conclusions they draw from them; these questions, labels and conclusions often provide a fascinating insight into the assumptions that the researchers bring to their projects, which in themselves are often a reflection of wider views about the issue under study.[1]

Anthropologists, particularly in the field of semantic anthropology or discourse analysis (Bloch 1975; Bourdieu 1991; Parkin 1978, 1984), have also examined how even the most essentialised of symbols are not immune from challenge and change. While the most powerful groups in society, especially the 'state,' may try to maintain their own definitions and explanations of symbols and slogans, other groups will also attempt to have them redefined to suit their own interpretations. Symbols, as Victor Turner (1967) put it, are 'multivocal' and in few areas is this as clear as in the politics of social policy. Family policy is especially susceptible to national histories and sensitivities, as can be seen if one compares recent policies on the family in France, Germany, UK and Japan. Each country has tried to introduce social policies to reverse its rapidly declining fertility rate, which is far below the replacement level of 2.1 children that women on average need to produce. The French and German populations seem to be fairly relaxed about state intervention in such a sensitive – and some might argue private – arena, though their approach has been quite different: in France, policies have been determinedly pro-natalist, even to the extent of encouraging the birth of children outside wedlock; while in Germany the emphasis has been on strengthening the family unit, in the hope that this will lead to a more secure basis for the development of larger families (Pringle 1998: 57). In the UK, however, attempts by the state to get involved in such personal family affairs as reproduction have been met with general hostility, in particular against the rally of the previous Conservative Government to go 'back to basics,' in which the 'back to' element involved a return to childbirth in marriage, in face of the fact that over 35 percent of children were, by the early 1990s, being born outside of wedlock (including some to the mistresses of Conservative Members of Parliament). In fact, in over 70 percent of cases where children were born to unmarried mothers, both parents were registered on the birth certificate as living at the same address. The Conservative Government was making what Robin Fox (1967) long ago described as the classic anthropological error of confusing reproduction with marriage in its attack on unmarried mothers being a drain on society.

In Japan, there has also been considerable ambivalence to state intervention in pro-natalist policies: in part, because of reminders of such policies in the 1930s when more men were needed to staff the army; in part, because of women's new-found freedom outside marriage. The mixed messages that the Japanese government has been sending out about its pro-natalist policies were well encapsulated in mid-1999 by the question directed at Posts and Telecommunications Minister, Noda Seiko – the only woman in the Cabinet – by Nonaka Hiromu, head of the government's Office of Gender Equality, during a meeting on measures to tackle the declining birth-rate: 'Why don't you set an example?' (*Japan Times International* 1–15 June 1999). Japan's collapsing fertility rate is a topic to which I shall return later in this introduction, since it is an underlying theme that links all of the chapters.

If the anthropology of social policy is the study of *meaning*, particularly the different meanings that are ascribed to slogans and symbols, it is also the study of practice – to use a classic anthropological distinction, *function*

– of what happens when policies are actually introduced and implemented. It is perhaps here that scholars in neighbouring disciplines have credited anthropologists, or at least the anthropological method, with making the biggest contribution to the study of social policy. Because of the distinction that it allows anthropologists to make between what people say they do, say they should do and actually do, participant observation has been seen as an important aid to policy-makers who wish to follow through the effect of policy implementation. Christensen, Hockey and James (1998), for example, explain why the take-up of available welfare benefits in rural farming communities in the UK appears to be so low: the title of their paper, 'You just get on with it,' expresses a stoic individualist philosophy that requires an independence from the welfare state that had simply been ignored by urban-based policy-makers.

Participant observation and the accounts that it produces – what Geertz (1973) calls 'thick description' – provide a context for understanding not only how social policy is produced but also how it is consumed. The deep knowledge of a particular context that results from extended immersion in it allows the anthropologist not only to describe actual situations involving real people but also to imagine hypothetical situations and anticipate reactions to them through 'understanding' the assumptions, values, expectations and feelings of the different groups involved. As policy-makers frequently discover, the introduction of policy can have unexpected consequences; the anthropologists may sometimes be able to anticipate these. In some ways, such 'thick description' is particularly important in comparative social policy, since it is here that the ideology of a foreign welfare system tends to be compared, unrealistically, with the 'reality' of the domestic system. This is a process which, elsewhere, Gordon White and I have called 'welfare orientalism' (White and Goodman 1998), the idea that policy-makers use idealised versions of the welfare systems of other societies as a means of introducing new policies into their own societies. Japan was particularly subjected to this approach during the 1980s when its economy was booming (see Goodman 2001).

A related way in which anthropology can influence policy-makers has been through its holistic approach to society. The anthropologist does not separate off the political, economic, religious, and kinship elements of social policy but sees them as intricately interconnected with each other. Policy is affected by both micro and macro forces, local and global, and this is reflected in anthropological accounts which generally move from micro-level analysis of the production and consumption of policy by specific individuals in specific places at specific times to the broader social, political, economic, demographic and other social forces and changes which directly and indirectly impinge on that policy. Hence, an anthropology of policy not only looks at those who produce policy

(Nader's – 1972 – idea of 'studying up') and those who consume policy (often Ardener's – 1972 – 'muted groups', i.e., those who are not given the political space to articulate their feelings about that policy publicly), but also the process of policy: the manner in which it is constructed, challenged, mediated, manipulated, ignored or accepted. As Edgar and Russell (1998: 12) put it: 'The anthropology of welfare is concerned with the human face of welfare provision, the realities behind the rhetoric, the people behind the policies.' Moreover, in looking at contemporary social policy debates in Japan, the chapters in this book respond to the charge that Ahmed and Shore (1995: 25) claim is often laid at the feet of anthropology: 'where anthropology is failing to come to terms with events in the modern world is its inability to deal with current events.'[2]

Social policy in Japan

The papers in this volume will be of interest to those who are not Japan specialists in that they provide important insights into how problems and issues that currently confront every industrial society are being tackled in Japan. The Japanese appear – by the standards that are taken as measures of 'success', at least by governments, in most industrial countries – to have had conspicuous success in dealing with such problems. Consider, for example, the following facts. Not only does Japan have the world's second largest economy, but it also has: the world's highest figures for longevity;[3] the lowest rate of infant mortality; rates of divorce between one-quarter and one-third those of north European and North American societies; by far the lowest rate of illegitimate births (less than one percent) of all OECD societies; probably the world's most highly educated and literate population; the lowest rates for serious crimes in the OECD and, between 1985 and 1997, a juvenile crime rate that declined significantly. Moreover, it has maintained all these figures in the face of trends that might have been expected to take it in the opposite direction over the past 40 years – continual urbanisation, rapid nuclearisation of the family – and since around 1990 it has been mired in its worst and longest recession of the post-war period when the economy has actually contracted and the official rate of unemployment has almost doubled.

The context of contemporary debates

The factor that has by far the greatest effect on the development of contemporary social policy in Japan is the changing demography of the country. This is an issue that lies behind all of the papers in this volume and hence needs to be examined here in some detail. In its plainest form, the current situation can be put very simply: Japan is rapidly becoming the world's oldest ever human population. If we accept the standard definition of aged as those of 64 years and over, the proportion of the aged in Japan will change from 4.9% in 1950 to 14.5% in 1995 to a projected 25.5% in 2020.[4] The US, by contrast, is projected to change only from 12.5% in 1995 to 16.1% in 2020. In Japan, the proportion of those 75 years or over will rise even more dramatically from 1.3% in 1950 to 5.7% in 1995 to a projected 12.5% in 2020 (Harada 1998: 176). It took Japan just 24 years to go from a society with seven percent of the population officially defined as aged (1970) to 14 percent (1994), a demographic shift that took 70 years in the US and 130 years in France; and it will take Japan only 22 years to change from a society with ten percent of the population defined as aged to one with 20 percent, a transition that it is estimated will take 50–60 years in countries such as Italy, Germany, Holland and Sweden.

There are two unconnected reasons for Japan's aging population. On the one hand, people in Japan are living longer than anywhere else in the world. Average life expectancies at birth increased from just over 50 for men and just under 54 for women in 1947 to 79 for men and almost 83 for women in 1999. To reach 100 in Japan is no longer exceptional; the number of centenarians increased from 3,625 in 1991 to 15,475 in 2001 (*Asahi Shinbun* 12 Sept. 2001).

At the same time as longevity has increased, the number of children being born in Japan has declined dramatically. The total fertility rate (the average number of children that women are expected to bear) dropped from 5.24 in 1920 to 4.32 in 1949 (the first post-war baby boom when 2.7 million babies were born) to 2.14 in 1973 (the second post-war baby boom when 2.09 million babies were born) to 1.57 in 1989 (when only 1.25 million babies were born). As Glenda Roberts describes in detail in her paper, at this point the Japanese government decided for the first time to raise public consciousness of the potentially calamitous effects of such a low birthrate. The media dubbed this the '1.57 shock.'

Japan's declining birthrate is an immensely complicated topic. Significantly, the average number of children that married women are having has remained at around 2.2 over the last three decades and the illegitimacy rate at around 1 per cent; the decrease in fertility is almost totally due to an increase in women of reproductive age not getting married and not having children. This is largely due to a conscious choice to stay in employment and not have children: the fertility rate for working women in the late 1990s was 0.60 against 2.96 for those not working (Harada 1998: 223). Whether such women will decide to have children at a much later stage still remains to be seen, and will determine the overall fertility rate over a much longer period than simply a single decade. Further, one of the ironies of increasing the birthrate in order to deal with Japan's aging population is that it will, in the short term at least, increase Japan's 'dependency ratio' (the number of those under 14 and over 64 in relation to the whole population), which with Japan's current low birthrate is not expected to be far out of line with that of its OECD competitors during the first half of the twenty-first century (Hill 1996: 301). Nevertheless, the subtleties of this debate, while recognised by the experts in Japan, have seldom been translated into the popular media where there remains the belief that Japan currently faces a 'population crisis.'

It should be pointed out that Japan's fertility rate in 1989 was not in fact uniquely low. Those of Italy and West Germany at the end of the 1980s were even lower, those of Britain, France and the US were not much higher and all were below the official rate of 2.1 that demographers give as the fertility rate needed for a society to maintain a constant population. It was, in Japan, the combination of decline in the fertility rate with rapidly increasing longevity that led to the sense that the country faced a demographic crisis. Also, unlike many other OECD countries, Japan had no plans for, nor history of, immigrant labour – despite the appearance for the first time in the post-war period of some foreign workers at the end of the 'bubble economy' in the late 1980s. This sense of crisis was expressed perhaps most vividly in the realisation that while in 1950 in Japan there was a ratio of over twelve people of (potentially) working age (15–64) for each aged person, in 1990 there were only 5.7, and in 2025 there would only be 2.4. Further, as Kwon (1999: 11) points out, there is a very low (and declining) level of financial support for the elderly in Japan by their own children (15.6% of their total income in 1981; 9.0% in 1988) compared to some other East Asian societies (Korea, 44.3% in 1994; Taiwan, 53.2% in 1994). Hence, the comparatively high reliance of Japan's elderly population on state pensions (already over 50 percent of their total income package at the end of the 1980s) will mean that the working population will have to transfer much more of its wealth to the elderly if the current system of intergenerational, pay-as-you-go pension payments persists.

It was in the light of the growing realisation of its changing demographic profile that, in the 1990s, the Japanese government set about seriously trying to develop welfare programmes to support its aged and aging population. While 60 percent of those over 64 in Japan continued in the early 1990s to live with at least one adult of a younger generation (compared to around eight percent in the UK and 14 percent in the US), the government recognised that this meant a large and growing – 72 percent had lived with an adult of a younger generation in 1980 – proportion of aged that did not do so, and hence it had to significantly increase the provision of home helps, daycare and short-stay community centres and nursing homes. This it did through its *Gold Plan* of 1990. The demand for such services proved so overwhelming (and the plan itself was so conscientiously implemented) that an enlarged *New Gold Plan* had to be introduced in 1994 and a further *Gold Plan 21* in 2000.

In order to tackle the problem of the declining fertility rate, the government introduced what it called the *Angel Plan* in 1994 to encourage women to have more children by making it easier to have a family while continuing to work. As Roberts explains, the plan involved a ten-year programme starting in 1995 to increase day nurseries, drop-in care for non-working mothers, centres to care for sick children, after-school care centres and counselling centres for parents with childcare problems. At the same time, it sought to remove the stigma from mothers who worked and replace it with the idea that the state should support such women to ensure they could have a full career and bring up their families. Unlike the *Gold Plan*, however, it seems the *Angel Plan* was beset by problems from the moment it was implemented and it failed to reach many of its targets as the economy stagnated. Many local governments were reluctant to implement its provisions in full, in part because so much of their expenditure was already committed to the various *Gold Plans*.

Social policy for whom?

One of the most notable and recurring themes in the papers in this volume is how an examination of the way in which social policy is implemented in Japan offers interesting insights into the nature of what it means to be Japanese itself. This is one of the main messages from Vera Mackie's paper. While social policy in Japan is presented as blind and impartial – and post-war Japan indeed has one of the world's most liberal constitutions – it both reflects and helps construct and legitimate differential categories of citizenship (defined around the reality of who has the right to call on the state's support services) and other social values. As Mackie (p.206) succinctly puts it, citizenship in Japan is a spectrum: 'Welfare policies and the taxation system are. ... organised around the assumption that ... people live in heterosexual nuclear families with a male breadwinner and female primary caregiver.' Politicians not only work on this assumption but they also help to legitimate, reinforce and even possibly construct it.

Social and welfare policies in Japan historically have been constructed so as to support the most productive elements of the society rather than to provide a safety net for those who would not otherwise be able to survive. While historians can point to individual examples of social welfare activity at certain points in the pre-modern period in Japan, the majority date the start of the development of a welfare system to the Meiji Restoration of 1868. The Meiji government followed a policy that state intervention was not only unnecessary but might, indeed, prove counter-productive by developing lazy and dependent attitudes in the population as a whole (Hastings 1995: 18). Social policy throughout the period was seen more as an instrument to control unrest – very much in the style of Bismarckian policies at the same time in Germany – than the means by which the state sought to provide a minimum standard of living for its citizenry. The idea that social policy should be seen essentially as a device for mitigating social tension continued to be important until the end of the Second World War.

The late 1950s and early 1960s saw the institution of universal health and pension insurance in Japan, and there was a plan in the late 1960s to introduce a welfare regime along the lines of those which had developed in Western Europe in the post-war period (Campbell 1992). This went into rapid reverse with the oil shock of 1973. In its place, there emerged a model that came to be known as the 'Japanese-style welfare society' (*Nihongata shakai fukushi shakai*). As Watanuki (1986: 265) says, '(t)he idea of a Japanese-style welfare society (was) rather confused' but, essentially, it was expected that the family, community and company, rather than the state, would take on the major burden of social welfare, and that government expenditure on social security would be maintained at a lower level than in the Western 'welfare state.' Indeed, as Harada (1998: 198–202) points out, the model was called a 'welfare society' as opposed to a 'welfare state' in order to emphasise that people should not come to depend on the state but on self-help, communal solidarity, the family and the firm. (See Baba Keinosuke, 1980, for the most cited account of what constitute the main features of the Japanese-style welfare system.)

If the state sees its role, in as much as it has a role at all, as providing support for the potentially most productive members of society, Mackie's paper suggests that its sense of responsibility is least in dealing with those – such as trans-sexuals, hermaphrodites and homosexuals – who either are, by definition, unable or, by choice, refuse to (re)produce. The problematic role of the state in its citizens' reproduction – surely one of the most personal of all issues in any society – is a common theme of many of the chapters in this volume. To what extent will individuals tolerate the state playing a role in this area? This topic is still particularly sensitive in Japan because of reminders of the wartime slogan (*umeyō fuyaseyō*) that encouraged women to bear children who could become soldiers on behalf of the nation. As Mackie points out, also, the state has particular problems when dealing with certain contradictory categories: Japan needs immigrant workers, it needs to increase its fertility rate, but it is extremely worried by immigrant workers who produce babies.

The issue of immigrant mothers is the main focus of the paper by Carolyn Stevens and Setsuko Lee. Their paper shows very clearly how the marginal person in Japan is affected by social policy that has been developed to support those who are considered the 'mainstream.' At the same time, by looking at how birth is experienced by marginal women in Japanese society, one gets a very clear concept of what constitutes a 'normal' birth in Japan. This is a crucial point, since, as Callaway (1978) points out, while birth might appear to be the most 'essentially female function of all,' it is in fact a cultural as much as a natural event. Stevens discovered this for herself as she, an Australian, prepared for her first birth in Japan and found the cultural 'norms' surrounding childbirth – that it was the child's experience not the mother's; that intervention to relieve the pain of childbirth was eschewed as far as possible; that the mother was not supposed to demonstrate any indications of pain; that men were not expected to be supportive of their partners; that women in childbirth were polluted and polluting; that breast-feeding was optional – all came into significant conflict with those expectations of childbirth with which she had grown up. As Stevens' experience suggests, if she, a white, well-educated, high-status, well-connected and well-integrated woman in Japan found these cultural expectations stressful, how much worse they must be for other 'marginal' women who shared none of the same advantages. It is small wonder, therefore, that birth outcomes for women from marginal groups in Japan are so much poorer than for the majority Japanese population.

The production and consumption of social policy

The poor birth outcomes of 'marginal' foreign women in Japan are despite, as Stevens and Lee point out, all the current rhetoric about the need for internationalisation (*kokusaika*). *Kokusaika* has been one of the key political slogans in Japan since the early 1980s (replacing the earlier rhetoric of *kindaika* or modernisation). It became particularly associated with the prime-ministership of Nakasone Yasuhiro (1982–6). As with all powerful political symbols (democracy, freedom), everyone has always been agreed that *kokusaika* is a 'good thing' for Japanese society – in the late 1980s the anthropologist Ebuchi Kazukimi pointed out, according to McConnell (2000), that 'to internationalise' in Japanese is always used intransitively – even though there have been many different ideas as to what it actually means in practice. According to Stevens and Lee, while in the medical field there have been those who have argued that *kokusaika* in Japanese medical practice should mean understanding and adapting to the cultural expectations of those from other societies, the majority view in Japan has been that *kokusaika* in this context means educating those 'others' about Japanese practices so that they can adapt to them more easily. There is little doubt that, at present, the majority view of the meaning of *kokusaika* in the medical arena prevails. Multivocal symbols, however, are flexible in their interpretation, and, as the number of foreign mothers in Japan increases, so it is possible that the concept of *kokusaika* in this field may become more sympathetic to new and different interpretations.

One of the ways in which the state most powerfully controls the definition of a normal or natural birth is through the document that all women must carry to every meeting with their obstetrician, gynaecologist, doctor, midwife and anyone else involved in an official capacity in the birth process – the *Boshi Techō* (Mother–Child Handbook). While this handbook – which was first introduced into Japan by Segi Mitsuo, a medical scholar who had been studying Nazi policies for the protection of maternal and childhood health in Germany between 1938 and 1941 (Takeda 2002: 134) – presents itself as a guide for mothers to monitor whether everything that they are doing and that is happening is 'normal,' to a very large degree it also constructs and legitimates those definitions of normality. This is a process that Eyal Ben-Ari describes very well in his account of the documentation of small children in Japanese daycare centres. As Ben-Ari demonstrates, documents are a very effective way of both standardising behaviour and recording that behaviour is standardised. According to him, documents relating to preschools are overwhelmingly written by so-called experts in Tokyo and are remarkably homogeneous in the message of normality that they present; what are presented as 'explanations' of childhood development have become prescriptive norms and do as much to construct childhood behaviour as to explain it. There can be little doubt that the documents which contain these assumptions are used not only to monitor children but also affect how their carers look at them.

As Ben-Ari points out, however, carers are not totally passive in the way they respond to these prescriptions. Indeed, there is an interesting distinction they clearly make in following the prescriptions in form, but not necessarily in content – a distinction, which is often summed up in Japan as one between *tatemae* and *honne* – and it seems that the forms are checked by officials as much for the way they are completed as for what they actually contain.

Even if the state philosophy of childcare is re-interpreted in the process of implementation, it still clearly provides an important element in the construction of the type of citizen the state wishes its education system to produce. Ben-Ari indeed links what is taught in preschools with what is expected, in terms of behaviour, from members of the labour force some 15–20 years later. In Japan, rather as in France, the centralised and highly standardised nature of the whole education process – from conception to adult education – has over the past hundred years focused on producing individuals to be of direct use to the state. In the 1980s, indeed, this approach was often used to explain Japan's apparently miraculous economic growth (see Lynn, 1988). After ten years of recession, however, many in Japan have begun to question whether such standardisation is actually good for the workforce of what is now a 'mature' economy, and recent years have seen strenuous efforts to liberalise and diversify the whole educational experience from preschools through to university (see Goodman and Phillips 2002).

The changes that are taking place throughout the education system will dramatically alter not only people's concept of education but also the role of such apparently 'natural' categories as '*sensei*' ('teacher'). These changes are likely to be quite gradual. The changes supported by the *Angel Plan*, described in detail by Roberts in her paper, are likely to be much more dramatic since they go to the heart of the issue of the gender division of labour in Japanese society. The *Angel Plan*, as discussed before, is an ambitious (and expensive) plan to increase Japan's rapidly falling fertility rate. Underlying it, however, are important social considerations which both explain its importance in Japan and why it is not only economic reasons that have made its implementation far from completely successful.

As Roberts explains, as well as a major increase in support services to allow women to both remain in the workforce and bring up families – by removing some of the burden of care and shifting it to the state and the market – the Angel Plan has also involved an attempt to change the balance between work and family for men in Japan. Not only should women with young children be allowed to think that it is all right for them to go to work but men are also encouraged to spend less time at work and more time with their families.

Significantly, while, according to Roberts, the 1997 *Kōsei Hakusho* (White Paper on Health and Welfare) supported it, the 1998 version included perhaps the most potent state attack ever in Japan on the *sansaiji shinwa* (myth that mothers must look after their children fulltime until they reach the age of three). This critique was significant on a number of counts. First of all, it suggested that the myth actually originated from research conducted in European and North American countries in the 1960s, but it took particularly firm hold in Japan where, by the early 1990s, 90 percent of mothers supported its main tenet that it was better for the child for them not to work during its first three years of life. Secondly, it suggested that despite the high level of support for the idea, the fact that it was of relatively recent origin meant that it should be treated with considerable caution and that there was no reason why fathers should not play a larger role in childrearing. Thirdly, it suggested that new research from Europe and North America showed that an excessively close relationship between mother and child in early years might actually be quite problematic (see *Kōsei Hakusho* 1998: 84).

The idea of men and women sharing the work of parenting on a much more equal basis goes right to the heart of the development of the nuclear family in post-war Japan where the responsibility for childcare has rested almost entirely on the shoulders of mothers and where fathers have often been expected to show their primary loyalty to their company rather than their family. This was particularly the case in the first three post-war decades as the society tried to rebuild and modernise. In the 1960s, terms such as '*maihōmuisumu*' (my-homeism) were used in a derogatory fashion to refer to male company employees who appeared to spend too much time with their families. It is clear from Roberts' account that companies in Japan, despite lip-service, have been reluctant to attack this ideology that has served them very well in the past 50 years; few industrial work-forces appear to have been as loyal or to have worked as conscientiously as that of Japan. At the same time, during the current recession in Japan, it might be argued that there has been little economic reason for companies to encourage women back into the labour force as soon as they have given birth; indeed, to some extent, it might seem logical that companies are keen to keep women in the home so as to help them protect the jobs of their male workers and, as far as possible, maintain the myth of lifetime employment, which has generally only pertained to men, aged 22–55, who work in white-collar jobs in the largest of companies. It is important to point out, however, that while the *ideology* of lifetime employment has been given much greater prominence in Japan than in many of its OECD competitors, the *reality* has been that the make-up of the Japanese workforce in this regard has not in the post-war period been nearly as different as much of the rhetoric might have suggested. For example, according to Koike (1996: 34–7), long-term white-collar employees have constituted about the same percentage of the workforce in Japan as in Western Europe, and the only distinctiveness of Japan in this regard is that about ten percent more blue-collar workers engage in long-term employment than in most of Western Europe. The Germans surpass even the Japanese in the proportion of long-term blue-collar workers. Nevertheless, while the economic outlook remains poor, there is little incentive for employers in Japan to attack the idea that a division of labour by gender is 'natural' and that women should stay at home to care for their young children.

The Japanese government, however, has recently come up with another significant argument as to why men should become more actively involved in the process of caring for children and this relates to the 'discovery' of child abuse, which is the topic of my paper in this volume. As I show (see Table 6.2), recent surveys have suggested that women are the main abusers of children. The interpretation of this by the government is interesting. According to the Japanese government in its 1998 *Kōsei Hakusho* (Annual Report on Health and Welfare):

In cases of abuse, excluding sexual abuse, natural mothers were the perpetrators twice as often as natural fathers, *reflecting the much greater burden of parenting that is placed on mothers* (1998: 110; italics added).

The 'discovery' of child abuse made it easier for the government to put in place more state-funded systems in the community to support women with families and thereby help both to ease their situation and to encourage other women in the belief that having a family could, in future, be rewarding.

One of the most surprising elements of the recent debate about child abuse in Japan is the speed with which it has allowed ideas about the nature of certain roles in Japanese society to change. In the early 1990s, parental rights were considered virtually inviolable, and a child was seen by and large as the property of the parent; by the end of the decade, the idea of children being endowed with their own rights had gained enormous ground, and it was even possible for children to receive legal and financial support to sue their parents for abuse. The idea that parents innately have the interests of their children at heart and are therefore incapable of abusing their children has rapidly become replaced by the perception that child abuse is virtually endemic.

The question, of course, is why has Japan discovered child abuse now? The role of the media has clearly been very important, as it has been in the development of other social panics in Japan, but the media cannot construct social problems out of nothing. The 'discovery' of child abuse has been part of a major attack on the whole institution of the family in Japan. Only ten years ago, the Japanese family system, along with many others of its social and cultural institutions from its education system to its management structures, was regarded as the reason for Japan's economic success. Ten years of recession, and exactly the same systems are being used to explain Japan's economic failure. There has been a sustained critique of all those values that in the post-war period have been presented as 'core Japanese values' – respect for seniors, the group prevailing over the individual, the importance of maintaining harmony. According to many commentators, both inside and outside Japan, these 'Japanese' values (some of which have previously been presented as the direct legacy of neo-Confucian influence on Japanese society) have to be shed in favour of individualism and an entrepreneurial spirit before Japan can fully recover economically and socially.

As Leng-Leng Thang shows in her paper, new rhetorics and approaches have also been emerging in the treatment of the elderly in Japan. Elders in Japan are less often referred to by the term '*silver*' (with its implication that they are irreversibly different and in a separate category from those who are 'not-silver') and more often by the term '*senior*' (which means they are simply somewhere on a spectrum of age). Increasingly, the elderly are being seen as a group with enormous potential political power. While there has been little evidence of this power being mobilised, Talcott (2001) believes that this potentiality explains why so many recent government reforms have benefited Japan's elderly.

At the same time as the state has been developing social services for the young and the elderly, there has emerged in Japan a new type of volunteer in the welfare field. The Hanshin earthquake saw a sudden upsurge in volunteer activity that caught many in Japan unawares and led to 1995 being described by some as 'the first year of volunteerism in Japan' (Nakano 1998: 3). According to the Hyōgo prefectural government, 1.17 million volunteers offered their services in the six weeks after the earthquake. Seventy percent of them had never been involved in volunteer activity before (Nakata 1996: 22). Most of them were young, enthusiastic and not bound to mainstream ideas of volunteer activity. As Nakata (1996: 23) put it: 'The youths flocking the ward office were different from the obedient and respectful "volunteers" that ward officers had known previously … for whom volunteer work meant … doing whatever they were told to do by the ward officers.'

As Victoria Bestor, in the paper which follows this introduction, explains, in the wake of the Hanshin earthquake, there was a sudden reconsideration of the role of volunteer activity in Japan and a new debate began about the development of civil society, based on a model of what many commentators describe as a Western concept of volunteer activity. As Nakano (2000: 93) puts it: 'The Japanese media in the 1990s have made volunteering a symbol of social transformation … Volunteers are portrayed by the media as the agents of a citizen revolution.' This has had a major impact on raising awareness about a host of welfare issues, including the care of the elderly. Adachi (2000) suggests that a new western-style volunteer type is currently actively in competition with previous models, such as the *minsei jidōiin* system (see Goodman 1998), which were based on community rather than individual participation.

If, in some ways, the system of care for the elderly in private institutions which bring them into contact with the young described by Thang draws on very recent discourses in Japanese society, it also draws on much older ones, in particular the idea that the elderly should be supported as far as possible in the community rather than by the state and that they are part of some large extended family of which, ultimately, all

Japanese are members. Even following the *Gold Plan* of 1990, the *New Gold Plan* of 1994 and the groundwork lain down for the *Gold Plan 21* of 2000, the proportion of elderly receiving home help services and the number of helpers per 1000 population still lags some way behind the UK (Kono 2000) and of respondents to a survey in 1997, 76 percent said that if a member of their household needed care, this would be provided wholly or principally by family members or relatives (*Kōsei Hakusho* 1997: 119).

The rhetoric of community care, as we saw earlier, was particularly important in the development of the Japanese-style social welfare society (*Nihongata shakai fukushi shakai*) in the 1970s. In his policy speech to the 151st session of the Diet in May 2001, the new Prime Minister, Koizumi Junichirō, drew on a very similar rhetoric when he announced that he was determined to base the three pillars of social welfare – pensions, medical care and nursing – on a 'spirit of self-help and self-sufficiency' and that he intended to reach out widely to local community residents, volunteers and non-profit organisations (NPOs) to create a society 'sustained through mutual assistance' in taking care of the sick, elderly and children.

As Yohko Tsuji shows in the penultimate chapter of this volume, the state has a role to play even in the way that death is dealt with in Japanese society. Death, like birth, is a culturally constructed experience on which there is also a rich anthropological literature. In every society, funerals are a source of potential conflict as much as they are a means of reorganising society following the departure of a member. Tsuji shows how, in the Meiji period, funerals were removed from the remit of the family and religious organisations and taken over directly by the state. They were placed under increasingly tight regulation in part as a means of raising money but also as part of the state's construction of a Japanese national identity organised around the concept of the *ie* or extended family. The Meiji authorities thereby simultaneously managed to take control over the two certainties of life – taxation and death. Ever since the Meiji period, there has been a constant struggle between the state and various interest groups which have tried to wrest back control over funerals. In the 1990s, individuals won important rights to conduct funerals in new ways, demonstrating that citizens are not simply passive consumers of social policy. Significantly, the new forms of funeral can only be understood in the context of the issue of declining fertility in Japan. It has been the growth in families without children, and hence no second generation to perform rites for the deceased, that has led to the demand for funerals to be performed in ways that no longer require these rites.

As this final example, hopefully, shows, social policy in Japan cannot be fully understood without a deep knowledge of Japanese history and social organisation. Social policies not only emerge from a particular context, but they also provide important clues to how social values are constructed, manipulated and changed. As such, as the papers in this volume set out to demonstrate, the study of social policy provides an excellent entrée into the study of contemporary Japanese society.

NOTES

1   See Okely (1999: 30) for a telling ethnographic example of how 'normality' among the 'aged' is tested in British society and how this test tells us as much about the assumptions of those applying it as it does about those being tested.
2   For a recent review of the practical ways in which anthropology as a field has contributed, and continues to contribute, to social policy research, practice and advocacy in the current international context, see Okongwu and Mencher (2000).
3   Particularly influential in the late 1980s and early 1990s (see, for example, Marmot and Davey Smith 1989; Wilkinson 1996) was the idea that Japan's rapidly increasing longevity in the post-war society was directly correlated with the relative social and economic equality of its population.
4   It should be pointed out that in 1950, which is generally used as the baseline in Japanese illustrations of its aging society, Japan had its youngest population during this century as a result of the post-war baby boom. More than five percent of the population was over the age of 64 at the beginning of the twentieth century.

REFERENCES

Adachi, Kiyoshi. 2000. 'The development of social welfare services in Japan,' pp.191–205 in *Caring for the Elderly in Japan and the US: Practices and Policies*, ed. Susan Orpett Long. London: Routledge.

Ahmed, Akbar and Cris Shore, eds. 1995. *The Future of Anthropology: Its Relevance in the Modern World*. London: Athlone Press.

Ardener, Edwin. 1972. 'Belief and the problem of women,' in *The Interpretation of Ritual*, ed. Jean La Fontaine. London: Tavistock.

Asad, Talal, ed. 1973. *Anthropology and the Colonial Encounter*. London: Ithaca Press.

Baba, Keinosuke. 1980. *Fukushi Shakai no Nihonteki Keitai (The Japanese-style Welfare Society)*. Tokyo: Tōyō Keizai Shinpōsha.

Beauchamp, Edward R. and Richard Rubinger. 1989. *Education in Japan: A Source Book*. New York and London: Garland Publishing Inc.

Ben-Ari, Eyal, 1999. 'Colonialism, anthropology and the politics of profession-alisation: an argumentative afterword,' pp. 384–409 in *Anthropology and Colonialism in Asia and Oceania*, ed. Jan van Bremen and Shimizu Akitoshi. Richmond: Curzon Press.

Benedict, Ruth. 1946 (repr. 1977). *The Chrysanthemum and the Sword: Patterns of Japanese Culture*. London: Routledge and Kegan Paul.

Bloch, Maurice, ed. 1975. *Language and Oratory in Traditional Society*. London: Academic Press.

Bourdieu, Pierre. 1991. *Language and Symbolic Power*. Cambridge: Polity Press.

Callaway, Helen. 1978. 'The most essentially female function of all,' pp. 163–85 in *Defining Females: The Nature of Women in Society*, ed. Shirley Ardener. London: Croom Helm.

Campbell, John Creighton. 1992. *How Policies Change: The Japanese Government and the Aging Society*. Princeton, NJ: Princeton University Press.

Christensen, Pia, Jenny Hockey and Allison James. 1998. '"You just get on with it": questioning models of welfare dependency in a rural community,' in *The Anthropology of Welfare*, ed. Iain R. Edgar and Andrew Russell. London: Routledge.

Cohen, Stanley. 1971. *Folk Devils and Moral Panics: The Creation of the Mods and Rockers*, London: McGibbon and Kee.

Cummings, William K. 1999. 'The institutions of education: compare, compare, compare!' in *Comparative Education*, 43/2: 413–37.

Dale, Peter N. 1986. *The Myth of Japanese Uniqueness*. London, Sydney and Oxford: Croom Helm and the Nissan Institute.

Dore, Ronald P. 1965. *Education in Tokugawa Japan*. London: Routledge & Kegan Paul.

Edgar, Iain R and Andrew Russell, eds. 1998. *The Anthropology of Welfare*. London: Routledge.

Esping-Andersen, Gosta. 1990. *The Three Worlds of Welfare Capitalism*. Cambridge: Polity Press.

Feldman, Eric A. 2000. *The Ritual of Rights in Japan: Law, Society and Health Policy*. Cambridge: Cambridge University Press.

Ferguson, James. 1996. 'Development,' pp. 154–60 in *Encyclopaedia of Social and Cultural Anthropology*, ed. Alan Barnard and Jonathan Spencer. London: Routledge.

Foucault, Michel. 1972. *The Archaeology of Knowledge*. New York: Harper and Row.

——. 1977. *Discipline and Punish*. Harmondsworth: Penguin.

Fox, Robin. 1967. *Kinship and Marriage*. Harmondsworth: Penguin.

Fujimoto Tetsuya. 1994. *Crime Problems in Japan*. Tokyo: Chūō University Press.

Garon, Sheldon. 1997. *Molding Japanese Minds: The State in Everyday Life*. Princeton, NJ: Princeton University Press.

Geertz, Clifford. 1973. 'Thick description,' in *The Interpretation of Cultures: Selected Essays*. London: Fontana Press.

Goodman, Roger. 1993. *Japan's 'International Youth': The Emergence of a New Class of Schoolchildren*. Oxford: Oxford University Press.

——. 1998. 'The delivery of personal social services and the "Japanese-style welfare state,"' pp. 139–58 in *The East Asian Welfare Model: Welfare Orientalism and the State*, ed. Roger Goodman, Gordon White and Huck-Ju Kwon. London: Routledge.

——. 2001. 'Images of the Japanese welfare state,' pp. 176–93 in *Globalizing Japan: Ethnography of the Japanese Presence in Asia, Europe and America*, ed. Harumi Befu and Sylvie Guichard-Anguis. London and New York: Routledge.

Goodman, Roger and David Phillips, eds. 2002. *Can the Japanese Change their Education System?* Oxford: Symposium Books.

Goodman, Roger, Gordon White and Huck-Ju Kwon, eds. 1998. *The East Asian Welfare Model: Welfare Orientalism and the State*. London: Routledge.

Goody, Jack. 1995. *The Expansive Moment: The Rise of Social Anthropology in Britain and Africa, 1918–1970*. Cambridge: Cambridge University Press.

Gould, Arthur. 1993. *Capitalist Welfare States: A Comparison of Japan, Britain and Sweden*. Harlow: Longman.

Gould, Stephen J. 1984. *The Mismeasure of Man*. Harmondsworth: Penguin Books.

Grillo, R. 1985. 'Applied anthropology in the 1980s: retrospect and prospect,' in *Social Anthropology and Development Policy*, ed. R. Grillo and A. Rew. New York: Tavistock.

Hann, Chris and Elizabeth Dunn. 1996. *Civil Society: Challenging Western Models*. London: Routledge.

Harada, Sumitaka. 1998. 'The ageing society, the family, and social policy,' in *The Political Economy of Japanese Society, Vol. 2: Internationalisation and Domestic Issues*, ed. Junji Banno. Oxford: Oxford University Press.

Hashimoto, Akiko. 1996. *The Gift of Generations: Japanese and American Perspectives on Aging and the Social Contract*. New York: Cambridge University Press.

Hastings, Sally Ann. 1995. *Neighbourhood and Nation in Tokyo, 1905–1937*. Pittsburgh and London: University of Pittsburgh Press.

Hendry, Joy. 1996. 'The chrysanthemum continues to flower: Ruth Benedict and some perils of popular anthropology,' pp. 106–21 in *Popularizing Anthropology*, ed. Jeremy MacClancy and Chris McDonaugh. London and New York: Routledge.

Hill, Michael. 1996. *Social Policy: A Comparative Analysis*. London: Prentice Hall.

Holmberg, A. 1960. 'Changing community attitudes and values,' in *Social Change in Latin America Today: Its Implications For United States Policy*, ed. R. Adams et al. New York: Published for the Council on Foreign Relations by Harper & Brothers.

Illich, Ivan. 1977. *Disabling Professions*, London; Salem, N.H.: Marion Boyars.

Izuhara, Misa. Forthcoming. *Social Policy in the Twenty-First Century: Anglo-Japanese Perspectives*. London: The Policy Press.

Jackson, Anthony, ed. 1987. *Anthropology at Home*. London and New York: Tavistock Publications.

Jones, Catherine, ed. 1993. *New Perspectives on the Welfare State in Europe*. London: Routledge.

Kawada, Minoru. 1993. *The Origin of Ethnography in Japan: Yanagida Kunio and his Times*. London: Kegan Paul International.

Koike, Kazuo. 1996. *The Economics of Work in Japan*. Tokyo: LTCB International Library Foundation.

Kono, M. 2000. 'The impact of modernisation and social policy on family care for older people,' *Journal of Social Policy*, 29/2: 181–203.

Kōseishō (Ministry of Health and Welfare). Various years. *Hakusho (Annual White Paper on Health and Welfare)*. Tokyo: Ministry of Health and Welfare.

Kwon, Huck-Ju. 1999. *Income Transfers to the Elderly in East Asia: Testing Asian Values*, CASEpaper 27 (London School of Economics: STICERD).

Kuper, Adam. 1997. *Anthropology and Anthropologists: The Modern British School* (3rd edition). London and New York: Routledge.

La Fontaine, J. S. 1988. 'Child sexual abuse and the incest taboo: practical problems and theoretical issues,' in *Man* (N.S.), 23/1: 1–18.

——. 1990. *Child Sexual Abuse*. London: Polity Press.

——. 1998. *Speak of the Devil: Tales of Satanic Abuse in Contemporary England*. Cambridge: Cambridge University Press.

Long, Susan O., ed. 2000. *Caring for the Elderly in Japan and the US: Practices and Policies*. London: Routledge.

Lynn, Richard. 1988. *Educational Achievement in Japan: Lessons for the West*. London: Macmillan Press in association with the Social Affairs Unit.

Malinowski, B. 1929. 'Practical anthropology,' *Africa*, (2), 1: 22–38.

McConnell, David L. 2000. *Importing Diversity: Inside Japan's JET Program*. Berekely: University of California Press.

McKechnie, Rosemary and Tamara Kohn. 1999. 'Introduction: why do we care who cares?' pp. 1–13 in *Extending the Boundaries of Care: Medical Ethics and Caring Practices*, ed. Tamara Kohn and Rosemary McKechnie. Oxford: Berg.

McVeigh, Brian. 1998. *The Nature of the Japanese State: Rationality and Rituality*. London: Routledge.

Marmot, M. G. and G. Davey Smith. 1989. 'Why are the Japanese living longer?' *British Medical Journal*, 299: 1547–51.

Mouer, Ross and Yoshio Sugimoto. 1986. *Images of Japanese Society: A Study in the Structure of Social Reality*. London: Kegan Paul International.

Mulvey, Howard. 1996. 'Patients' rights: organ transplantation and brain death in Japan,' pp. 184–221 in *Case Studies on Human Rights in Japan*, ed. Roger Goodman and Ian Neary. Kent: Japan Library (Curzon Press).

Nader, Laura. 1972. 'Up the anthropologist – perspectives gained from studying up,' in *Reinventing Anthropology*, ed. Dell Hymes. New York: Random House.

Nakano, Lynne Yukie. 1998. 'Civic volunteers in a Japanese neighborhood: negotiating status in a marginal place.' PhD thesis. Yale University.

——. 2000. 'Volunteering as a lifestyle choice: negotiating self-identities in Japan,' *Ethnology*, 39/2: 93–107.

Nakata, Toyokazu. 1996. 'Budding volunteerism,' *Japan Quarterly*, 43/1: 22–6.

Okely, Judith. 1999. 'Love, care and diagnosis', pp. 19–48 in *Extending the Boundaries of Care: Medical Ethics and Caring Practices*, ed. Tamara Kohn and Rosemary McKechnie. Oxford: Berg.

Okongwu, Anne Francis and Joan P. Mencher. 2000. 'The anthropology of public policy: shifting terrains,' in *Annual Review of Anthropology*, 29: 107–24.

Parkin, David. 1978. *The Cultural Definition of Political Response: Lineal Destiny among the Luo*. London: Academic Press.

——. 1984. 'Political language,' *Annual Review of Anthropology*, 13: 345–65.

Pringle, Keith. 1998. *Children and Social Welfare in Europe*. Buckingham and Philadelphia: Open University Press.

Riviere, Peter. 1985. 'Unscrambling parenthood,' *Anthropology Today*, 1/4: 2–7.

Robertson, A. F. 1984. *People and the State: An Anthropology of Planned Development*. New York: Cambridge University Press.

Said, Edward. 1978. *Orientalism*. Harmondsworth: Penguin.

Shimizu, Akitoshi. 1999. 'Colonialism and the development of modern anthropology in Japan,' pp. 115–171 in *Anthropology and Colonialism in Asia and Oceania*, ed. Jan van Bremen and Shimizu Akitoshi. Richmond: Curzon Press.

Shore, Cris and Susan Wright, eds. 1997. *Anthropology of Policy: Critical Perspectives on Governance and Power*. London: Routledge.

Siaroff, Alan. 1994. 'Work, welfare and gender equality,' pp. 82–100 in *Gendering Welfare States*, ed. Diane Sainsbury. London: Sage.

Spector, Malcolm and John I. Kitsuse. 1977. *Constructing Social Problems*. California: Cummings Publishing Company.

Takahagi Yasuji et al. 1982. *Kaigai.Kikokushijo ni Okeru Culture Shock no Yōin Bunseki to Tekiō Programme no Kaihatsu Seikō* (The Trial and Development of a Programme for Adaptation and Fundamental Analysis of Culture Shock among Overseas and Returnee Children). Tokyo: Tōkyō Gakugei Daigaku Kaigaishijo Kyōiku Centre.

Takeda, Hiroko. 2002. The Political Economy of Reproduction in Japan: Between Nation-State and Everyday Life. PhD thesis. Graduate School of East Asian Studies, University of Sheffield.

Talcott, Paul David. 2001. 'Respect for the elderly's votes: theories of interests and the elderly in Japanese healthcare policy, 1995–2000.' Harvard University Program on U.S.–Japan Relations Occasional Paper 00–14.

Therborn, Göran. 1986. *Why Some People Are More Unemployed Than Others*. London: Verso.

Turner, Victor. 1967. *The Forest of Symbols: Aspects of Ndembu Ritual*. Ithaca: Cornell University Press.

van Bremen, Jan and Shimizu Akitoshi, eds. 1999. *Anthropology and Colonialism in Asia and Oceania*. Richmond: Curzon Press.

Watanuki, Jōji. 1986. 'Is there a "Japanese-Type Welfare Society,"' *International Sociology*, 1/3: 259–69.

White, Gordon and Roger Goodman. 1998. 'Welfare Orientalism and the search for an East Asian welfare model,' pp. 3–24 in *The East Asian Welfare Model: Welfare Orientalism and the State*, ed. Roger Goodman, Gordon White and Huck-Ju Kwon. London and New York: Routledge.

Wilkinson, Richard G. 1996. *Unhealthy Societies: The Afflictions of Inequality*. London and New York: Routledge.

2 Toward a cultural biography of civil society in Japan

Victoria Lyon Bestor

Since 1989, when civil society was credited with providing the space within which democratic reforms emerged after the fall of communism in Eastern Europe, the role of civil society has been the subject of an enormous amount of social science discourse. Japan's experience with both civil society and democracy has been vastly different from that of the states of the former Soviet bloc, yet the role of civil society in Japan has also become a major topic of discussion.

In Japan, the recent discourse on civil society emerged not from a fallen political philosophy but from the rubble of a disastrous earthquake. Early on the morning of January 17, 1995, a massive temblor hit the Hanshin region of central Japan. Initially, the government did almost nothing. It seemed frozen in a state of bureaucratic ossification caused by ministerial turf wars and disputes over jurisdiction between the central government and local authorities. With no systematic relief efforts in sight, small voluntary groups, small firms and their employees, and individual citizens, totalling approximately 1.2 million individuals, stepped in to fill the void by providing rescue, relief, and shelter. The earthquake starkly revealed both the inadequacies of the Japanese government's response to the disaster and the power of voluntary action to aid quake victims. Post-quake press on the volunteer effort produced more press coverage that brought more volunteers and yet more press. New volunteer groups sprang up and older unincorporated nonprofits (NPOs) grew more active.

That apparently spontaneous mobilisation of volunteers from all walks of life sparked widespread discussion and debate about the past, present, and future of 'civil society' in Japan. To illustrate the reconceptualisation or reimagination of the civil sector that is taking place today, this chapter has three goals: to provide a brief history of the employment of the notion of civil society in the post-war period; to examine the role that translation and Western models of civil society play in shaping the debate; and to briefly review recent trends in the study of civil society both in the Japanese popular press and among foreign observers of Japan.

This chapter therefore is an attempt to begin to sketch a 'cultural biography' of civil society. That is, to borrow the term from Igor Kopytoff (1986) who coined it, I examine how the concept of civil society has developed layers of meaning and association, both internal and external to Japanese society, as it has gained currency and has migrated from one discursive sphere to another in discourses about the changing political and social dynamics of Japanese life during the last several decades.

The evolution of post-war notions of civil society in Japan

The possible roots of Japanese civil society have been traced variously to early Buddhist acts of benevolence (Yamaoka 1998), to Japan's Confucian traditions (Tucker 1998), to the theories of John Locke (Deguchi 1999), to Meiji era popular rights movements (Irokawa 1964), and to Western models of philanthropy and concepts of social responsibility (Deguchi 1993, 1999, 2000; Bestor 1999a, 1999b). But as historian Andrew Barshay notes, 'the history of civil society in Japan – that is, as a "self-conscious" and "self-aware" history – belongs to the postwar era' (Barshay forthcoming).

Japan's post-war discourse on civil society can be roughly divided into four periods:

1. the period during the Occupation (1945–52) when notions of civil society were tied closely to efforts to bring American-style participatory democracy to Japan, through 1955 when the Japanese economy 'took-off;'
2. the period of citizens' movements and popular protests during the 1960s and 1970s when progressive intellectuals and liberal politicians gave voice to the need for minimum standards of well-being and when the effects of unbridled industrial growth produced mass protests against pollution;
3. the era of Japanese corporate philanthropy in the 1970s and 1980s when Japanese multinationals thrived and made charitable giving a strategy for success abroad and at home; and
4. the current post-bubble, post-earthquake era when Japan's continued economic decline has diminished prospects for all age groups; a period characterised by government ossification and its inability to reform from within. This has also been a time when natural and social disasters have starkly brought the shortcomings of the political establishment into focus, creating the opportunity, indeed the necessity, for Japanese citizens to redefine civic participation and voluntary action.

The occupation period and the early 1950s

At the end of World War II, Japan lay in ruins, its industry and infrastructure destroyed by a series of Allied incendiary air strikes and the first atomic bombs dropped on Hiroshima and Nagasaki. Initially, the US Occupation of Japan, described as Japan's short-lived eight-year experience of colonialism by Roger Goodman in his introduction to this volume, undertook to completely remould Japan on an American democratic model. The 'Occupationaires' were a mixed collection of American career military officers and very idealistic young civilians. Together, they sought to radically change Japan through a process of 'induced revolution' with a programme of modernisation and American-style democratisation. Among the goals were to establish a responsible government in accordance with the freely expressed will of the people and strong civil institutions operating outside the sphere of government. Initial efforts included the constitution, drafted in 1946, with a bill of rights that ostensibly guaranteed individual freedoms broader than those guaranteed by the American constitution, laying the groundwork for a fully participatory democracy ensuring individual rights and freedoms. Occupationaires saw a strong American-style democracy as challenging, discrediting, and replacing the ideologies that had brought Japan into the war. Western philanthropists like the Rockefellers also played important behind-the-scenes roles in the reinvigoration of cultural and civic organisations which have played major roles in the evolution of Japanese notions of the civil sector ever since (Bestor 1998b).

After the defeat of the Nationalist Chinese and the establishment of the People's Republic of China in 1949 and the outbreak of the Korean War in 1950, many of the reforms originally envisioned by the Occupation were quickly revised or forgotten. Occupation policy refocussed on efforts to bring Japan firmly into the Western bloc as a client state and an ardent anti-communist ally. Emphasis on promoting civil society and broad individual freedoms declined. Democratic concepts of civil society and larger civic involvement were put aside in the midst of American paranoia about the communist threat.

Reinvigorating Japan's economy and making Japan 'America's unsinkable aircraft carrier' in the Pacific became the central motivations of Occupation policy. The Japan that resulted was a market-led, 'developmental state' (Johnson 1995, 1999) with the overarching objective of creating a strong industrial and economic sector at the expense, if necessary, of a broader range of personal liberties and social welfare. Accompanying these initiatives was a narrowing of political options that included the suppression of communist and leftist groups and the concentration of power in the hands of a group of conservative leaders who had been quickly 'rehabilitated' by the Occupation to take over the reins of government.

However, the idea of civil society was not entirely lost as a political concept or ideal. Among Japanese intellectuals, the discourse on civil society continued as an important theme both in post-mortem evaluations of the wartime experience and in discussions of how post-war democratic institutions in Japan could best evolve. After US policy changed abruptly, notions of civil society and discussions of ways to promote it were largely restricted to intellectual circles. During much of this era, Japan's intellectuals were predominantly of the progressive or Marxist camp. Leading among them were Uchida Yoshihiko, Hirata Kiyoaki, and Maruyama Masao (1969) whose works were widely translated in the West (Barshay forthcoming). In Japanese, the discourse was published widely in leftist monthly journals such *Sekai* or *Shisō*. Social commentators like Sakamoto Yoshikazu, Hani Gorō and Kuno Osamu believed in historical progress and were convinced that it was leading toward a socialist society in which the leading role would be played by the *shimin*, or citizens. From the end of World War II until the 1980s, the term *shimin shakai* was most commonly used in this progressive sense, to point toward an idealised socialist state in contrast to Japan's market-led enterprise state (Deguchi 1999).

The 1960s and the growth of citizen participation

The 1960 revision of the US–Japan Security Treaty (AMPO) became an important focus for citizens' action. Reacting to Prime Minister Kishi's high-handed ramming of the AMPO Treaty through the Diet, opposition from Diet members and leading liberal and leftist intellectuals promoted the formation of a citizens' movement that mobilised a sizable protest. Those efforts eventually led to the cancellation of President Eisenhower's proposed visit to Japan in June 1960 and eventually resulted in Prime Minister Kishi's downfall, although the AMPO Treaty itself survived the crisis.

The aftermath of the 1960 AMPO riots further pushed discussions of promoting civil society to the periphery. However, the anti-treaty riots also demonstrated the potential for citizens' action that began to take hold as official policy more intensely emphasised market-led growth, industrial development and expansion of the corporate sector at the expense of grass-roots needs and initiatives. While national prosperity through the 1960s and 1970s was enormous, little emphasis was placed on the individual, nor was attention given to the needs of urban neighbourhoods or rural communities. As the wealth of Japanese corporations became more conspicuous, local interests began to demand spreading the wealth and creating accepted minimum standards of living. Again, Uchida was a key spokesman along with Hirata who coined the term 'enterprise state' (Barshay forthcoming). Another important leftist political theorist, Matsushita Keiichi (1964), argued for a 'civil minimum' of quality of life, access to resources, and public services (Matsushita 1964). His views were later influential on the progressive politician Minobe Ryōkichi who was elected Governor of Tokyo in 1967 by a coalition of communist and socialist supporters. Governor Minobe strongly promoted 'community consciousness' and 'citizen participation' to make Tokyo a city truly 'managed by the people themselves' (Snow 1973).

Governor Minobe was also one of the first elected officials to take action on the environmental front. In 1970, he supported Diet legislation that passed 14 environmental ordinances to curb pollution in the Tokyo area. Enforcement was not an easy task and both industrial and labour interests resisted full implementation of the initiatives. Minobe was in the forefront of the issues but he had to rely heavily on the press and public opinion because he lacked the support of the conservative political-bureaucratic establishment (Snow 1973).

By the early 1970s, pollution had become a serious problem in many parts of Japan. During the 1950s, Japan was still struggling to recover from the war and the prospect of industrial growth seemed to present future opportunities tantalising enough to quell opposition despite the lack of much evident direct benefit to the average citizen. Two decades later, serious and widespread incidents of industrial pollution such as those in Tokyo, the mercury poisoning of fisheries stocks that became known as Minamata Disease, and severe air pollution and endemic lung disorders in such industrial cities as Yokkaichi in Mie Prefecture, led to local environmental awareness and activism throughout Japan. The mid-1960s and early 1970s' opposition to environmental hazards produced by unbridled industrial growth began to create a ground swell of locally based citizens' movements (*shimin undō*).

Residents of rural areas affected by specific sources of industrial pollution joined with members of the urban middle classes whose consciousness had already been raised by urban pollution and Minobe's efforts to highlight such issues through the press. A broad range of middle-class professionals, doctors, scientists, lawyers, school children, teachers and the media mobilised public interest and support, both to aid the pollution victims in their long legal battles with polluters and to demand that preventative measures be taken to insure that industry behave more responsibly. The continued and intense focus of the media was particularly important in holding domestic Japanese attention on the problem and bringing the issue into the international spotlight (Simcock and Krauss 1980).

Other movements expanded simultaneously, including the anti-nuclear movement and a range of vigorous and diverse consumer movements, mostly made up of housewives. These movements focussed broader attention on consumer needs, on food safety, on environmental hazards as they relate more broadly to the general populace, and, most importantly, on the excesses of corporate Japan and its disregard of the consumer.

Contemporary citizens' movements and popular protests also stimulated interest in the history of the 'Freedom and People's Rights Movement' (*Jiyū Minken Undō*) of the 1880s, including its challenges to the centralised authority of the Meiji State (Irokawa 1964). This contributed to an intellectual climate in which a popular version of civil society could be seen in the past as well as in the present-day political, environmental, and consumer movements.

Pressure continued for implementation of social reforms, and by the late 1960s and early 1970s, concrete plans were being made for the creation of a broad range of social programmes. However, the so-called 'Oil Shock' of 1973 severely jolted Japan (which was dependent on foreign sources for 98 percent of its energy needs) and derailed policies that were leading toward the creation of a Western European-style welfare state. Instead, what was created came to be known as the Japanese-style welfare society (*Nihongata shakai fukushi shakai*, see Goodman, this volume, pp. 16, 23). This offered far fewer entitlements than Western models and relied heavily on traditional Japanese support networks (although these traditional social elements were seen not as autonomous elements of civil society, but rather as subsidiaries of state policy).

In due course, the economy recovered and as prosperity spread throughout the Japanese populace and economic growth seemed unending, complacency seemed to settle over much of the Japanese middle class. During the 1970s and 1980s, the good life seemed within reach, and many Japanese concentrated their energies on better educating their children to get top jobs, investing in the booming real estate market, savings, and conspicuous consumption of luxury goods. Indeed, such an enormous percentage of Japanese thought of themselves as firmly middle class (roughly 85 percent) that they were called 'the New Middle Mass' (Murakami 1982). While consumer action, civil militancy and social involvement continued, for the most part it was concentrated in smaller, more factionalised or specialised movements.

The era of Japanese corporate philanthropy

Throughout the late 1960s and early 1970s, Japanese corporate philanthropy grew dramatically. During that period, most Japanese corporate giving was domestic and overwhelmingly supported projects aimed at facilitating continued economic growth, including Japanese rural development, improvement of medical care, student scholarships, and technical and scientific research funding. Government regulation of philanthropic activities ensured that most giving supported government projects and policies.

The formation of philanthropic organisations was based on the Meiji Civil Code of 1898. Article 34 of that code allowed for the creation of '*kōeki hōjin*' (public benefit corporations): 'incorporated associations or foundations relating to worship, religion, charity, science, art, or otherwise related to public interest and not having for their object the acquisition of gain' (Yamamoto 1998). That statute allowed for the creation of juridical persons (*hōjin*), which are legal corporations granted permission by the government to operate for a specific purpose under the administrative oversight of a given ministry, regional governmental agency or other governmental administrative body. The creation of a *hōjin* requires a considerable endowment or annual revenue from dues or other sources amounting to ¥300 million (approximately $3 million). In addition, very strict guidelines outline the focus of giving, for example, *gakkō hōjin* (educational), *shūkyō hōjin* (religious) *shakai fukushi hōjin* (welfare), and *iryō hōjin* (medical), as well as *zaidan hōjin* (philanthropic foundations). Strict geographical restrictions are often applied and approximately three-quarters of all Japanese *hōjin* have extremely local or regional spheres of activity.

By the 1970s, Japan's economic growth had become global, and Japanese corporate and government leaders began to see the need to improve Japan's image abroad (Rockefeller 1971, 1973). Particularly in Asian countries that were increasingly becoming the sources of raw materials, the sites of plants, pools of cheaper labour, and markets for Japan's industrial production, there was a need to try to erase lingering memories of World War II. And in the West, there was the need to enhance Japan's profile as a world leader, to keep pace with its obvious economic strength and to promote an image of Japan as more than simply an economic powerhouse.

Beginning in the early 1970s, Keidanren (the Federation of Economic Organisations), a major business organisation, took the lead in coordinating Japanese corporate support for foreign institutions by working directly with institutions abroad for whom Keidanren agreed to act as the fund raising agent. Over the years Keidanren led fund raising for Japanese studies centres at major North American and European universities, Japan wings at leading museums, and the presentation of Japanese culture abroad (e.g. cultural festivals, art exhibitions, and tours of performing artists) (Bestor 1998a).

Japanese corporate philanthropy's move abroad coincided with the expansion of Japanese multinational corporations, following them into major new markets. Similarly to the way that the government had provided the impetus and a template for earlier domestic corporate support, Keidanren pointed the way for new corporate philanthropies abroad. Consequently, the late 1970s and 1980s witnessed an explosion in the number and range of internationally focussed corporate giving organisations.

At the same time, tensions between the US and Japan over trade imbalances and market access continued to increase. Japan's growing international role, major corporate takeovers, conspicuous real estate investments and dramatic gifts to leading American research universities increasingly became the subject of criticism in the US (van Wolferen 1989; Choate 1990). Japan's US-focussed philanthropic activities led critics to question the goals and motivations of Japanese corporate giving. And some saw Japan's support as dangerous: buying American basic research and brainwashing the public (Epstein 1990).

Throughout the period of mounting trade tensions, the Japanese government, Keidanren, JCIE (the Japan Center for International Exchange), the Japan Chamber of Commerce, and Japan affinity groups (like the National Association of Japan–America Societies) worked consistently in the US to promote positive dialogue on issues related to Japanese philanthropy and corporate citizenship. Keidanren, with JCIE, conducted study missions for Japanese corporate and foundation leaders to study corporate social responsibility in the US. Those efforts led to the creation in Japan of the 'One Percent Club' in 1989 to encourage corporations to commit at least one percent of profits to philanthropic purposes. The same year, the Council for Better Corporate Citizenship (CBCC) was founded by Keidanren to promote good corporate citizenship in the US by Japanese affiliates. In connection with those efforts, in 1990, the Japan Chamber of Commerce and Industry of New York published *Joining In! A Handbook for Better Corporate Citizenship in the United States,* a guide to grass-roots volunteering in the US. (I believe that the volunteer experience first gained in the US by many in the expatriate Japanese community later provided a possible template for voluntary action among corporate returnees, many of whom eventually found themselves unemployed or underemployed when Japan's economy contracted in the 1990s.)

While Japanese philanthropy was skyrocketing abroad, an enormous range of philanthropic and quasi-philanthropic efforts in the arts, music and culture was expanding in Japan. Whereas earlier domestic philanthropy had been largely devoted to efforts that supported the national infrastructure, such as scientific and technological advancement, health-care and education, in the 1970s, 1980s and early 1990s, philanthropic activity increasingly focussed on the arts. There was an eclectic proliferation of museums of every kind, size, and focus; corporate-sponsored concert halls became engines of public relations; and, organisations known as 'mecenat' were established to funnel corporate support to the arts. (The term 'mecenat' (*mesena* in katakana) grew out of private Franco-Japanese dialogue exploring strategies for increasing support to the arts; the name was coined from the name of the Roman minister, Caius Maecenas, who protected the arts during the reign of Emperor Augustus.)

The burgeoning of this sector in Japan also led to the beginning of a professionalised corps of managers specialising in cultural and nonprofit organisations. Many of these managers were trained in or influenced by the professional norms of Western philanthropic organisations. In 1997, the GAP Group published the book *Kokusai Puroguramu Ofisā* as a guide to the professionalisation of the field. Since then, a series of exchanges and internships between programme officers from Japanese nonprofit organisations and American counterpart organisations has been funded by the Japan Foundation Center for Global Partnership.

No sooner had this infrastructure been firmly put in place and the professionalisation of the field of corporate philanthropy begun, than the Japanese economic bubble burst, effectively gutting Japanese philanthropies in the early 1990s.

Civil action after the bubble burst and the ground shook

The quake that hit Kobe on the morning of 17 January 1995 registered 7.2 magnitude on the Richter scale and has since come to be known as the great Hanshin–Awaji Earthquake (*Hanshin–Awaji Dai Shinsai*). More than 6,000 lives were lost, 350,000 people were made homeless, and damage ran to many billions of dollars. Kobe, one of Japan's major international harbours, came to a standstill.

Initially, the Japanese government seemed frozen, unable to respond. Bureaucratic wrangling and turf wars prevented cooperation or even the coordination of basic information. Government relief efforts were paralysed, and disputes among government agencies over jurisdiction prevented effective, coordinated crisis management (Pekkanen 2000, forthcoming).

The quake generally awakened many Japanese to the inability of the government to act in the face of such an emergency and dramatically demonstrated the ability of a spontaneously formed coalition of local and regional voluntary, philanthropic and religious groups. Accurate totals are unknown but reliably estimated at more than 1.2 million individual volunteers in the first two months following the quake, reaching a total of possibly 2 million in following months.

Media attention focussed on the volunteers from the beginning, no doubt encouraging even more participation. Donations from individuals and groups around the world streamed in to aid earthquake victims. Over the days and months that followed the quake and the marvellous outpouring of voluntary effort that followed, people began to imagine again (or anew) the potential of civil society in Japan. Barely six months after the earthquake, Kyōdō Tsūshin, one of Japan's major wire services declared 1995 the 'Beginning of Japan's Volunteer Era' (*borantia gannen*) (Kyōdō Tsūshin, July 13 1995).

Examples of the surge in volunteer activity that followed this declaration include the huge turnout of volunteers to mop up following a major oil spill that threatened wildlife off the Japan Sea Coast of Fukui Prefecture in 1997 after a Russian tanker sank and the outpouring of monetary and other support in the aftermath of a major quake in Taiwan that same year. Recognition of the considerable mobilisation of monetary and human capital required for these efforts produced a widespread realisation that Japan lacked the necessary legal framework for the growth of civil society now conceived as this new form of voluntary relief activity. The accounts of volunteers aiding in these crises were followed closely in the media, and public discussion of the importance of civil society and the voluntary sector and the need for a stronger legal framework for that sector continued to grow.

Finally, the government spoke publicly of the need to draft legislation to aid the nonprofit sector. Nonprofit leaders and Diet members began to discuss legislation that eventually produced the NPO Law passed in March 1998. In Japan, where bureaucrats draft almost all legislation, the submission and passage of a bill drafted jointly by ordinary citizens and Diet members set a new precedent (Pekkanen, 2000). The objective underlying the NPO bill was to confer legal status on NPOs that were too small to incorporate under the old civil code. While the manner of bringing the law to the Diet was path-breaking, instead of amending the civil code fully the resulting law only created a patchwork solution that allowed NPOs to operate more easily within the pre-existing framework. Disputes among Diet factions prevented the full implementation of the law as originally planned. The new law fell far short of redefining the provisions of 1898 Civil Code but it did establish a range of newly defined activity eligible for corporate status, without conferring any special tax breaks, at that time.

Talking the talk

This section examines the multiple uses of terms related to civil society, to help distinguish the ways 'civil society,' 'voluntary action,' 'NPO,' and

'NGO' are understood in the contemporary Japanese context both by Japanese and non-Japanese observers, and to understand their relationship to the shifting boundaries between 'public' and 'private' domains that are key to understanding the scope of 'private' action within Japan's 'public' sphere.

It is not merely a question of varying disciplinary perspective or different theoretical frameworks: the question of how terms related to civil society are translated into Japanese is key. At first glance, many of the terms – 'civil society,' 'volunteer,' 'NGO,' and 'NPO,' 'public' and 'private' – seem easily understood and translated. However, all are either directly translated or are foreign 'loan words' written in katakana.

Translation, at its most basic, is the act of privileging one definition or a range or definitions over others. As those translations become more broadly used and accepted they further crystallise and reify essentialised meanings attached to a phenomenon. In the keynote speech given at the Japanese Ethnology Society annual meeting in 1998, American anthropologist Richard Fox spoke about 'Cultural translation as craft and politics' (Fox 1998). As part of his discussion of the politics of translation, particularly as it relates to current debates within anthropology and cultural studies, Fox focussed on a number of types of translation including 'domesticating' or 'familiarising' translations, which he defines as effacing differences of language and culture. He contrasts these translations with 'foreignising' translations, those that have the effect of emphasising difference and accentuating the exotic qualities of foreign influences. While Fox speaks much more broadly about translation as cultural critique as articulated in current anthropological debates, his discussion might equally be applied to discussions of civil society in Japan today and hence the trajectory of the concept's 'cultural biography.' Often, without ulterior motives, a translation is made merely to arrive at a rough approximation in both languages. But, in an increasingly globalised world, these translations also place Japanese social trends more securely within the discourse of universalist definitions of transnational civil society.

A brief overview of key terms used to describe civil society in Japan illustrates some of the social and cultural contexts, resonances, and interpretations at work in these processes of linguistic and conceptual translation.

The word *shakai*, now freely translated as society and completely understood as a Japanese word, is a borrowed concept, first adapted to Japanese in the mid-nineteenth century by the influential educator-philosopher, Fukuzawa Yukichi (Fukuzawa 1866). Civil society, *shimin shakai*, both the term as translated and the concept as broadly defined, has been, until recently, more easily imagined in theory than in practice in Japan's post-war developmental, enterprise state. Indeed, the often constructed opposition between the state and civil society in discourses about post-Soviet economies is all but impossible to imagine in a Japanese context, characterised by state activism and state targeted support of development in all sectors (Schwartz and Pharr forthcoming).

The term 'civil society' itself is foreign to Japanese and if literally translated, *shimin shakai* means a society of (urban) citizens. A man I interviewed in Kyoto commented that his mother, who lived in a remote village in Shikoku, wondered how she could be a *shimin*, since she lived in a tiny village (*mura*) not in a city (*shi*). The Kōjien defines civil society as a 'modern society composed of free and equal individuals, having abolished all privileges, control by status or relations of subordination' (translated by Barshay forthcoming). Elsewhere, I have defined civil society as 'the space, real or imagined, between government and business – nation–state and corporate domain – in which individual and private agency can play an important role in organising consciousness, bringing change, providing services, and working for the common good.' And Susan Pharr has employed a more encompassing gloss in her new edited volume *The State of Civil Society in Japan,* by referring to Japan's 'associational landscape' (Schwartz and Pharr forthcoming).

Another concept that has become an increasingly important part of Japan's associational landscape in recent years, that of the *borantia* (volunteer), is sometimes confusing. The act of volunteering has arguably become an increasingly popular pastime with various age groups (Nakano 2000). Nonetheless, what being a volunteer entails is still unclear to many Japanese. Prior to the Kobe earthquake, perhaps the most common characterisation of individual 'voluntary action' was that prompted by Christian religious altruism. Since Christians make up approximately one percent of the Japanese population, however voluntarily active they may be as individuals, their numbers remain small. A valuable ethnography of Christian volunteers before the Kobe quake is contained in Carolyn Stevens' study of volunteerism in Yokohama's Kotobuki-chō slums (Stevens 1997).

'Voluntary associations,' not to be confused with voluntary action, have existed in Japan for centuries. Common examples in recent decades include *chōnaikai* (neighbourhood associations) and their rural counterparts. *Chōnaikai* fell into disrepute for the roles they played in providing local, neighbourhood-based control in Japan's war effort, but they continue to be important organisations in many urban neighbourhoods today (T. Bestor 1989). Other perspectives on voluntary associations include Sally Hastings' history of their social and political roles during the 1920s and 30s (Hastings 1995), Ralph Braibanti's liberal (and completely ignored) interpretation of their democratic potential during the Allied Occupation (Braibanti 1948), and anthropologist Edward Norbeck's study of rural community organisations (Norbeck 1962, 1977). Other important voluntary organisations on a community level include *shōtenkai* (shopkeepers' guilds), *shōbōdan* (volunteer fire brigades), PTAs, *kōenkai* (politician support groups) (Curtis 1970, 1971), alumni groups, and religious organisations.

Okpyo Moon (2002) has offered further discussion of the conceptualisation of voluntary associations by noting various Japanese anthropological discussions of the term and how that discourse has evolved (Moon unpublished paper). Yoneyama Toshinao, she notes, coined the term *shaen* to define modern associational ties as opposed to blood ties (*ketsuen*) and territorial ties (*chien*), both of the latter non-selective traditional ties binding the individual to their kin and to their local community however defined. Moon notes that subsequently Ueno Chizuko has argued that one should push the definition of *shaen* ties to differentiate between those that individuals are free to choose and those that are thrust upon them. For the purposes of this discussion, it is the truly voluntary ties that are the primary focus of current discussions of *borantia katsudō*, voluntary action in Japan. Such voluntary and grass-roots organisations have long been a mainstay of anthropological research in Japan and elsewhere, although, oddly, the subject seems to have been slower in coming to the centre stage of current ethnographic inquiry than it has in other social sciences. More anthropological participation in the discourse on Japanese civil society in studies of volunteers in all settings and in comparative studies of the volunteer sector with past anthropological studies of voluntary groups will greatly contribute to the completion of a cultural biography of civil society in Japan.

Another term that is particularly problematic is *dai san sekutā* (literally, 'the third sector'), which refers not in a Western sense to a third sector beyond the domains of the business world and the government, nor to a nonprofit or voluntary sector as it is understood in the West. Instead, the term *dai san sekutā* refers to hybrid institutions that are essentially half public and half business. To many Japanese, such organisations are virtually indistinguishable from the government (Yamamoto 1991, 1995, 1998). The *dai san sekutā* presents a problem both for these Japanese citizens who confuse the roles of such organisations and for foreign observers who accept its seeming familiarity. Those who assume it means the same as the third sector in the West and rely wholly or in part on government statistics, without clear understanding of the institutions that might fall under this umbrella classification, cannot make any meaningful comparisons across societies.

The term 'NGOs,' non-governmental organisations, is used to describe border-crossing institutions that work internationally and 'NPOs,' nonprofit organisations, describes a domestically oriented organisation. NPOs in particular have increased in number enormously since the Kobe earthquake. Before the new NPO Law was passed in 1998, such organisations were officially constituted under the provisions of the Meiji Civil Code of 1898. Many small NGOs and NPOs had no legal status whatsoever and unincorporated NPOs were not legally able to have a bank account or phone number listed in their name. To operate, they often relied on accounts listed in the name of an officer of the organisation, creating a potential legal liability for that individual. It is principally unincorporated organisations that experienced the most dramatic growth after the Kobe earthquake, and it was those organisations that the 1998 NPO law was intended to promote and regularise.

Further confounding one's understanding of Japan's civil sector are interpretations of 'public' and 'private.' The Japanese character '*kō*,' which is generally defined as 'public' and is used in compound words such as '*kōeki*' (public service) and '*kōen*' (public park), is also used in combinations such as '*kōji*' (government business), and '*kōgi*' (imperial court). In the dictionary, the character alone is defined first as a prince, duke or lord; the second definition includes all of the following – the public, the state, the government, and the community. Much of the work of organisations in the *dai san sekutā* mentioned above is considered public works, and the term *kōeki hoji*' (public benefit corporation) includes a much broader range of organisations than might be included in a Western interpretation of the concept.

The term 'private' is equally problematic, and much has been made of Japan's purportedly less well developed sense of the individual. Private is generally conveyed in compounds with a character pronounced '*shi*' read also as '*watakushi*' (I, myself). The popularity in the Meiji period of the literary style the 'I-novel' (*watakushi shōsetsu* or *shi shōsetsu*) is partly attributed to the novelty of a genre depicting a hero speaking from an individual perspective. Anthropologist Hamaguchi Eshun has problematised the Japanese self by arguing that, for the Japanese, the self only comes into play through interaction with others, as opposed to being a 'self-contained' entity (Hamaguchi 1985). The critic Yamazaki Masakazu has recently added his perspective on the changing role of the individual when he coined the term 'soft individualism' to suggest a form of individualism that takes shape through social interaction and mutual influence (Yamazaki 1994).

The concepts of civil society, volunteerism, NPOs, NGOs, the *dai san sekuta*, and the meanings of public and private are all fertile ground for linguistic and cultural unpacking and should be the topic of further anthropological research.

Popular domestic images of Japan's associational landscape

Civil society – that associational landscape, real and imagined, between government and business, nation–state and corporate domain – in which individual and private agency can play an important role in organising consciousness, bringing change, providing services, and working for the common good may not have fully caught on everywhere, but there is no doubt that the concept is being examined and employed in Japan. What is taking place, I believe, is a process of reconceptualisation or reimagination of Japanese civil society, echoing the phrase made famous by Benedict Anderson (1983) in *Imagined Communities*, the milestone book which examined how nations and nationalities were conceived anew as collectivities throughout the world during the nineteenth century, an important phase in the cultural biography of the concept of nationalism.

At the level of policy makers and opinion leaders, there is great discussion of both domestic and international civil society. Civil society has become a major topic of discourse among Japanese scholars, journalists, politicians, and *hyōronka* (social critics and pundits), as well as among Western scholars of Japan. However, what I found most intriguing in my research on civil society in Japan (conducted on a Fulbright during 1997–8) was the variation between the interpretations of the person on the street and the definitions expressed by dominant 'expert' voices. All those voices need to contribute to a full cultural biography of Japanese civil society.

Though Japanese publishers bemoan declines in readership, even in the age of the cell phone, the palm pilot, and the game boy, Japan is still a nation of readers, and publishers rapidly produce an enormous range of books on any topic imaginable. Benedict Anderson (1983) identified the combined forces of 'print capitalism' – journalists, rhetoric, and mass media – as key elements mobilising the imagination of nationalism and creating discursive spaces in which the new ideology of the nation could create the nation–state as a 'natural' entity, inevitable in its centrality. Japan is a perfect case for examining Anderson's concept of 'print capitalism' in the digital age where media has been a major force in the contemporary mobilisation of civil society. In particular, the new media of the Internet and cell phones have transformed communications and removed many barriers to open discourse, real and imagined. In the wake of the Kobe quake, and increasingly since, the Internet and on-line discussion groups have created a range of discursive spaces in which Japanese civil society is being mobilised.

New forms of mass media and communication have speeded up the dissemination of new ideas, concepts, and trends, making it easier to broaden the imagination of larger numbers of people. The Internet has created opportunities for new interest groups and discourse unmediated by conservative Japanese publishers, business leaders and government agencies, as well as by physical, cultural and political boundaries worldwide. Cell phones, too, are everywhere in Japan today, and in the hands of virtually every age and sector, creating a sense of unlimited connectivity. Through the popular media, the Internet and cellular communications, civil society is being reimagined into an indigenous Japanese concept to bring about changes that are barely being considered by increasingly marginalised bureaucrats, elected leaders, and corporate elites.

Since 1985, articles in newspapers and weekly magazines on civil society have become increasingly more plentiful (Yamauchi 1997; Bestor 1998a, 1999a). Yamauchi Naoto, an economist, has looked at the use of terms and the proliferation of substantive stories on the civil sector over the last 15 years in four major papers (*Mainichi, Yomiuri, Nihon Keizai,* and *Sankei*). My own research has looked in particular at articles in the *Asahi Shinbun*, one of Japan's leading newspapers. Each of us has found dramatic increases in stories that laud the activities of volunteers, promote interest in civil society, and explain the activities of NPOs and NGOs. Stories on those subjects have risen consistently from the mid-1980s, spiking dramatically in 1995 following the Kobe quake and continuing to the present.

Civil society has also made it to the Japanese popular press with such books as Saeki Keishi's *Shimin to wa dare ka?* (Who are the citizens?) and dozens of other books that crowd the shelves. There are guides to becoming a volunteer (*Borantia Wārudo e Yōkoso* – Welcome to the Volunteer World (Gurupu Kan 1997)); introductions to the concepts of NPOs (*NPO to wa nani ka?* – What is an NPO? (Dentsū 1997), *NPO Ai wo Chikara ni Kaeru Shisutemu* – NPOs The System for Transforming Love into Strength (Asakura 1997), *NPO to Machizukuri* – NPOs and Community-Building) and NGOs (*NGO Handobukku* – The NGO Handbook, *NGO to wa nani ka?* – What is an NGO? (Isezaki 1997)); and other 'how-to tips' for those thinking about getting involved. Together, old and new media, popular literature, and the organisations they discuss have created the discursive space for involvement in a newly imagined community of individual and private action, analogously invoking and drawing upon the spontaneous activism that arose after the earthquake.

Civil society is also being reimagined by various governmental, business, or quasi-governmental groups, such as Keidanren (the Federation of Economic Organisations), JCIE (the Japan Center for International Exchange), and CGP (the Center for Global Partnership) that in 1999 made civil society one of its five thematic clusters for further exploration. The CGP Winter 2000 Newsletter summarised the group's interest as follows:

In October 1999, CGP announced its new priorities in the field of civil society. The three areas of focus are the evolution of civil society, international civil society, and issues related to nonprofit organizations in the development of civil society. CGP hopes that these priorities will encourage further research and the development of new policies in this area over the next several years.

These groups have been among the principal actors and heirs to the growth of Japanese philanthropy and its internationalisation. They have actively participated behind the scenes in mobilising discourse on the need for new civil legislation.

The reimagination of Japanese civil society as a dynamic process is being negotiated by a growing federation of NPOs and NGOs working with these older organisations, along with a new constellation of academic and 'think tank' organisations (Shimokobe, 1996) that now focus on Japan's civil sector. New leaders in the field include the Japan NPO Center (founded in 1996), academic programmes such as those of Sōkendai (Sōgo Kenkyū Daigakuin Daigaku – the Graduate University for Advanced Study), its Scope Project (Study Center on Philanthropy), which utilises both traditional and internet publishing, and programmes at major universities such as Tokyo, Keiō, Osaka and others. Joining them are regional and local groups that focus on the needs of their own communities. Together, through their actions, their services, and the growing involvement of Japanese from many walks of life, there is a broadening and redefining of the appropriate spheres in which policy can be implemented (Pekkanen 2000) and services distributed by individual actors and private groups rather than through the actions of the state and its clients.

Such organisations are increasingly taking major roles in lobbying for and re-defining social policy in Japan and are expected to assume even larger roles in the future. Joining these representatives of the old and new Japanese civil sector is a new breed of politicians (*seikaku shinjinrui*), more interested in being involved in the policy process and in networking broadly within the government.

Anthropological scholarship and the reimagination of civil society

To appreciate foreign discourse on civil society in Japan, it is important to note the strongly Western models that mould the debate about civil society more broadly. So as to not privilege those 'Western' definitions as applied to Japan, it is essential to look at how non-Western models of civil society differ and need to be interpreted. Briefly, Chris Hann, who argued for more anthropological examination of the field in *Civil Society: Challenging Western Models*, offers a useful dichotomy between 'universalist' and 'relativist' approaches (Hann and Dunn 1996). Universalists draw from a Western liberal-individualist model, employ a rather 'hard' definition and hold that comparisons can be drawn across cultures. 'Universalists tend to see this civil society as a concrete and quantifiable thing ... They often confuse their analysis of what *is* with what they think *ought to be.*' Relativists 'recognize that other societies have organized their social and political life in terms of different, often incommensurable ideals (Hann and Dunn 1996: 17–18).' Hann argues for a broader examination of civil society by political anthropologists. I would argue that anthropological research on civil society should not be limited to anthropologists who focus on politics. Hann's is a useful duality to keep in mind in examining how different groups within Japan articulate civil society and also how scholars from different disciplines may interpret the role of civil society and its actors in Japan.

The majority of what is being written in English about civil society in Japan has been by political scientists and policy analysts. The focus of these studies has provided a wealth of information on the structural components of Japanese civil society including on the regulatory framework (Pekkanen forthcoming), on the partnership between state and society in Japanese welfare policy (Estevez-Abe forthcoming), and on state response to consumer activism (Maclachlan forthcoming). All of these are contained in a new volume *The State of Civil Society in Japan* edited by Frank Schwartz and Susan Pharr of Harvard University, which also contains chapters by several sociologists, historians, a religions scholar, and a social psychologist. Unfortunately the volume has no contributions from anthropologists, and focusses heavily on the role of the state, as the title might imply.

Developing a cultural biography of civil society in Japan

Since 1989, when civil society was credited with being a potent force in bringing about the resurgence of democracy following the collapse of communism in Eastern Europe, the notion of civil society has received considerable attention worldwide. The community imagined as the nation–state is not unlike the notion of civil society as it is being imagined today. Lester Salamon, a leading theorist of the civil sector, has drawn a parallel when he identified the 'New Associational Revolution,' that 'upsurge in organized voluntary activity and the creation of private, nonprofit or nongovernmental organizations' as being as significant in the late twentieth century as the rise of nationalism was in the late nineteenth (Salamon 1994; Salamon and Anheier 1997). The parallel is apt. But the Japanese variant of Salamon's 'associational revolution' is quite different from other models, both Western and Eastern European, just as Japan's concept of nationalism differed from what other 'nations' imagined in the late nineteenth and early twentieth centuries.

Susan Pharr's reconfiguration of Salamon's concept to that of the 'associational landscape' may be more appropriate for those examining Japan's experience with civil society. Her concept retains the focus on the importance of associational relations however constituted. But rather than seeing a 'revolution' in Japan, Pharr employs the concept of landscape, envisioning the contours, perspectives, shades, crevices, and streams that flow metaphorically through all human relationships. Describing much of Japan's civil society as having recently experienced state-led targeted growth as a sector provides a useful framework for envisioning Japan's new 'associational landscape' (Pharr forthcoming).

The scholarship on the field is in need of more ethnographic accounts from Japanese who are working within all sizes of organisations in the civil sector and from Japanese workers in international NGOs abroad. It should examine those who discuss the role of global civil society; and interview Japanese not yet involved and wondering what all the talk of civil society is about. Given that anthropology has always been a discipline that has studied aspects of civil society – voluntary associations such as merchants guilds, fire brigades, housewives organisations; grass-roots initiatives like consumer protests and environmental movements; and, religious, political, and fraternal associations – it is a mystery why anthropologists have not been more in the forefront of current research on the evolution of civil society in Japan today.

Anthropologists have studied 'civil society' for a long time, many perhaps without even thinking of it in such terms. John Embree (c. 1939), Richard Beardsley (Beardsley, Hall and Ward 1959), Robert Dore (1965), Robert Smith (1978; Smith and Wiswell 1982), Bill Kelly (1985), and Ted Bestor (1989) (to name only a few) have examined aspects of civil society through their research on the formal and informal networks and institutions that exist (or existed) at the local level of society. The contributors to this book all have looked at aspects of Japanese social policy. However, few anthropologists have looked explicitly at Japan's civil sector after the earthquake and since the new NPO Law. One exception among them is Lynne Nakano, who studied volunteer identities as a lifestyle choice in a Yokohama neighbourhood (Nakano 2000). Nakano looks particularly at the rise in volunteerism among men and woman at different life stages in order to try to understand how that lifestyle choice has provided new strategies for negotiating identity.

The statistical reasons for the rise in voluntary action are numerous. In the corporate environment, grass-roots volunteerism was heavily promoted abroad, and many now retiring Japanese men first became volunteers while working abroad. Once they returned to Japan, opportunities for voluntary action have dovetailed with the numbers of retiring or redundant employees who now seek new meaning in life. My own research in the early 1980s looked at the end of 'lifetime' employment and at corporate

and government strategies for older workers (Bestor 1986). Since that
research, the Japanese economy has experienced a decade of major recession and finding meaningful and paid employment is even harder for older
citizens. Increasingly, volunteer activities have become popular among
members of this age group, particularly among men, as Lynne Nakano
(2000) notes. Within some companies the promotion of volunteerism has
been further encouraged, perhaps replacing the role of the *madogiwa zoku*
(those who sit by the window away from the action – the middle
managers who exhausted their employment options within the firm before
they reached mandatory retirement.) Whether men in their 40s, 50s, and
60s are underemployed, unemployed, or retired, as Nakano found, being
a volunteer can provide new meaning and definition to their lives.

For women, employment options are even worse than for men. The
glass ceiling for well-educated Japanese women was barely beginning to
crack when the bottom fell out of the Japanese economy. The first to lose
positions, as in the past, were non-permanent employees and women,
many of whom were not in 'permanent' career tracks. Dwindling career
options, the decline in the birth rate, and the increased popularity of
volunteerism has created the peer status that motivates women to use
their organisational and nurturing skills in the increasingly valued
volunteer realm.

Nakano has provided important insights into the choice made by a
small group of volunteers in Yokohama. Yet, much more anthropological
research is needed on the role of NPOs, the formation of policy, the
participation of ordinary citizens in the policy process, and the new breed
of volunteers in all social settings and age groups. Further examination of
the ways that identity is constructed and defined by voluntary action, of
the changing Japanese articulation of self and other and of public and
private will benefit greatly from anthropological research. Such inquiry is
needed to project the individual and collective voices through which civil
society is being reimagined in Japan and to provide a textured ethnographic understanding of how civil society is being mobilised in Japan at
the beginning of the twenty-first century.

To become meaningful to all Japanese, civil society requires further
familiarisation and domestication through the mass media, political
action and word of mouth, so that more people can recognise their own
potential to create and be part of civil society. Such a familiarisation – a
reimagination – is not simply to label something that is already occurring,
but to create the conscious space in which these people can recognise
their own potential to effect positive change in society.

Chapters in this volume demonstrate how ethnography can contribute
to the study of civil society in Japan. While they may not focus explicitly
on the role or understanding of civil society, each addresses the discourse
on key social issues in which civil society is identified as increasingly

instrumental. Among the social problems that civil society is being reimagined to 'address' as it evolves are the problems of Japan's aging population (discussed by Leng Leng Thang); questions of handling Japan's sizable immigrant, transient, and marginal populations (examined in different ways in the chapters of Setsuko Lee and Carolyn Stevens and in the concluding chapter by Vera Mackie); growing social and educational inequities that will increase as the financial crisis deepens (no doubt contributing to the discovery of child abuse, which Roger Goodman addresses, and altering the ease with which the state can articulate 'normal' educational standards, discussed by Eyal Ben-Ari in Chapter five); the problems of the baby boomer generation, many of whom now think of themselves more as baby busters (certainly contributing to the decline in birthrate, examined by Glenda Roberts, which has itself contributed to changes in funeral patterns, discussed by Yohko Tsuji); and the crying need for administrative and government reform in the face of bureaucratic ossification, corruption, and paralysis. These are only a few of the domestic initiatives in which civil society is being reimagined to serve, and all are rich sites in need of ethnographic research.

REFERENCES

Anderson, Benedict. 1983. *Imagined Communities: Reflections on the Origin and Spread of Nationalism*. London: Verso.

Appadurai, Arjun. 1986. *The Social Life of Things*. Cambridge: Cambridge University Press.

Asakura Shoko. 1997. *NPO: Ai wo chikara no kaeru shisutemu* (NPOs: The System for Transforming Love into Strength). Tokyo: Buronzu Shinsha.

Azumi Koya. 1974. 'Voluntary associations in Japan,' pp. 15–26 in *Voluntary Action Research 1974: The Nature of Voluntary Action Around the World*, ed. David Horton Smith. Lexington, MA: Lexington Books.

Barshay, Andrew. Forthcoming. 'Capitalism and civil society in postwar Japan: perspectives from intellectual history,' in *The State of Civil Society in Japan*, ed. Frank J. Schwartz and Susan J. Pharr. Cambridge: Cambridge University Press.

Beardsley, Richard K., John W. Hall and Robert E. Ward. 1959. *Village Japan*. Chicago: University of Chicago Press.

Bestor, Theodore C. 1989. *Neighborhood Tokyo*, Stanford: Stanford University Press.

Bestor, Victoria Lyon. 1986. 'The Short Life of Lifetime Employment in Japan and the Long Life Thereafter.' MA thesis. University of California, Berkeley.

——. 1998a. 'Shimin shakai to wa nani ka: is civil society a transnational phenomena or a translational dilemma in Japan?' Unpublished paper presented at the Kansai Forum on US–Japan Relations, Osaka American Center, June 16. Osaka.

——. 1998b. 'The Rockefeller Legacy: Cultural Diplomacy, Area Studies and the Growth of American Studies in Japan and Japanese Studies in the United States.' Unpublished paper presented at the Center for American Studies, Doshisha University, 20 June. Kyoto.

———. 1999a. 'Reimagining "civil society" in Japan.' *Washington–Japan Journal* (special issue, spring): 1–10.

———. 1999b. 'The Rockefeller legacy in Japan: philanthropy, politics, and the molding of Japan's nonprofit sector.' Paper presented at the Annual Conference of ARNOVA, 4 November, 1999, Washington DC.

——— and Reiko Maekawa. Forthcoming. 'The philanthropic roots of the voluntary and nonprofit sector in Japan: the Rockefeller legacy,' in *The Voluntary and Nonprofit Sector in Japan: An Emerging Response to a Changing Society*, ed. Stephen P. Osborne. London: Routledge.

Bob, Daniel E. 1990. *Japanese Companies in American Communities*. New York: Japan Society, Inc.

Braibanti, Ralph J. D. 1948. 'Neighborhood associations in Japan and their democratic potentialities.' *Far Eastern Quarterly*, 7(2): 136–64.

Center for Global Partnership. 2000. 'New Priorities in the Field of Civil Society.' *CGP Newsletter*, 24: 2–8.

Choate, Pat. 1990. *Agents of Influence*. New York: Knopf.

Curtis, Gerald L. 1970. 'The *Kōenkai* and the Liberal Democratic Party.' *Japan Interpreter*, 6(2): 206–19.

———. 1971. *Election Campaigning Japanese Style*. New York: Columbia University Press.

Davis, Glen and John G. Roberts. 1996. *An Occupation without Troops: Wall Street's Half-Century Domination of Japanese Politics*. Tokyo: Zen Books.

Deguchi, Masayuki. 1993. *Firansoropii: Kigyo to Hito no Shakai Kōken* (Philanthropy: The Social Contribution of Companies and People). Tokyo: Maruzen Library.

———. Spring 1999. 'A Comparative View of Civil Society.' *Washington–Japan Journal*: 11–20.

———. 2000, 'Not for Profit: A brief history of Japanese nonprofit organizations,' in *Look Japan* (January). Tokyo: Look Japan, Ltd.

Dentsū Institute for Human Studies. 1997. *NPO to wa nani ka* (What is an NGO)? Tokyo: Nihon Keizai Shinbunsha.

Dore, Ronald P. 1965. *Education in Tokugawa Japan*. London: Routledge & Kegan Paul.

Embree, John F. c. 1939. *Suye Mura: A Japanese Village*. Chicago: University of Chicago Press.

Epstein, Stephanie. 1990. *The Buying of the American Mind*. Washington DC: Center for Public Integrity.

Estevez-Abe, Margarita. Forthcoming. 'State–society partnerships in the Japanese welfare state,' in *The State of Civil Society in Japan*, ed. Frank J. Schwartz and Susan J. Pharr. Cambridge: Cambridge University Press.

Fox, Richard. 1998. 'Cultural translation as craft and politics.' Keynote speech from the meeting of the Japanese Association of Ethnology, Fukuoka, Japan, 13 March.

Fukuzawa Yukichi. 1866 [1960]. *The Autobiography of Fukuzawa Yukichi*, trans. Kiyōka Eiichi. New York: Schocken Books.

GAP Group. 1997. *Kokusai Puroguramu Ofisā* (International Programme Officer). Tokyo: Kokusai Kōdan Katsudō Kenkyūkai.

Garon, Sheldon. 1997. *Molding Japanese Minds: The State in Everyday Life*. Princeton: Princeton University Press.

Gordon, Andrew, ed. 1993. *Postwar Japan as History*. Berkeley: University of California Press.

Gurupu Kan, ed. 1997. *Borantia Wārudo e Yōkoso* (Welcome to the Volunteer World). Tokyo: Asahi Shinbunsha.

Hamaguchi, Eshun. 1985, 'A contextual model of the Japanese: toward a methodological innovation in Japanese studies.' *Journal of Japanese Studies*, 11(2): 289–321.

Hann, Chris and Elizabeth Dunn. 1996. *Civil Society: Challenging Western Models*. London: Routledge.

Hardacre, Helen. 1991. 'Japan: the public sphere in a non-Western setting,' in *Between State and Market: The Voluntary Sector in Comparative Perspective*, ed. Robert Wuthnow. Princeton: Princeton University Press.

——. Forthcoming. 'After Aum: religion and civil society in Japan,' in *The State of Civil Society in Japan*, ed. Frank J. Schwartz and Susan J. Pharr. Cambridge: Cambridge University Press.

Hastings, Sally Ann. 1995. *Neighborhood and Nation in Tokyo, 1905–1937*. Pittsburgh: University of Pittsburgh Press.

Hayashi Yujiro. 1980. *Nihon no Zaidan* (Japan's Foundations). Tokyo: Chuokōron Shinsho.

—— and Yamaoka Yoshinori. 1993. *Firansoropii to Shakai* (Philanthropy and Society). Tokyo: Daiyamondosha.

Irokawa Daikichi. 1964. *Meiji Seishishi* (Meiji Political History). Tokyo: Tokyo University Press.

Isezaki Kenji. 1997. *NGO to wa nani ka* (What is an NGO)? Tokyo: Fujiwara Shoten.

Japan Chamber of Commerce and Industry of New York. 1990. *Joining In! A Handbook for Better Corporate Citizenship in the United States*. New York: JCCI-NY.

Japan Foundation Center, ed. 1997. *Directory of Grant-Making Foundations in Japan*. Tokyo: Japan Foundation Center.

Johnson, Chalmers. 1995. *Who Governs: The Rise of the Developmental State*. New York: W. W. Norton.

——. 1999. 'The developmental state: odyssey of a concept,' in *The Developmental State*, ed. Meredith Woo-Cummings. Ithaca: Cornell University Press.

Kelly, William W. 1985. *Deference and Defiance in Nineteenth-Century Japan*. Princeton, NJ: Princeton University Press.

Kopytoff, Igor. 1986. 'The cultural biography of things: commoditization as process,' in *The Social Life of Things*, ed. Arjun Appadurai. Cambridge: Cambridge University Press.

Kyōdō Tsūshin, Kyōdo News Service, release of 13 July 1995.

LeBlanc, Robin M. 1999. *Bicycle Citizens: The Political World of the Japanese Housewife*. Berkeley: University of California Press.

Lebra, Takie Sugiyama. 1984. A review of 'Kanshin-shugi no shakai: Nihon by Hamaguchi Esyun.' Tokyo: Tōyō Keizai Shimpō-sha.

——. 1992. 'Self in Japanese Culture,' pp. 105–20 in *Japanese Sense of Self*, ed. Nancy Rosenberger. New York: Cambridge University Press.

London, Nancy R. 1991, *Japanese Corporate Philanthropy*. New York: Oxford University Press.

Maclachlan, Patricia. Forthcoming. 'The struggle for an independent consumer society: consumer activism and the state's response in postwar Japan,' in *The*

State of Civil Society in Japan, ed. Frank J. Schwartz and Susan J. Pharr. Cambridge: Cambridge University Press.

McKean, Margaret A., 1981. *Environmental Protest and Citizen Politics in Japan.* Berkeley: University of California Press.

——. 1993. 'State strength and the public interest,' in *Political Dynamics in Contemporary Japan*, ed. Gary D. Allinson and Yasunori Sone. Ithaca: Cornell University Press.

Maruyama, Masao, 1969. *Thought and Behavior in Modern Japanese Politics*, trans. Mikiso Hane. London: Oxford University Press.

Matsushita, Keiichi. 1964. 'Present-day problems in Japanese politics.' *Journal of Social and Political Ideas in Japan*, 2(2): 65–9 (originally published in *Sekai*, January 1964, pp. 198–206).

Moon, Okpyo. 2002. 'Voluntary associations in Japan: a functional factor in the system or a changing force?' in *The Culture of Association and Associations in Contemporary Japanese Society*, ed. Hirochika Nakamaki, *Senri Ethological Studies 62*, Minpaku.

Murakami Yasusuke. 1982. 'The age of new middle mass politics: the case of Japan.' *Journal of Japanese Studies*, 8(1): 29–72.

Nakano, Lynne, 2000. 'Volunteering as a lifestyle choice: negotiating self-identities in Japan.' *Ethnology*, XXXIX(2): 93–107.

Noda, Pamela, ed. 1998. *Globalization, Governance, and Civil Society.* Tokyo: JCIE.

Norbeck, Edward. 1962. 'Common-interest associations in rural Japan,' pp. 73–85 in *Japanese Culture: Its Development and Characteristics*, ed. R. J. Smith and R. K. Beardsley. Chicago: Aldine.

——. 1977. 'Changing associations in a recently industrialized Japanese community.' *Urban Anthropology*, 6(1): 45–64.

Pekkanen, Robert. 2000. 'Japan's new politics: the case of the NPO law.' *Journal of Japanese Studies*, 26(1): 111–48.

——. Forthcoming. 'Molding Japanese civil society: state structured incentives and the patterning of civil society,' in *The State of Civil Society in Japan*, ed. Frank J. Schwartz and Susan J. Pharr. Cambridge: Cambridge University Press.

Pharr, Susan. Forthcoming. 'Targeting by an activist state: Japan as a civil society model,' the conclusion to *The State of Civil Society in Japan*, edited by Frank J. Schwartz and Susan J. Pharr. Cambridge: Cambridge University Press.

Rockefeller, John D. 3rd. 1971. 'The challenge of the quality of life.' Speech delivered in Tokyo at International House of Japan, 14 May 1971. Rockefeller Archive Center, R.G. 5 (papers of JDR 3rd), series 3, box 95, folder 776.

——. 1973. *The Second American Revolution.* New York: Harper and Row.

SCAP (Supreme Commander for the Allied Powers). 1948. *A Preliminary Study of the Neighborhood Associations of Japan.* Tokyo: SCAP, Civil Information and Education Section, Public Opinion and Sociological Research, 23 January.

Saeki Keishi. 1998. *Shimin to wa dare ka? Sengo Minshushugi o toinaosu* (Who are the citizens? Problematizing Postwar Democracy). Tokyo: PHP.

Salamon, Lester, 1994. 'The rise of the nonprofit sector.' *Foreign Affairs*, 73(4): 109–22.

—— and Helmut K. Anheier. 1997. *Defining the Nonprofit Sector: A Cross-National Analysis.* Manchester: Manchester University Press.

Schwartz, Frank J. and Susan J. Pharr, eds. Forthcoming. *The State of Civil Society in Japan.* Cambridge: Cambridge University Press.

Shimokobe, Atsushi. 1996. *Seikaku Keisei no Sōshutsu: Shimin Shakai ni okeru Shinkutanku* (The Development of Personality Formation: A Civil Society Think Tank). Tokyo: Daiichi Shorin.

Simcock, Bradford L. and Ellis S. Krauss. 1980. 'Citizens' movements: the growth and impact of environmental protest in Japan,' in *Political Opposition and Local Politics in Japan*, ed. Kurt Steiner, Ellis S. Krauss, and Scott Flanagan. Princeton, NJ: Princeton University Press.

Smith, Robert J. 1978. *Kurusu: The Price of Progress in a Japanese Village, 1951–1975*. Stanford, California: Stanford University Press.

—— and Ella Lury Wiswell. 1982. *The Women of Suye Mura*. Chicago: University of Chicago Press.

Snow, Crocker, 1973. 'Tokyo's Governor Minobe.' *Japan Interpreter*, 8(2): 185–94.

Steiner, Kurt, Ellis S. Krauss, and Scott Flanagan eds. 1980. *Political Opposition and Local Politics in Japan*. Princeton, NJ: Princeton University Press.

Sternau, Cynthia, ed. 1999. *Civil Society: Japanese Experiment and American Experience: A Report on Japan Society's Study Mission*. New York: Japan Society, Inc.

Stevens, Carolyn. 1997. *On the Margins in Japanese Society: Volunteer Work with the Urban Underclass*. London: Routledge.

Tocqueville, Alexis de. 1969. *Democracy in America*, trans. George Lawrence. New York: Anchor Books.

Tsuji Kiyoaki, ed. 1984. *Public Administration in Japan*. Tokyo: University of Tokyo Press.

Tsujinaka Yutaka. Forthcoming. 'Japan's civil society organizations in comparative perspective,' in *The State of Civil Society in Japan*, ed. Schwartz and Pharr. Cambridge: Cambridge University Press.

Tucker, Mary Evelyn. 1998. 'The neo-Confucian roots of Japanese philanthropy,' in *Philanthropy in the World's Tradition*, ed. Warren F. Ilchman, Stanley, N. Katz, and Edward L. Queen II, Bloomington: University of Indiana Press.

Van Wolferen, Karel. 1989. *The Enigma of Japanese Power: People and Politics in a Stateless Nation*. New York: Knopf.

Weintraub, Stanley. 2000. *MacArthur's War: Korea and the Undoing of an American Hero*. New York: Simon and Schuster.

Yamamoto, Tadashi. 1995. *Emerging Civil Society in the Asia Pacific Community*. Tokyo: Japan Center for International Exchange (JCIE).

——. ed. 1998. *The Nonprofit Sector in Japan*. Manchester: University of Manchester Press.

——, with Hiroshi Peter Kamura and Hideko Katsumata. 1991. *International Philanthropy Project of the Japan Center for International Exchange (JCIE)*. Tokyo: JCIE.

Yamaoka, Yoshinori. 1998. 'History of the nonprofit sector in Japan,' in *The Nonprofit Sector in Japan*, ed. T. Yamamoto. Manchester: University of Manchester Press.

Yamauchi, Naoto. 1997. *Nonpurofitto Ekonomii* (The Non-Profit Economy). Tokyo: Nihon Hyōronsha.

Yamazaki, Masakazu. 1994. *Individualism and the Japanese: An Alternative Approach to Cultural Comparison* (translated by Barbara Sugihara). Tokyo: Japan Echo, Inc.

3   Pinning hopes on angels: reflections from an
     aging Japan's urban landscape[1]

Glenda S. Roberts

When I lived in Japan in the beginning of the 1990s, it seemed I could
hardly open a newspaper without reading an article about the rapidly
greying society and the economic toll this would take on Japan's citizens
in the future. Much ink flowed in this discourse of the aging society as
national policymakers and pundits struggled to determine who would
care for the elderly in the future and how this would be paid for. Now, at
the start of the twenty-first century, newspapers still give extensive
coverage to the 'aging society,' but in the past few years, a new, com-
plementary yet competing discourse has been added to Japan's population
dynamic: the *shōshika mondai*, or 'problem of a low-birthrate society.' In
fact, in recent years the two terms are often combined, as it has become
recognised that the two are of a piece, in danger of being frayed as each
side pulls in a tug of war over funding new programmes.

In this paper I seek to analyse the *shōshika mondai* by examining a
range of public opinion from the media and scholarly publications as well
as by discussing several programmes within the 'Angel Plan,' the governmental policy to address this 'problem.' Shore and Wright (1997: 7) note
that policies both 'codify social norms and values and articulate fundamental organising principles of society, [but] they also contain implicit
(and sometimes explicit) models of society.' Through the Angel Plan and
through the windows of its implementation, we can discern a number of
conflicting models of how families should be constructed in contemporary
Japan, how couples should interact in production and reproduction, and
how institutions from daycare centres to corporations should behave to
respond to these models. The *shōshika mondai* as public discourse, at
least, is quite new to post-war Japan. The population has been declining
steadily since 1974, but only after the so-called '1.57 shock' of 1989 (when
the total fertility rate fell to 1.57) did it get taken up by the government
and the media as a problem. While we can follow the government's policy
response to it, we cannot yet know what the outcomes of these policies
will be. Each year brings new perspectives on the issue. To me, the value

of studying this current process, however, lies in what it communicates about how Japanese citizenry and elites interpret their society, and how they attempt to shape it through policy incentives. It shows us what is being contested; it reveals the models that are being held up for future behaviour. More perhaps than any other issue, this process of defining the problem and then casting about for remedies illustrates the anxiety around the rapidly changing landscape in gender relationships, employment, and family patterns in Japan today. In this chapter, I seek to accomplish three objectives. First, I lay out the parameters of the low-birthrate society and introduce the discourse surrounding its debut. Second, through analysis of some government programmes intended to make the future society a better one in which to rear children, I demonstrate some of the 'fault lines' where policy and practice are out of sync, and identify some of the voices that are influencing the shape of policy as it is made and carried forward. Finally, through the latter analysis, I make observations on the nature of changing social norms in contemporary Japan and the place of policy in urging on change or reining it in.

The coming up-ended triangle: elders

First let me drop a few historical and numerical anchors. Japan's population in 1920 was 55,960,000. It broke one hundred million for the first time in 1967, and arrived at near peak in 1995 at 125,570,000. In the post-war period, the total fertility rate peaked at 4.32 births per woman in 1950, fell rapidly to just over two births by 1955, and levelled off there until 1974 (Ministry of Health and Welfare, hereafter Kōseishō 1998: 9, 18). This first post-war drop in birthrate was caused by the prospering economy, improved sanitation, and access to birth control, and was not related to a change in the age of marriage – that came later (Kōseishō 1998: 18).

A second descent in the birthrate came in the mid-1970s. The Kōseishō notes that this coincided with an increase in married women working, a consequent drop in the percentage of fulltime homemakers, and a trend toward later marriage. In 1989 Japan the term '1.57 shock' was coined, when the birthrate plummeted below the one-time sudden dip of 1966, the *hinoeuma*, 'Special Year of the Horse,' because girls born that year were to be especially strong-willed, and parents did not consider that a desirable trait for a girl to exhibit. Hence people simply refrained from planning babies to be born that year. By 1995, 48 percent of women aged 25–29 were unmarried, as were 66.9% of their male counterparts (Kōseishō 1998: 24). This has serious implications for the size of the future population, as Japan has not shown a trend toward increases in births outside of marriage, unlike many other OECD countries. In 2015, one in four Japanese will be 65 years old or older, and in 2049, the rate will be nearly one in three (Jinkō Mondai Shingikai 1997: 2). The blame for this rapid greying of society is laid on the plunging fertility rate, down to 1.42 in 1995, and the ever-increasing life expectancies. It was predicted the fertility rate would drop to 1.38 in the year 2000. This prediction came true a bit early: as the total fertility rate actually reached 1.38 in 1998 (*NW* 28 June 1999: 18). Although the extent of the low-birthrate differs depending on region and population density (Kokudochō Keikaku/ Chōseikyoku, eds 1997), here I will not dwell on regional variations, except to note that the low birthrate is particularly acute in the most urban areas. The number of children under the age of 15 in Japan has been declining now for 20 years in a row, to reach 18.34 million, or 14.4% of the nation's total population. This child-percentage figure is the world's lowest, with Italy at 14.5%, Germany at 15.8%, France at 19 percent, Britain at 19.1% and the US at 21.4% (*JT* 5 May 2001: 2).

The big question on the agenda, as the government has framed it, is who is to do the work of reproduction in the present so that production and pension disbursement can continue in the twenty-first century. As with many European governments facing similar crises (see *IHT* 8 Jan. 2001: 8), Japan's government sees the drop in population as an economic threat, and they are trying to encourage people of childbearing age to produce offspring. Of particular interest is the push to establish a framework for a 'gender-equal' society, where women do not feel compelled to quit their jobs at childbirth, and men feel free to take childcare leave and spend time with their children. What they have found so far, however, is that this is a difficult task to accomplish, partly due to fiscal constraints imposed by the costs of the rapidly growing elderly population, and also for a lack of agreement in society on the desirability of the 'gender-equal' model and the radical changes in social patterns it would entail.

Neither the government nor the media have framed the 'low-birthrate problem' as a phenomenon to be welcomed; yet some environmentalists and scholars see benefits to a smaller population, as it could be a more environmentally sustainable one. Paul Erlich was featured in an article in *The Japan Times*, where he stated. 'I think that what the government should be doing is to encourage small families and working longer (in life)' (*JT* 13 Nov. 1999). While there would be some budget problems during the initial years when workers were insufficient in number to shore up the pensioners, Erlich notes this problem would be transitional. Furthermore, with increasing technological advances, there are fewer physical barriers to older people working, so the healthy elderly might be encouraged to delay retirement. Last, welcoming migrant workers could also remedy future problems of labour shortage.

Higuchi Keiko, a feminist scholar who has been instrumental in for-mulating the Nursing Care Insurance programme put into place in April 2001, came out in 1997 with the view that it is only natural that the birth-rate should decline, since Japan has reached the status of an aged society, and women's lives are changing. She asserts, 'We should welcome such an aged society as the first society of happiness and well-being that we have really experienced in history and seek to build the future from this standpoint' (Higuchi 1997: 46).

Finally, Gotō Junichi of Kobe University argues that it is too late now to increase fertility in order to decrease the burden on the working population in the early twenty-first century; this should have been consid-ered over 40 years ago. In his words, '... the rapidly aging society in Japan in the early 21st century is the natural outcome of the structural change in the Japanese fertility rate in the 1950s' (Gotō 2001:9). He also feels that increasing labour productivity and female labour force participation could offset the adverse impact of the aging society. Of course, prolonged recession would also accommodate a lower work force.

The Angel Plan

In December of 1994, four government ministries put together a policy plan called the 'Angel Plan' (*Enzeru Puran*) to respond to the problem of the 'low-birthrate society of the twenty-first century.' The plan was to be carried out over a ten-year period, from 1995, by the Ministries of Health and Welfare, Labour, Construction, and Education, to give support to childrearing from a 'comprehensive social perspective.' Along with this plan, the MHW joined with the Ministry of Finance and the Ministry of Home Affairs to mark policies for daycare centres as ones they wished to urgently address within the first five years, with plans to extend the spaces for infants in centres, to increase the number of centres offering extended daycare (2,230 to 7,000), temporary daycare services (450 to 3,000), daycare for children recovering from illnesses (30 to 500), and after-school clubs for school children in the lower grades (generally grades 1–3)(4,520 to 9,000), to refurbish daycare centres for multi-purpose activities, and to create local childrearing centres for giving advice and support to childrearing (236 to 3,000) (Kōseishō, Jidōkateikyoku 1996).

Where did the name come from, one might ask. Although I have queried several bureaucrats on this, I have not received a definitive reply. One MHW official did say, however, that the name probably derived from the cute angel on the Morinaga Caramel box, as well as the associa-tion of children with angels, as in, '*kodomo wa tenshi*' (children are angels). This certainly makes symbolic sense, fitting with Edward's (1989) analysis of sweets in Japan as associated with fertility.

In an interview in September 2001, a Ministry of Health, Labour and Welfare (MHLW – the MHW merged with the Ministry of Labour in 2001) official explained to me that the Angel Plan was initially conceived because the Ministry of Health and Welfare was implementing the Gold Plan (a ten-year plan from 1989 to improve welfare services for the elderly) and thought they should probably do something for children as well. This was after the '1.57 shock,' but before the population projections of the Council for Population Problems noted above. It also followed the ratifying in 1994 of the Convention on the Rights of the Child (Goodman 2000). Peng (1997a, 1997b) discusses the Gold Plan in relation to the Angel Plan, noting that along with this initiative came a decentralisation of funding that increased the burden of local governments to provide the new service. Less wealthy areas are suffering a 'tremendous financial strain' under the mandates to finance both Gold and Angel Plans, she noted (1997b: 27).

Actually, public daycare for children in Japan is nothing new. Public and government-subsidised, private, licensed daycare services have been provided in Japan since the Child Welfare Law of 1947. While they were initially intended to serve the working poor and children whose mothers were unable to care for them, nowadays they are a mainstay for dual income families, and the working poor are the minority. The problem, then, is not that there is no publicly funded daycare; the problem is there is not *enough* of it to meet the demands of women's changing lifestyles. Fees at licensed centres are on a sliding-scale and quite affordable, while the quality of care is high. According to the Japan Institute of Labour, 1,788,000 infants and children (one-quarter of all under school age) were enrolled in licensed centres in 2000(JIL 2001: 5). Of babies and toddlers, 5.6% under the age of one and 19.2% of those aged one to two are cared for at licensed centres. For these age groups, demand for places is greatest and supply short, as they require more staff and hence more expense (JIL 2001: 3, 5). For instance, at a public centre in Shibuya Ward in Tokyo in 2001, for the highest tax bracket, the fee for a child under three was ¥57,500, or about $450 per month. The second child in the same centre is given a discount (¥40,250 per month) (Shibuya Kuyakushō 2001). Unlicensed centres generally cost more than twice as much as they do not receive the state subsidies of licensed centres, although this is now under consideration. Fees decline with the age of the child. While relatives often provide daycare, casual babysitting by teenagers or unrelated others is uncommon in Japan. Professional, insured babysitting services are available in major urban areas, but the cost for a day runs well over $150 and is not an option for most families. (For an excellent overview of the history of daycare in Japan, see Uno 1999.)

A five-year plan for emergency childcare was funded by the national government at ¥18 billion in 1995. The planners anticipated ¥600 billion in additional funds over the ensuing years to 1999. They ran into difficulties, however, as the interest rates fell, the economy remained stagnant, and local governments were not eager to embrace the full plan. The news media criticised the execution of this five-year emergency childcare plan, noting that in many categories it was far from meeting its goal and would probably be scaled back. One MHW official complained in an interview in 1997 that the problem of the rapid aging of society was taking up all the attention, while people were much slower to grasp the necessity of funding programmes to make child bearing and rearing less burdensome. Since then, heavy media coverage on *shōshika* and the problems young families face today in raising children has made people more aware of these issues.

An editorial in the *Nikkei Weekly* that discussed the population projections noted that if social conditions deteriorate, the fertility rate could continue to slide. Stating 'it is not a sound society that discourages women from having children,' the *Nikkei* urged that steps be taken to stem the falling birthrate. What measures did they propose? Noting that increasing the number of childcare facilities and providing financial incentives for children are inadequate, they urged more fundamental change: an overhaul of the tax system, changes in personnel management and employment policies of companies, and a shift toward less gender compartmentalisation in housekeeping, childcare and the education system. 'Social policies must make it easier to raise children,' they stated (*NW* 1997: 6). These comments appear to be a thinly veiled barb against a perceived inadequate policy response to the '*shōshika mondai*.' A *Tokyo Shinbun* reporter dubbed Japan a society unfriendly to children, where childcare leave is unpaid (not strictly true, as workers taking childcare leave could recover 25 percent – raised to 40 percent in 2001 – of their salary through social insurance, provided they returned to their job and remained in it for at least ten months), the child allowance is only to age three (it has since been raised to age six), and the daycare system is inadequate (*TS* 12 February 1997). The *Mainichi Shinbun* echoed this sentiment, stating that the image people have of childrearing is 'hardship' not 'joy,' citing such problems as the strictly gendered division of household labour, the absence of fathers or grandparents, anxieties that one's children may refuse to attend school or may be bullied, inadequate social welfare programmes to cover children's illnesses and accidents, the high costs of education, housing problems, and worries over future environmental degradation. They also criticised the notion that Japan needs children in order to pay for the legions of future elderly. Children are not 'resources,' stated the *Tokyo Shinbun*, and the society in its entirety should take on the 'hardships' of childrearing, and enjoy its pleasures, they exhorted. Will the Angel Plan assist in bringing about such a society? How is the government planning to address the prospect of a future population distribution that may resemble an upside-down triangle? Will policies be effective in making childrearing and work activities more compatible? Before we discuss some of the actual programmes, let us look further into the background of *shōshika*, asking, why are there so few angels?

Why so few angels?

The reasons behind the low birthrate have been studied extensively of late. In October of 1997, the Council for Population Problems of the Government of Japan issued a report concluding that for both men and women, marriage rates had fallen, and age at first marriage was becoming increasingly late, causing the population projections to plummet. It attributed this to:

1. the variety of lifestyles now found in a maturing society;
2. women's entry into society, made difficult by a strict consciousness of a division of labour by sex and the corporate culture that supports it;
3. a hesitation to give up one's enjoyable life (the 'parasite single' phenomenon noted below); and,
4. unease about Japan's future (Jinkōmondai Shingikai, 1997).

A more recent survey by the Prime Minister's Office found that 20 percent of women aged 20 to 30 feel that one need not have a child even if one marries, and over 30 percent of the men and women surveyed felt that marriage is a burden. The survey was conducted nationwide in February 1999 to a sample of 5,000 men and women aged over 18, with a relatively high response rate of 70.6% (*AS* 7 July 1999). Still, there is dissent in the scholarly camps over the fundamental reasons behind young people's delay in marriage. Roughly, one could divide the debate into two camps: those who blame the consciousness of 'parasitic' young people, dubbed 'parasite singles,' who supposedly fear losing their high and easy living standard if they marry and leave the comfort and low-cost security of their parents' home; and those who blame the lack of social infrastructural support for childrearing and work in a society where the young are aiming to change the strictly gendered division of labour. The former camp's chief proponent is sociologist Yamada Masahiro, author of *The Age of Parasite Singles* (1999); the latter view has been propounded in various forms by economist Yashiro Naohiro (1999; see also Hurd and Yashiro, eds 1997; Yashiro et al., eds 1982), and is strongly in evidence in recent government programmes for work/life harmonisation. Actually both scholars have been featured in government-sponsored symposia on the low-birthrate. The government ministries, as I mentioned above, have been trying to boost the infrastructure. Let us turn now to the Angel Plan itself and view some of its programmes in action.

The projects associated with the Angel Plan are numerous and wide-ranging. Each ministry has carved out its own jurisdiction, and operates within those boundaries. The segments do connect, although the emphases tend to follow the contours of each ministry's prerogatives. What they share in common is a notion that the reason for the low birthrate is the increasingly late age of marriage, and that this is largely due to women's dissatisfaction with the burdens placed upon them under the marriage contract, including expectations that they will quit their jobs to raise children and care for the elderly of the family. This view was made explicit in the 1998 White Paper of the MHW, entitled 'Thinking about the problem of a low-birthrate society.' This report garnered much public attention, as it located the reasons for the low birthrate in the heavy burden placed on mothers, and called strongly for more participation on the part of fathers in childrearing (YS 13 June 1998: 11). Angel Plan initiatives hence revolve around lessening the burdens of childcare through counselling services, creating infrastructures to support working parents, and encouraging attitudinal change away from the professional homemaker–corporate warrior model toward one more supportive of dual parenting and sharing of domestic responsibilities. This need not suffice for married couples to have the third child they always longed for. But the presumption is that working couples who want a second child might go ahead, while single women might hesitate less at the altar if they thought they would not have to sacrifice their careers.

The Ministry of Health and Welfare

While most of the Ministry of Health and Welfare's Angel Plan initiatives (i.e. the Five Year Plan for Emergency Childcare) have to do with supporting the needs of working parents through daycare services, one that does not is quite striking in its capacity to frame and respond to an increasing (or increasingly recognised) urban social problem: the isolated and beleaguered fulltime homemaker who is home alone with her small child. (For further discussion of mothers' childrearing problems, especially *ikuji noirose*, 'childrearing neurosis,' see Peng 1998 and Jolivet 1997.) The project aims to open certified daycare centres to mothers and children of the local community even if they are not enrolled in the centres. This is a kind of revolutionary concept, as in Japan the walls of schools, including daycare centres, really indicate their separation as entities apart from the community (Tobin 1989; Rohlen 1983). Furthermore, until recently, daycare centres have been regarded as social welfare institutions for children who are lacking in family supervision. (Roberts 1994; Peng 1998). Hence, the children of fulltime homemakers were not under the purview of daycare centres.

The first example of this project in Tokyo is that of the Shin'ai Nursery School in the Koto ward, a private, government licensed daycare centre that offers care from babies through age six, plus extended hours. Shin'ai actually took the initiative to start a childrearing seminar before the Angel Plan was in place. In 1986 they instituted a telephone hotline twice a week, as they had noticed the changing character of their neighbourhood, with more and more high-rise apartments crowding the landscape. They thought the newcomers might need some assistance. To their surprise, many of the calls coming in were from young mothers totally lacking in common sense about infant care, and ignorant of neighbourhood medical and social resources. They continued the hotline, and in 1989 they began getting more serious calls, mostly from the high-rises, from women complaining of loneliness or fear that they would resort to child abuse, or complaints of intense physiological reactions against their children's presence. Most of the women's husbands were salaried employees who were rarely home but to sleep and spend the weekend, and who left all domestic chores and childcare to their wives. There were also calls about spouse abuse.

In reaction to these calls, Shin'ai began a seminar programme for neighbourhood mothers, with centre personnel looking after the children while the women attended the childrearing seminars. The Ministry of Health and Welfare heard of the programme, and eventually lent financial support to it. This allowed Shin'ai to expand their programme, so they could open their doors every morning to local mothers and children. The mothers sit and talk, while the children roam around the centre and play. The Centre also offers counselling services and continues to hold seminars. In 1995, the daily drop-in programme saw 1,180 adults and 1,382 children. The programme seems to go to the heart of the urban problem: the strictly gendered division of labour, the lack of time together as a family, and the dearth of kin or friends. It seems to offer women a space for belongingness in a welcoming atmosphere, with opportunities to actually break the ice and discuss problems. While local parks are reported to be daunting to the newcomer, this programme makes efforts to create friendship networks. Moreover, it is useful to women who are on childcare leave as well as those who have quit their jobs.

The Centre director noted that it has proved difficult to establish such a programme in areas other than *Shitamachi* (downtown) Tokyo, that lack the ethic of community responsibility for children. Even in Koto Ward, it was not easy to establish. Staff members reported that there was a lot of resistance at first on the part of working parents, who thought their own children would be neglected if additional children came in from the neighbourhood. This problem was eventually solved by hiring more staff to assist, and by convincing the parents through contact and practice that it was indeed beneficial to all concerned.

A private daycare centre in Kanagawa has established a similar programme, and the National Federation of Private Daycare Centres indicated in an interview (7 March 1997) that the Federation is very interested in promoting this programme.

The Ministry of Education initiatives

The Ministry of Education's (hereafter ME) policy focusses on providing support services for home education and childrearing nationwide. It rests on four pillars:

1. home education, that is, a system for counselling, hotlines, and media programmes to assist parents and grandparents in rearing children;
2. creation of networks for childrearing;
3. promotion of opportunities for parents and children do things together; and,
4. promotion of opportunities for fathers to participate more in their children's lives.

In Japan's central gender role paradigm of the modern era, the ME deemed mother to be the educator-parent (Nolte and Hastings 1991; Uno 1999), so I was particularly curious to see how the ME was re-creating fatherhood. I looked at their in-company programme for fathers, called 'Support Project for Fathers to Participate in Home Education,' (*Chichioya Katei Kyōiku Sanka Shien Jigyō*), which ostensibly seeks to increase fathers' understanding of their children's development and encourage them to participate more in the life of the household. This project started in 1994, and has been implemented through the Boards of Education in localities that express an interest in the subsidised programme.

In 1996, 17 local governments held 32 seminars with 2,046 participants in all. The instructors chosen ranged from university professors to NGO representatives, physicians, occupational instructors, nutritionists, educational counsellors, and so on. The content of the seminars ranged widely, from child development to parenting skills, to community involvement, to education in the 1990s, to the psychology of bullying, to dad's PTA participation and role in education, to fieldtrips to dad's workplace, to the father's role in creating a bountiful home life, and so on. I attended one seminar held in Kyoto at a local bank. It was the last in a series of five two-hour seminars for these employees. All were scheduled between six and eight at night on weekdays, with the exception of one Saturday morning session for fathers and children, entitled 'Dad is a famous chef.'

Lifelong learning was the topic the evening I was there. Along with about 35 male employees of the bank, I listened to a two-hour lecture by a professor from Bukkyō University who is an education specialist. The lecture was light-hearted and humorous. She noted that education has changed; no one can any longer afford to draw a line to say this is where my education ends. She emphasised that education is a lifelong process that increasingly calls for identifying problems and solving them rather than memorising and spitting back answers. She urged men to make a life plan that would reach to age 80, and start now to develop and expand their interests lest their wives request a divorce at retirement. She asked men to balance work and home, telling them that some children cannot draw their fathers' faces because they see them so seldom. She cautioned them against dying from overwork. She also urged fathers to communicate with their children, and cautioned that they should not rely on *juku* tutorials to teach children everything. She furthermore asserted that since children develop at different speeds, one should not judge them by graded steps, but respond to one's own child's level and needs.

The men sat attentively throughout the lecture, but they hardly cracked a smile at her jokes. There was no time for questions at the end, nor was there a chance for me to talk with the audience. The lecturer told me later that a smaller group with built-in discussion format would be better, but it would require much more time. The Kyoto city bureaucrat whom I met the next morning told me that it was very difficult getting businesses to agree to hold five two-hour seminars during the workday, even after hours. This was their third and last year of the programme; from next year they planned to go through the Chamber of Commerce and the PTA to schedule three or four one-and-a-half-hour seminars on alternate Saturday mornings when children are in school. This way, they would be gathering employees from a variety of companies, rather than targeting one company for a ten-hour sacrifice, he explained. Neither this bureaucrat nor the professor thought these seminars were very effective in changing mindsets, but both noted it was better than nothing. The overwhelming problem, according to them, is the rigidity of the work environment, which continues to demand 'service' overtime from its employees long after official work hours are over. One ME official told me that as long as this remains unchanged, these programmes would be of little practical use. What employee could spend more time with his family, given the current pressures to remain late at work?

After hearing this line of argument several times, I asked a manager of the Japan Institute for Workers' Evolution whether she thought men who were not employed as salaried workers, and who may have more flexibility in their schedules, are more likely to participate in childrearing and housework. She replied that was not the case, and she believes men's lack of participation in the household stems from the gender role paradigm, not from the work ethic per se. In other words, given less demanding jobs, men might still choose to spend their leisure time away from home and family. Doing away with *sābisu zangyō* ('volunteered over-time') is a necessary but not sufficient condition for increasing men's participation in the household.

Ministry of Labour initiatives

The second set of policy initiatives I will consider are those by the Ministry of Labour (hereafter ML), and its arm, the Japan Institute of Workers' Evolution. Broadly speaking, the Ministry's Angel Plan policies focus on three areas:

1. creating an environment that is conducive to employees' taking childcare leave or eldercare leave, including making their re-entry to work smooth;
2. creating a work environment that makes it easy to continue working; and,
3. providing support for re-employment to those who quit their jobs because of childcare or eldercare responsibilities.

The first category includes grants to companies that provide re-entry training to employees returning from leave, and offers employees, men or women, on childcare leave 20 percent of their salary during leave, and the remaining five percent ten months after their return. This was increased to a total of 40 percent in 2001. It also provides counselling and guidance to employers and workers to speed the introduction of the childcare–eldercare leave system. Finally, it offers financial aid to small-to-medium-sized firms that are planning to make the work environment more conducive to reconciling home and work.

The second category offers financial aid to companies that assist their employees in paying for babysitters or home helpers; pays grants to companies that establish on-site daycare centres; provides a telephone hotline in 21 locations throughout the country[2] to respond to questions about daycare facilities, babysitters, home helpers, eldercare services and so forth in the locality; holds seminars to encourage people and provide the know-how to make work and home responsibilities compatible; provides aid to localities that establish family support centres for children's emergency illnesses, sudden overtime assignments or other unpredictable work needs; and, offers financial grants to locales that build facilities that support the working and family lives of workers.

The third category has two programmes: one that promotes re-entry to employment by offering financial incentives; and, the other that offers information to those who quit work on account of childcare or eldercare responsibilities. Thus far, the programme I have studied is the seminar programme for those with children who wish to return to work – the *ryōritsu shien* seminars, balancing childcare and work. There are two types: one, the *kosodate ryōritsu shien seminā* (support seminar for balancing childrearing and work) aims at informing people of the programmes and public facilities and strategies to help them to work while being a parent; and the other, the *saishūshoku seminā* (re-employment seminar), aims to encourage people to think over what sort of job they would like to have after they finish childrearing and gives them the encouragement and practical information needed to land the job. It also provides financial aid for skills-related training.

These seminars have been in place since 1995, sponsored by the Japan Institute of Workers' Evolution, which has branch offices in every prefecture of the country. The Japan Institute of Workers' Evolution [21 Seiki Shokugyō Zaidan] formerly the Foundation for Women's Employment, was established in 1986 to promote the Equal Employment Opportunity Law (EEOL). In 1993, the foundation's name was changed to its current one to reflect the change in policy that was embodied in the Childcare Leave Law, that is, to encourage men to become more involved in doing housework and childrearing (lecture at *Ryōritsu shien seminā* and 21 Seiki Shokugyō Zaidan, '*Hito to Kigyō no Mirai wo Hiraku*' [Opening the Future for People and Corporations]). As with the ME sponsored seminars, a variety of people are invited to give talks, from educators to corporate managers to women who have returned to work and give accounts of their personal experience. What messages do they convey?

Support seminar for balancing childrearing and work

I attended a support seminar for balancing childrearing and work in March of 1997. It was held in Ikebukuro, in a large meeting room of a new high-rise office and mall complex near the train station. About 60 women were in attendance. Childcare services were offered. The speaker, a professor from a prestigious university, was an education specialist in his early 40s. He had been asked to tell the audience his experiences of raising three children with his wife, who worked fulltime herself until the second child was born, quit after the second child but who now had become a university student. His main points were:

1. No one lifestyle is 'right;' you need to figure out what is right for yourself.
2. You should not berate yourself for not wanting to be a professional homemaker. If you sacrifice yourself for your child, things may not turn out so well. To illustrate this, the professor noted that his second child, for whom his wife reluctantly quit work to devote herself to rearing, developed severe asthma and other problems. The child you have may not be the one of your dreams, he told us; fulltime childrearing may not be what you thought it would be, and your spouse may change. Being always by the child's side may be stressful for both mother and child, which is not productive.
3. The stress of the fulltime parenting mother may lead to child abuse, when the husband does not understand his wife's stress, and she has no close friends to tell her real feelings. Citing a European study that found that it is more healthy to have children raised at daycare centres from four months old, the professor stressed that we are no longer living in an age when having mother at home will guarantee that a child will be well raised.

From this prelude, the speaker went on to discuss his own situation, and described how he and his wife managed to balance home and child-care, mainly through making networks with neighbours and other parents at the daycare centre and through creating an independent parents' group from daycare centre parents, which met on a weekly basis to go on outings and socialise together. He also emphasised the importance of communication with one's spouse, including putting up a fight if the husband does not agree to share the childrearing. In this professor's case, he purpose-fully decided not to work so hard during his 30s, so that he could rear his children with his wife. While he heard comments deriding his choice (just think of how much you could have published had you worked harder), he felt it was worth it.

This lively lecture was followed by a question session. After much prompting, one woman in her 40s spoke up and said her husband was a very busy and pressured salaried employee, who said he could not possibly cut down on the amount of time he spent at work. Furthermore, his mother had become ill, and he expected his wife to go to take care of her in the countryside. She asked for advice. The speaker admitted that academics have more leeway than salaried employees, but he thought there must be some room for compromise. He suggested she tell her husband she has only one life to live and advised her to leave him once to show him she meant business. He also noted that no one has the right to foist the care of his parents on his spouse, unless the spouse wants to do it. In response, the questioner said that many men expect their wives to care for their aged parents, and the lecture should be directed to men.

Another questioner worried that if she went out to work, her two-year-old would eventually suffer in academic performance. The speaker responded that a warm family atmosphere is the key to children's success, not mother's presence. He also noted the importance of getting away from the paper test performance mentality, and instead providing opportunities for children to feel curiosity about learning.

This lecture was certainly not the standard fare, and I heard from a few of the women present that they had enjoyed it. The professor's message that women won't ruin their children by going out to work may have boosted their confidence, and his practical suggestions regarding creating networks of daycare parents and neighbours in lieu of family support would also be useful. But how many of these women's husbands would have the flexibility in their business environments that he had in academia? While it took courage for this professor to buck the system at the university, there is a legitimating discourse, especially in his field, that he could hook into to explain his behaviour.

At present, Japanese corporations do not support childrearing involvement by their male employees, and the only discourse that legitimates it is the one the ME and ML are pushing, through the seminar series that companies so reluctantly sign on for, and through the childcare leave that men may take but in fact very seldom do. Moreover, in his testimony, the speaker told the audience that his son, in junior high, had decided not to continue on in the Japanese education system, but convinced his parents to allow him to finish his education in England. They had consented. His account of his warm family environment that ended in his child dropping out of the Japanese education system probably came across as a cautionary tale to many in the audience, and may well have prompted the question from the woman who was worried about the effect of mother's employment on the child's school performance. How many people could afford the alternative that the professor's family chose?

The seminar was followed by the personal testimony of a woman in her 30s who is currently working part-time and has had her two children in a variety of daycare arrangements over the years. On marriage, she had quit her job, as many women do, and then took some computer coursework to prepare for her next employment. She had had various part-time and contract jobs, but could not go into fulltime work as she had no relatives to support her in childcare, nor could she afford a fulltime babysitter or housekeeper (In 1998, the basic hourly charge for a babysitter was ¥1,400 per hour, plus, in most cases, additional registration and annual membership fees, NW 20 July 1998.) Her spouse was a salaryman who was often sent on business trips, so she could not rely on him to drop off or pick up the children. She was a veteran of daycare centres, both licensed and unlicensed, and advised the audience to avoid the latter, as the facilities were not adequate and the location often undesirable, such as above a liquor shop. She praised the after-school care system for students in the lower grades.

This woman also advised the audience that private daycare centres were better than public ones, as public employees gave parents a hard time when they were late picking up the children. This is a litany I have often heard from mothers with children in public centres as well as from the management of private centres and Ministry of Health and Welfare bureaucrats. They say that public daycare employees are more interested in getting home to pick up their own children rather than staying to care for their charges, and that they lack enthusiasm for the new directive to increase daycare centre hours and to increase the numbers of infants, because they are public servants and lack a service mentality.

The speaker finished by noting that it is very important to continue talking to one's spouse, even if he is against one's going back to work. Her husband was opposed as he thought it would mean an additional burden on him, but she started gradually, first from home, and built up the work over time. This advice – to ignore one's spouse's objection, to say 'yes, yes' and then do as one pleases – is the same advice I heard at another childcare seminar, where it was described by a woman lecturer as the way Japanese women always handle men. It is also a technique many of my co-workers at a lingerie factory employed when they initially set out to work or tried to remain employed after marriage (Roberts 1994). The problem with it is the burden of fatigue it imposes on the woman worker, who essentially ends up doing the 'double shift.' The professor's advice – to fight, and to leave home if that's what it takes to convince the spouse – is certainly more drastic, and women may fear the consequences of such a direct tactic. That is, if it led to divorce, divorce settlements are generally very low in Japan (according to a 1998 survey by the MHW, only one-third of all divorced women had received a share of property or any form of compensation), and child support or a decent pension cannot always be counted on. For mothers returning to the workforce, jobs are usually part-time and poorly paid. Add to this the loss in one's social status from divorcing one's husband – especially if it was not for a culturally acceptable reason – and one might hesitate to push too strongly (Wijers-Hasegawa 2001).

There was not time for a showing of the videotape that the Foundation had made expressly for these seminars, but it is a regular feature of these programmes, I was told. The video, 'Working while raising children,' portrays a fictional working couple who, by availing themselves of their Childcare Leave Law rights and by using public services such as the childcare hotline, babysitters, public daycare centres with longer hours, and centres for children recovering from illness, overcome various

obstacles to reconcile work and childrearing. The husband in the video is
in total agreement with his wife's desire to continue work, and he vows to
support her in this. The wife, well informed of her rights vis-à-vis
maternity and childcare leave, happily notifies her employer well in
advance of the upcoming event. He greets the news with a congratulatory
smile, encourages her, and says he will be looking forward to her taking
over her important project full speed ahead when she returns from leave.
Meanwhile, he notes, he will divide up her work between two of her co-
workers. The husband decides he will take childcare leave after his wife
returns to work, and when he approaches his boss about this, the boss
says he wished such a system had been in place when he was young; he
would have gladly taken it. After each scene, a commentator's voice is
dubbed in, explaining the exact requirements of the law or content of the
social programme being made use of in the drama. The last cut shows the
couple playing in a park with their son, now a student in the lower grades.
A neighbour's child comes up and comments how cool it is that Taro has
two working parents. End of scene.

How does this portrayal of the happy working couple measure up to
reality? The Childcare Leave Law was put into effect in April 1992.
Under the law, until a child turns one, workers are allowed to take leave
from work for childcare. Either father or mother may take the leave, or
they may divide it between themselves. Employers may not refuse to
allow employees to take the leave, and it is illegal to dismiss a worker
because he or she has taken the leave. Firms with fewer than 30 employees
were exempted from this law until 1995. The employer is not obliged to
pay wages during the leave, but if a worker has insurance and has worked
for two full years, he or she is able to recover 20 percent of his/her wages
for the duration, and an additional five percent ten months following
return to work (Rōdōshō Fujinkyoko, 1996b: *Ikuji Kyūgyo Kyūfu no Naiyō
oyobi Kyūfu Shinsei Tetsuzuki ni Tsuite*) The amount of recompense has
recently been raised to a total of 40 percent.

A 1996 survey by the ML found that among people working in private
enterprises with Childcare Leave policies, 49.1% of those women eligible
took the leave (Rōdōshō Fujinkyoku 1996c: 30, 31), while 0.12% of men
eligible took it. This improved by 1999, when 56.4% of eligible women
(in firms with CCL policies) took it, and 0.42% of eligible men took it
(Kōseirōdōshō 2001a: 443). As in other countries, male workers who take
the leave are rare. Although in principle, companies cannot deny workers
the right to use this law, in fact, workers hesitate to be the initiators in a
company where no one has taken childcare leave before.

At a symposium sponsored by the ML, the MHW, and the Foundation
for the Evolution of Work on 30 October 1999, a male employee of
Procter & Gamble discussed his fear of being the first man in his

company to take childcare leave. He noted that once he returned to work, he had become something of a celebrity for it. In an interview that took place in 1998, I was told by a working mother who had become re-employed after having children that so far no one in her workplace, a semi-governmental agency, had yet taken maternity leave, let alone childcare leave. She was waiting for the environment to improve before she tried to have a third child.

It takes a brave soul to set the precedent. Even workers who wish to take maternity leave, which has been guaranteed by the Labour Standards Law in place since 1947, and which is more easily enforceable because it is under the jurisdiction of the Labour Standards Office, are sometimes denied by their bosses their right to take it.[3] It seems fair to say that the video is closer to fiction than reality at this point. At least they are trying; when I interviewed a Ministry of Health and Welfare official in 1997, his first comment to me was that despite the necessity to increase the variety of daycare options, the Ministry's basic orientation is that children are best raised by their mothers until age three. (This is commonly referred to as the *sansaiji shinwa*, or, 'myth of the three-year-old' – see Jolivet 1997; Makino 1999.) While it is certainly true that the Ministry is putting a good deal of effort into expanding daycare services for young children under the Angel Plan, one should keep in mind that their mandate as a Ministry has been health and welfare. Some officials at the Ministry are, understandably, I think, not happy with the prospect of babies and toddlers spending very long hours in group daycare. On the other hand, I never heard ML officials express negative views on extended hours of daycare to accommodate working parents' overtime duties.

Reemployment Support Seminar

Tokyo Women's Plaza was the venue for the re-employment support seminar of 4 March 1997. This three-hour seminar was composed of four parts: a lecture by a Japan Travel Bureau former career employee and upper-level manager, who is now in semi-retirement; a question and answer session; a break; and then, an opportunity to enrol in the seminar as a member. Those who enrol receive a copy of the quarterly magazine *REBE,* a publication of the Foundation that provides information on employment trends, gives advice on workers' legal rights, and offers human interest stories that encourage re-entry to employment. They are also put on the list to be informed of related seminars and events. Aside from the lecture, each participant received a thick packet of materials on employment, including a tax and insurance guide, a book on working as a *pāto*[4] and a pamphlet on *pāto* statistics, information on Foundation support projects, a self-diagnostic employment pamphlet, copies of their

PR magazine, *REBE*, and a flyer entitled 'Lady's hello work purie' from the unemployment office, which described in detail how a woman should dress and act for a job interview.

Before the lecture began, the head of the Foundation's Tokyo office gave a short speech where she explained the Foundation's purpose, and then read from a newspaper clipping of that day, where the top official of the Women's Bureau of the Labour Ministry had been quoted as saying that in this new age, men must also participate in childrearing and housework along with their wives. The lecture focussed on how to become re-employed, although the speaker admitted she had never faced that problem herself, as she had started and finished her long career at one company.

First, the lecturer explained what she called the harsh reality of working in Japan: that is, once you quit one job, your experience will not be recognised at the next job. She then emphasised the necessity to do market research and obtain skills that are in demand. Office work may have been common up to a few years ago, but it is now mostly automated, and companies are certainly not hiring mid-career entrants to do simple office work. Her next points concerned the importance of having a purpose to working, as it is not always enjoyable. She urged the women not to quit at anything, but to endure the rough times. To do this, it was important to be willing to adjust, to maintain good personal relationships and to know how to prioritise your work.

In the future, the speaker noted, Japan will have a labour shortage, and it will be the age for women. Everyone will be working, because men's salaries will be headed down. Indeed, she said, women and the healthy elderly should be working, rather than foreigners who came into the country illegally. Finally, the Head of the Tokyo Foundation office added a few words, encouraging women to work as *pāto*, and noting that the Labour Law for Part-time Workers was made to keep *pāto* from being exploited, and that many *pāto* will be needed in the future. She also remarked that not every couple could manage to have each partner work fulltime.

The questions from the audience were quite revealing. One 40-year-old woman, who had a two-year-old at home, stated she had not been able to seek fulltime employment although she wanted to, because she could not afford the daycare fees for infant care.[5] She further stated she was becoming discouraged about age discrimination, as she had been told that anyone her age was too old to gain regular employment, or even *pāto* employment. Another woman in the room echoed her statements. The speaker downplayed the age discrimination, saying that even older women could get their foot in the door if they acted knowledgeable and interested.[6]

At about 3:45, the large group disbanded into three smaller ones, with some women enrolling as members while others sat in circles and discussed their strategies with each other, the speaker, and facilitators. By 4:30, when it was time to go home, people seemed quite caught up in discussion and reluctant to leave.

The re-employment seminar programme is popular, and certainly gets a more engaged response from participants than the Ministry of Education's initiative with male employees in corporations, where the men, after a long day of work, were then required to listen to a lecture that probably either frustrated them as it kept them from the service overtime that awaited, or just made them feel worse about their inability to extract themselves from the salaryman box. With the re-employment seminar, the Foundation is emphasising the importance of work in women's lives, yet it is not encouraging women to insist on regular employment. There may be several reasons for this. Perhaps foremost, even if such programmes encouraged regular employment, the job offers would not be forthcoming. The Japanese employment structure, which features an internal labour market, offers few opportunities for re-entry at mid-life, and because the seniority-based wage remains a feature of most workplaces in Japan, age discrimination is commonplace. Women seeking re-employment are faced with this reality. They must also challenge the well-entrenched notion that a woman with children causes inconvenience to the employer. While irregular status, low-paid work might be available, secure jobs with regular status are the gems that newly unemployed men are also pursuing in this ongoing recession. Furthermore, the Ministry seems not to want to go too far out on a limb to reject totally the paradigm of the woman as nurturer and man as primary breadwinner.

Are women equal economic partners to men, or supplementary wage earners? A Foundation official remarked to me that women still think they can always rely on their husband if need be, without working. In fact, she said she still carries that attitude within herself, somewhere. Furthermore, continued emphasis on women's primary role as family nurturer allows local governments to be conservative in building community care support centres or nursing homes for the elderly.[7] As I see it, the Ministry of Labour wants to encourage re-employment in *pāto* work as women's role in the household as their husbands' wage packets head downward and their husbands' job security becomes less stable. They want to encourage women to work at least to this extent so that they will not need to further open the labour market to foreign workers in the future. The view of the Foundation official who exhorted women to get out and work lest Japan have to turn to foreigners can be found in many government documents as well as in scholarly publications. For instance, Takayama

Noriyuki, in a special issue of *Economy Society Policy*, writes, 'If we cannot leave things up to births and support for childrearing, in the end we will come to rely on foreign workers. When that happens, it is likely that the unique culture and traditions of Japan will gradually be lost' (Takayama 2000: 27). At the same time, however, the Ministry of Justice has made a new draft of its Basic Plan for Immigration Control, and while its thrust is very cautious in regard to loosening current restrictions on the immigration of unskilled foreign workers, the document does make mention that some feel that, due to the fear of a coming labour shortage, acceptance of foreign workers in such fields as eldercare should be studied. It is not known how long in coming such a decision will be (Ministry of Justice 2000).

The draft Plan also calls for an increase in the number of occupations in the technical internship category, to include agriculture, marine products processing, and hotel management. One suspects that, through such measures, some of the necessary labour will be admitted, in the guise of technical transfer rather than immigration. The numbers thus admitted, however, would not be sufficient to make much of an impact in a future labour shortage. This also makes the migration temporary, as internships are for limited terms only. Certainly, judging from the tone of this Basic Plan, migrant workers are not the government's desired solution to the problem of the low birthrate.

While a large-scale re-structuring of employment to rid the current system of gender bias and encourage more flexibility for both male and female workers could help to ensure the labour force as well as put brakes on the sliding birthrate, the ML has not yet gone after industry in any thoroughgoing, aggressive way. For instance, while the EEOL has been strengthened in its revisions of 1999, it still carries no stiff penalties for corporations that disobey its mandates. There is no Affirmative Action provision, nor any laws to eliminate age discrimination. While the MHW is beginning to require daycare centres to stay open for later hours to accommodate working parents, with weekend and late night hours also being planned for some centres, this does not question the standard of long hours of 'volunteered' overtime, but merely makes children share the burden.

In the present economic doldrums, the spectre of a future labour shortage casts too dim a shadow for most corporations to get onto the gender equality bandwagon, especially to move in the direction of family-friendly policies. Corporations welcomed the revisions in the Labour Standards Law, in effect from April 1999, to lift restrictions on night work and overtime for women workers (*AS* 27 Feb. 1999). In this sense, they rally to the cry of 'gender equality,' since it does not require any alterations in the current male work standard. They are less enthusiastic about instituting family-friendly work policies, such as shortening the work week or work day, instituting flex-time, or encouraging male employees as well as females to take childcare and eldercare leave.

Recent initiatives

The Ministries of Education, Health, Labour and Welfare have been active since 1997 in promoting a gender-equal society that would lessen women's burdens as childrearers, caregivers and homemakers, while allowing them to maintain themselves in the labour force, or to return to it. Besides the Angel Plan, several pieces of legislation have been passed that support gender equality in society and promote the 'harmonisation of work and family life.' The most salient recent laws are:

The Childcare/Familycare Leave Law (1999)

Childcare leave was established in 1992 and Familycare followed in 1999. CCL allows a one-year childcare leave after childbirth for mother or father or shared; 25 percent of salary is paid by social insurance (raised to 40 percent in 2001). FCL allows three-months leave to care for family members in need of care (Rōdōshō Joseikyoku 1999).

The Basic Law for a Gender-Equal Society (1999)

The law obliges the government (including local self-governing bodies) to devise a 'basic plan for a gender-equal society.' Furthermore, it requires the government to establish a procedure for handling complaints concerning its measures to establish a gender-equal society and to aid those whose human rights are violated (JIL 9/1999: 4).

Revised EEOL

The law, enacted in June 1997, enforced April 1999, prohibits employment discrimination against women workers; provides for settlement of disputes; punishes corporations that violate the law by publishing their names; and, provides measures against sexual harassment. Hanami Tadashi (2000: 8), however, noted 'discriminatory policies, particularly in recruitment, hiring, job assignment and promotions remain essentially unchanged.'

Revised Child Welfare Law (1997)

The law rendered parents clients with 'choice' in daycare services, rendered local governments service providers ('privatisation' of daycare);

required daycare centres to respond to the childcare concerns of people in the locale; altered fee scales to reflect varied costs depending on age level of children; raised the position of after-school care programmes (Kōseishō, Jidōkateikyoku 1997).

The council on shōshika

In 1998 the MHW and the Prime Minister's Office sponsored an *ad hoc* advisory council on the problem of *shōshika*, and it is from this council that much policy has developed. The 'Council of Concerned People to Think about Responses to the *Shōshika* Society' was composed partially of volunteers from the public who were selected through an essay contest. The council came up with a number of proposals for the government to implement, one of which I discuss below. This open solicitation of members to form an advisory council was an unprecedented step for the ministries and was regarded by them as a success. An official at the MHLW noted that they made the council open in order to include local people to create a good policy to address childrearing anxiety (*ikuji fuan*) (interview, 13 September 2001). The council was composed of members from all walks of society – businessmen and women, scholars, professionals, homemakers, retirees, etc. – and their suggestions for plans were said to be quite useful. I would venture to guess, too, that the decision to include volunteered members from the public may have also been motivated by a desire to demonstrate that the 'government' was not one-sidedly foisting population policy on the citizens, as it did during World War II.

Furthermore, the ML has designed a programme to publicly bestow prizes upon those firms that actively pursue 'family-friendly,' flexible work policies (Josei Rōdō Kyōkai 1999). This is another example of an idea that came out of the Council's recommendation (Shōshika e no Taiō wo Kangaeru Yuishikisha Kaigi 1998: 8). Although it is too large a topic to deal with in this paper, suffice it to say that encouraging flexibility in the workplace is a small step in the direction of nudging corporations to lighten the workload and respond to the needs of employees. Let us turn now to one of the MHW's more revolutionary initiatives, to which society's response spoke volumes to the contested field of family and work life in Japan today.

The Sam campaign

In an unprecedented move, in March of 1999 the MHW carried out a major campaign on TV, radio and print, to back up the 'hands-on' fathering stance they took in the White Paper of 1998. This campaign was the government's first large-scale attempt to seek to rectify the entrenched gender paradigm by urging fathers to spend more time caring for their children. They put a full-page advertisement in 48 major newspapers nationwide (see photo on page 78). One million posters were printed for display in train stations and daycare centres, and an additional 5,000 were printed to meet the demands of people who called in requesting a copy. Some ¥500 million were spent on the campaign (interview with Matsuoka Masaki, MHW 14 Jan. 2000). The poster portrays 'Sam,' the artist/entertainer husband of the then 21-year-old popular rock star, Namie Amuro, affectionately holding their baby boy. Sam is dressed casually with his long hair tied back. The baby looks out at us happily. The large print down the right margin reads, 'Men who don't do child-care we don't call dad.' In the upper left of the poster is written, 'A society that can hold the "dream" of family and childrearing.' The message under the picture reads, 'Spend more time with your kids.' It continues:

Seventeen minutes a day. That's the average amount of time men spend on childcare. Although it takes two to make a child, it seems as if Mother is raising the child all by herself. It's no wonder women don't think they can easily bear children. If pregnancy and childbirth are work only women can do, isn't childcare also an important job for men? We want fathers to better know the joys and difficulties of childrearing. We want them to think more about the children who will carry [the responsibility] of the twenty-first century for us. Please become a wonderful dad who has the time to gaze deeply into his child's heart.

To the left, a section entitled 'Aiming for a childrearing support society' reads:

The basis of childrearing is the home, but of course, the topic of building a system to support childrearing is one in which the entire society should get involved. In order to arrange an environment whereby the entire society can support childrearing and people who desire children can easily give birth and rear them, our society is preparing a cooperative system in many different areas.

At the very bottom of the poster are selected comments on the problem of the low-birthrate society, from members of a symposium on the topic held in February 1999, sponsored by the Foundation for the Children's Future, an arm of the MHW. The members are Iwao Sumiko, a renowned sociologist; Suzuki Koji, an author; Watari Sugi'ichiro, the vice-director of Nikkeiren; and Murakami Tadayuki, Department Head of Comprehensive Policy at the Rengo labour union. They offer additional comments about the social reasons behind the low birthrate and suggestions for change.

Response to this campaign was strong and varied. The Tokyo-based activist group Ikujiren (Childcare Hours for Men and Women Network)

3.1 Poster put out by Ministry of Health and Welfare captioned 'Men who don't do childcare, we don't call dad.' (March 1999)

noted those who support gender-equal childrearing were generally in favour of it, and women in particular were happy to have the government coming out publicly with this position. In their monthly newsletter, the men of Ikujiren voiced the opinion that the poster acted to validate men who are already involved in childrearing. They also claimed that Fukouin Akiko, a childcare activist, head of the group Hoikuen wo Kangaeru Oya no Kai (Parents Concerned about Daycare Centres) and member of the above-mentioned Council, was the genetrix of the idea for the campaign (*Ikujiren Nyūsu* 8 June 1999: 3). It was she who suggested to the Council that men needed to be able to imagine themselves in childcaring roles. In an interview, Ms. Fukouin herself told me that Japanese media are full of images of women performing housework and childcare, but bereft of images of men doing this work. She felt men needed an image lift, and apparently the result was this campaign[8]. Ms. Fukouin noted the campaign was overall a good one, and that she expected it to have a ripple effect. Indeed, the MHW was pleased with the campaign all in all, especially savouring the response of women aged under 40, who told them, 'You really went to bat for us (*Yoki daiben shite kureta yo!*'; interview, 13 September 2001, MHLW).

Nevertheless, there were some criticisms of the poster, from progressive activists as well as conservatives. Some Ikujiren members noted that rather than asking Sam, an entertainer with money and a flexible schedule, to be the poster dad, the message would have been much stronger had the poster man been your average salary man. In other words, the MHW should be targeting men in mainstream employment and especially their employers who frown on men taking childcare leave and keep them toiling away for long hours of 'voluntary' overtime (*Ikujiren Nyūsu*, no.73: 8 June 1999: 6. Such ideas prompted a spin-off poster created for May Day by other Ikujiren childcare activists, the Wakitas. Their poster featured a father in casual attire, holding his child, with the caption, 'Men who don't do childcare don't get called dad? Then let us do childcare without constraints!' The subtitle reads, 'Companies that don't let their employees go home, we don't call corporate citizens. A country that doesn't bear responsibility for childcare, we don't call a rich country.' (See photo on page 80). Indeed, many groups took up the slogan and used it for their own purposes. At a prestigious private university, the union proclaimed, 'A president who does not grant childcare leave, we don't call President!' Mr. Matsuoka related that the MHW itself had a taste of its own medicine, with people telling them 'A MHW that doesn't thoroughly carry out social welfare, we don't call the MHW.'

Others, however, objected to the poster for its undermining the conventional values of who a father is. In other words, a father's job is fulfilled if he brings home the bread. He toils away at this job day in, day out; what

私たちは、少子化対策で育児をしているのではありません。
自分が責任を持つ小さな命と、豊かな時間を過ごしたいから育児をしているのです。
そして、社会人として当たり前のように働きたいのです。
少子化対策もいいけれど、本当に子育てと仕事を両立できる社会になってほしい。
家庭責任と社会責任、働く権利と家族で過ごす権利。当たり前の権利・責任を果たせる社会を目指していきませんか？
そんな気持ちを伝えたくて、私たちは活動しています。

TEL/FAX:045(434)7519
http://www.eqg.org/

男も女も育児時間を！連絡会　E-mail: welcome@eqg.org

3.2   Poster put out by campaigning group Ikujiren captioned 'Men who don't
do childcare don't get called dad? Then let us do childcare without
constraints!' (May 1999)

nerve the government has to suggest that this sacrifice is insufficient to prove one's worth as a father. This sort of opinion was voiced by Inoue Ki'ichi, a 66-year-old Diet member from the Jiyūto (Liberal Party), who complained to the MHW saying,

There are mothers who are shirking on housework and childcare. [Such a campaign] will further that trend, and only strengthen types such as those female activists. How should we divide the childcare? Each household has its own circumstances, and the government should not be butting in.

The news article in which this appeared noted that Mr Inoue, a father of three, had had a career at the Ministry of Agriculture and Fisheries. He claimed never to have helped with household chores or childcare. He noted, 'My wife is a professional homemaker, so naturally she did it.' (*AS* 21 April 1999). Mr Matsuoka admitted the MHW was prepared for such criticisms but wanted to go ahead with the campaign anyway. He said that in general, men aged over 40 were quite critical, but the younger men liked the message. They felt a big gap in generational response, he noted (interview, 14 January 2000).

One indication of the effects of the Sam campaign is that months after-ward, it was still resonating. In an article recounting letters from readers responding to a recent sensational murder, the *Asahi* noted, '…Even if men want to participate in childrearing, the reality is that this is not possible in corporate society.' (*AS* 11 Dec. 1999: 27). This is followed by the comments of a 31-year-old Yokohama salaryman, who notes that it takes a lot of nerve and effort to leave work at the end of normal business hours. Then, from a 36-year-old salaryman from Tokyo, we hear further about long hours and cynicism over the Sam poster:

Under the current circumstances, I think 'Father's participation in childcare' is a castle in the air. The MHW created a stir with their poster of a popular entertainer holding his child, but it's a joke. Can't they [reduce working hours by] strictly enforcing the Labour Standards Law or legally prohibiting overtime, with no exceptions?

Obviously, the battle over appropriate gender roles is far from finished, but the lines are being drawn. As a result of the poster uproar, the liberal newspaper *Asahi Shinbun* started a special series of its own, called 'Absent Dad.' Since 2000, they have also devoted one half-page of news every Friday to columns related to *shōshika*.

On April 20 2000, Nikkeiren and Rengo, the Japan Trade Union Confederation, issued an unprecedented cooperative appeal for work–life balance, prompted by a request from then Chief Cabinet Secretary Aoki Mikio for the two groups to consult on the issue of the declining birthrate and take joint action (Nikkeiren [the Japan Federation of Employers' Association], 2000). I was surprised that two such unlikely bedfellows would be boosters of the Plan. After all, as of 1999, seven years after the Childcare Leave Law was passed, 46.5% of companies with five or more employees, and 23 percent of companies with thirty or more employees, had not put in place any formal policies for childcare leave (Josei Rōdō Kyōkai 1999: 8), and the stringent and gender-biased working environment in Japan is often noted as a prime reason for the *shōshika* problem. While it may appear to be a triumph of labour over management to see the major labour union and the major corporate organisation coming together to improve the work environment, one should not read too much into this joint appeal; labour unions in Japan have been losing strength vis-à-vis management since the 1970s, and it is unlikely that this appeal represents their having taken a strong stand against management on the issue of work–life balance.[9] Indeed, an MHLW official remarked to me that Nikkeiren's interest in the Angel Plan can be explained by the Plan's efforts to create an environment that allows parents to work longer hours without inconveniencing business; in other words, by extending daycare centre hours and keeping them open on weekends and holidays, by arranging for childcare for sick children, and so on (interview, 13 September 2001).

The campaign in retrospect

The government heeded the advice of its Council and took the lead in a strongly worded campaign. Since then, however, there have been no major follow-up campaigns on fathers' participation in parenting. Conservative politicians have considerable influence over Ministerial objectives, and the spectre of a society with few children doesn't seem to be enough to curb the anger of some elder statesmen whose feathers this poster ruffled. If there are conservative politicians such as Mr Inoue, there surely are some conservative constituents who are just as appalled at the MHW's attempt to 'educate' its citizens about proper gender roles in contemporary society. On the other hand, the MHLW is certainly going ahead with the Angel Plan initiatives, and the Sam campaign did set a progressive feminist agenda.

The responses to the campaign highlight a lack of consensus on how to solve the problem of the low birthrate. Should men spend more time with their children? Should women work fulltime throughout their childrearing years? Those who agree with this lifestyle are actually a minority. In January 2001, the Foundation for the Children's Future surveyed 1,140 people, of whom 877 were parents of children under age 15,with 499 mothers and 378 fathers in their childrearing years. Fifty-seven percent of the mothers and 55 percent of the fathers felt that mothers should stay home when the children were young. Thirty percent of the mothers felt it best that mothers continue working straight through marriage and childbirth. Only 23 percent of the fathers surveyed agreed to this, while of those men whose wives did not work, only 13 percent were in favour of mothers continuing their careers without interruption (*AS* 3 May 2001: 19). Furthermore, of the fathers surveyed, only half thought that men should take Child Care Leave.

Should the problem of an impending decline in population be solved through opening the gates to migrant workers? Or perhaps a small society will be a better one? This lack of consensus itself seems to indicate a divide on the desirability of the gender paradigm of the 'corporate warrior and the professional housewife' of the post-war period.

Some government advisory councils themselves are taking the lead in defining a gender-equal society that harmonises work and childrearing and are disappointed in the lack of progress they see to date. This is particularly true of the Specialists Survey Committee on Family–Work Harmonisation Policy, operating under the Council for Gender Equality of the Prime Minister's Office. This committee was quickly formed in the spring of 2001 with Higuchi Keiko, current Director of the Centre for the Advancement of Working Women, who spearheaded the drive for the Long-term Care Insurance Law, as the Chair. Among gender equality issues, it was *shōshika* alone in which Prime Minister Mori took a keen interest, and he asked that the committee be formed and begin work. When Mr. Koizumi took over as PM in late April of 2001, in preparation for his debut speech in the Diet, he was briefed by various ministers as to current programmes. Bando Mariko, Managing Director of the Bureau of Gender Equality, spoke with him for three hours. As a result, Mr. Koizumi decided to use 'positive action' and *shōshika* as his salespoints. Since the elections were only a short time away, he needed to have the Specialists Survey Committee produce their report as soon as possible so that he could make a 'plan with some backbone to it' (*honebuto no hōshin*) before the elections. Given the Committee's horizontal mandate, its report, 'On Policies in Support of Work and Childrearing Harmonization,' has some clout with the ministries and will be taken into consideration in policymaking (interview with Osawa Mari, 12 October 2001).

While the Council strongly supports Angel Plan policies that foster gender equality, their goal is just that – gender equality – not population growth. Their Report, issued in June 2001 and approved by all the Ministries involved in the Angel Plan as well as by the Kōmeitō (Clean Government Party) and the Jimintō (Liberal Democratic Party), has already had an impact on policymaking. The Committee states: 'The rigid employment system that takes men for its model has not changed.

Even with the legal system in place, people did not feel they could utilise it' (Shigoto to Kosodate no Ryōritsushiensaku ni Kansuru Senmon Chōsa Kai 2001: 4). In the same report, they mention that there is a need to reconstruct the whole social system itself toward a model that would support work–family harmonisation (ibid.: 3). The report later states that in order to imbue the people with new values, it would be desirable to make mandatory a five-day parental leave for fathers (ibid.: 24).

In other words, the Council of Gender Equality is pulling along a reluctant system by the nose. They do have the ear of Prime Minister Koizumi, however, himself a former minister of the MHW. As a result, he authorised a new campaign to completely eliminate daycare centre waiting lists (*AS* 19 June 2001: 28). There is some scepticism among bureaucrats as to how this will be accomplished, however, as whenever new spaces in centres are created, women's hopes to go out to work are raised, and waiting lists are created anew from the latent demand (Interview at the Ministry of Health, Labour and Welfare 13 September 2001). Among other items on the agenda of the Survey Group to push for in 2001–2002, or at latest, 2004, are reforms at the workplace for work–family harmonisation, provision of varied and high quality daycare services, a policy to provide after-school clubs wherever they are needed, and plans to draw communities into childrearing initiatives (Danjo Kyōdō Sankaku Kaigi 2001: 9).

The first Angel Plan ended in 1999, by which time it was clear that the 'problem of the low birthrate society' had not yet been alleviated. A New Angel Plan was then put in place for the next five years, with new targets but a similar overall thrust in policy. One difference is that a new goal has been added, perhaps indicating that the Ministries have decided to take seriously the advice of the above-mentioned Council of Gender Equality's Committee: that of 'Correcting the corporate culture [exemplified by] a fixed division of labour by sex that assigns priority to the workplace' (Kōseirōdōshō 2001a: 251). The Ministry of Health and Welfare and the Ministry of Labour merged in January 2001, so the Angel Plan pro-grammes that were formerly under two different jurisdictions are now in the same office. Officials reported they hoped this would mean better coordination in practice. There are new programmes, among them counselling programmes to deal with the behavioural problems and stress children nowadays are perceived to be exhibiting. These targets are shown in Table 3.1.

The MHLW is currently operating a budget of ¥315.3 billion for its programmes in the above Plan except for childcare service projects. It plans to request ¥337.5 billion for the 2002 budget (Kōseirōdōshō, 2001b: 4). Childcare service projects are currently funded at ¥449.438 billion; in 2002, the budget request will be ¥487.525billion. Of course,

Table 3.1   The New Angel Plan, 2000–2004

Ministry of Health, Labour and Welfare (amalgamated from 2001) initiatives

Category	1999	2004
Nursery spaces for babies aged 0–2	580,000 spaces	680,000 spaces
Extended daycare	7,000 centres	10,000 centres
Holiday daycare	100 centres	300 centres
Temporary care for infants	450 centres	500 centres
Multi-function daycare centres		2,000 centres
Local childrearing support (centres offering advice on childcare, childrearing circles, etc.)	1,500 centres	3,000 centres
Temporary daycare (to give care for children of part-time workers, for relief for homemakers who are ill, stressed, etc.)	1,500 centres	3,000 centres
Family support centres (membership-based local support network for childcare)	62 centres	180 centres
After-school care for elementary school students (lower grades)	9,000 clubs	11,500 clubs
Telephone referral	35 locales	47 locales
Support for re-employment	222 locales	47 prefectures
Pre-natal medical care network	10 locales	47 locales
Emergency care facilities for infants and small children	118 locales	360 (by 2001)
Infertility counselling	24 centres	47 centres

Ministry of Education, Sports, Science and Technology (amalgamated from 2001) initiatives

Child recreation centres	365 centres	1,000 centres
Children's public broadcast programme support	1300 stations	5,000 stations
24-hour counselling hotline on children	16 locales	47 locales
24-hour counselling hotline on household education	16 locales	47 locales
Comprehensive education (topic-oriented courses rather than subject-oriented)	124 schools (2001)	500 schools
Junior–senior high school combined schools	4 schools (2001)	500 schools
Schools with 'heart classroom' (to deal with problematic behaviour)		5,234 schools (half of all junior high schools)

Note: I have only listed categories with targets. The Ministry of Construction continues its efforts toward subsidizing building affordable spacious housing in urban areas and creating safe environments where children can play. No targets as such are listed in the New Angel Plan, however.
Source: Kōseishō Jidōkateikyoku, 2000: 24–7.

whether these levels of funding will be achieved or not depends on the coming state of the economy and political will. On the heels of the Angel Plan funding, there is always funding for the Gold Plan. In April 2001, Japan put in place an ambitious and costly Long-term Care Insurance Plan. Although it is intended to provide services for people in need of care rather than pay families to provide the care themselves, for a variety of reasons, this goal will take a long time to achieve fully (Morikawa, 2001). As Maeda (2000: 66) notes, in a society that is aging faster than any other first world country, and where institutional support for eldercare has been slow off the starting blocks, women and family will still be expected to be the mainstays of eldercare. This, of course, runs counter to encouraging women to remain in the labour force. Maeda remarks:

We should pay attention to the fact that in our country, there exist in parallel both the expectation on the part of the labour administration that women will be workers for the labour market, and the expectation on the part of the welfare administration that family (women) will be caregivers.

Japanese women themselves are fully aware of the weight of these expectations.

Conclusion

Government initiatives to solve the 'low-birthrate society' point to a panoply of contradictions in social institutions. Women are encouraged to become highly educated but are not encouraged to use this human capital in long-term employment. They are urged to become homemaker mothers, yet, until recently, there has been no framework to provide psychological, emotional and physical support and relief from the solitary role of child-minder. While women desire to marry some day, they delay it out of the knowledge that marriage severely curtails a woman's autonomy, and few young men are ready or able to be equal partners in the endeavour, as they themselves see their autonomy evaporating. Marriage, child bearing and rearing are difficult for women, whether or not they wish to remain active in the labour force. It is women, through their increasingly late marriages and work and leisure-oriented lifestyles, who have pushed demographics to the point where the government has seen the consequences of inaction in gender equality programmes. As Harada Sumitaka puts it,

... the declining birthrate may be taken as an unconscious or tacit resistance against the society by the family, which has been forced to bear various burdens to sustain the country's economic growth – and especially by women, many of whom, while holding jobs of their own, have been doing a large portion of the domestic work to sustain the 'self-support principle of the family' (1996: 56).

In a column in the *Asahi Shinbun*, former Diet member and former Vice Prime Minister Gotoda Masaharu noted that much more in the way of funds, coordination and goal-setting is needed in order to make an adequate support infrastructure to halt the slide in the birthrate (*AS* 6 November 1999: 7). By now, this is beginning to take hold. But the funding is the easy part.

As I understand it, the foremost problem is that the Angel Plan lacks the social consensus necessary to put in place the funding and comprehensive programmes, including penalties for violations of laws such as the Childcare Leave Law. As the Ikujiren citizens' group notes, nothing much will change without corporations changing to allow employees to have the flexibility to respond to family as well as work needs. This view is echoed by Takayama Noriyuki (2000: 27), when he says,

At present, as policies to address the low birthrate, childcare leave and the daycare system are the only two policies really functioning ... we must raise a 'third pillar' for childrearing support, of reconsidering traditional labour practices and the overly long, restrictive work hours.

Work is incompatible with family life due to corporations' demands on employees' time. So far, government ministries are not addressing this core issue aggressively enough. This is quite in line with Japan's 'soft' approach of using administrative guidance rather than strict disincentives when trying to make changes in society that are ahead of public opinion, as in the EEOL legislation of 1986 (Upham 1987; Parkinson 1989; Boling 1998).

Meanwhile, the average family is still muddling along, and the recession is now official with the unemployment rate over five percent (*NW* 5 November 2001). The bad economy, lack of confidence in the future, and the looming weight of the senior generation are all of a piece. As Osawa (2000: 18) notes, '... no amount of well-meaning policy statements on gender can offset the impact of dwindling income and mounting job insecurity on people's willingness to have bigger families.' Nevertheless, one effective stimulus toward stronger support for gender equality in the workplace and at home is coming from women themselves. If younger women continue to vote with their feet by veto, delaying or resisting the marriage contract that carries with it the burden of maintaining the household and rearing the children, and if middle-aged women refuse to carry the full burden of eldercare, they will push social institutions to change. Whether or not the *shōshika mondai* is actually alleviated by the Angel Plan programmes, *shōshika* may end up to be just what Japan needs to give women and men more options in their lifestyles and make gender-equality more than simply rhetoric.

NOTES

1   I have been pursuing research on the Angel Plan since 1996, first while as a
    Visiting Professor at the Institute for Social Science at the University of
    Tokyo, and since 1998 while Associate and then full Professor at the Institute
    of Asia-Pacific Studies, Waseda University. I would like to thank Jim Nickum,
    Ito Peng and Patricia Boling for their helpful comments on earlier versions of
    this manuscript.
2   Hokkaidō, Miyagi, Fukushima, Ibaragi, Saitama, Chiba, Tokyo, Kanagawa,
    Niigata, Nagano, Gifu, Shizuoka, Aichi, Kyoto, Osaka, Hyōgo, Okayama,
    Hiroshima, Aichi, Fukuoka, and Kumamoto.
3   Personal communication from Professor Osawa Mari of University of Tokyo
    Institute of Social Science, 12 October 2001.
4   *Pāto*, from the English 'part-time,' refers to irregular employment, paid by the
    hour, usually with few benefits and low wages. The number of hours worked are
    not necessarily less than those of regular employees, although they usually are.
5   In view of this mother's comment, it is interesting to note Peng's comment
    on the increase in number of daycare spaces through Angel Plan initiatives:
    '...many of the proposed day care spaces will be provided by the private for-
    profit sector and hence will not help mothers with low-paying part-time jobs
    (Peng 1997a: 30).'
6   The Employment Measures Law was revised and took effect in October 2001.
    In the revisions, it is stated that employers are no longer able to restrict jobs
    to people within certain age ranges, but the *Asahi Shinbun* reported that since
    the MHLW 'has issued guidelines setting out some broad-ranging exceptions
    when the law will not apply,' it will be of little use (Suzuki Yoshiko 2001: 25).
7   For a thorough discussion of women's burden in eldercare in Japan, see Ito
    Peng, 1997b.
8   This interview with Ms. Fukouin, on November 4, 1999, concerned the
    current directions of government policy in regard to child welfare issues, and
    the responses of the activist group that she leads to these initiatives. I con-
    ducted this interview together with Patricia Boling.
9   I say this from an interview with Osawa Mari on 12 Oct. 2001, but it is also
    true from my experience of research on unions in Japan that the keenest
    issues are wages and job stability. I would be surprised to see 'Family-friendly'
    policies on the front burner.

REFERENCES

Newspapers cited in the text:
AS: *Asahi Shinbun* (Asahi Newspaper)
IHT: *International Herald Tribune*
JIL: *Japan Institute of Labour*
JT: *Japan Times*
MS: *Mainichi Shinbun* (Mainichi Newspaper)
NW: *Nikkei Weekly*
TS: *Tokyo Shinbun* (Tokyo Newspaper)
YS: *Yomiuri Shinbun* (Yomiuri Newspaper)

Boling, Patricia. 1998. 'Family policy in Japan.' *Journal of Social Policy*, 27(2): 173–90.

Danjo Kyōdō Sankaku Kaigi, Shigoto to Kosodate no Ryōritsushiensaku ni Kansuru Senmon Chōsa Kai. 2001. 'Shigoto to kosodate no ryōritsu shiensaku ni tsuite (On the policies for harmonisation of work and child-rearing)'. Prime Minister's Office: Office of Gender Equality.

Edwards, Walter. 1989. *Modern Japan through its Weddings: Gender, Person and Society in Ritual*. Stanford, California: Stanford University Press.

Goodman, Roger. 2000. *Children of the Japanese State: The Changing Role of Child Protection Institutions in Contemporary Japan*. Oxford and New York: Oxford University Press.

Gotō, Junichi. 2001. 'Aging society and the labor market in Japan: should the fertility rate be raised now – No!' *Japan Labor Bulletin*, 40(9).

Hanami, Tadashi. 2000. 'Equal employment revisited.' *Japan Labor Bulletin*, 39/1: 5–10.

Harada, Sumitaka. 1996. 'The aging society, the family, and social policy.' *University of Tokyo Institute of Social Science Occasional Papers in Law and Society*, 8.

Higuchi, Keiko. 1997. 'Toward a bright and cheerful aged society with fewer children,' pp. 45–53 in *What is Needed for a Rapidly Aging Society*, ed. Foreign Press Center, Japan. *Reference Reading Series 26* (March).

Hurd, Michael D. and Naohiro Yashiro, eds. 1997. *The Economic Effects of Aging in the United States and Japan*. Chicago: University of Chicago Press.

Jinkō Mondai Shingikai. 1997. 'Shōshika ni kansuru kinhonteki kangaekata ni tsuite – jinkō genshō shakai, mirai he no sekinin to sentaku (On the basic viewpoint regarding the trend towards fewer children – a society of decreasing population: responsibilities and choices for the future).' Tokyo: Policy Planning and Evaluation Division, Ministry of Health and Welfare.

Jolivet, Muriel. 1997. *Japan: The Childless Society?* London and New York: Routledge.

Josei Rōdō Kyōkai. 1999. *'Fuamirī-Furendorī' Kigyō wo Mezashite* (Aiming for 'Family Friendly' Corporations). Tokyo: Josei Rōdō Kyōkai.

Kokudochō Keika/Chōseikyoku, eds. 1998. *Chīki no Shiten kara Shōshika wo Kangaeru: Kekkon to Shussei no Chīki Bunseki* (Looking at the Low Birthrate from a Regional Perspective: A Regional Analysis of Marriage and Birth). Tokyo: Okurashō Insatsukyoku.

Kōseirōdōshō. 2001. *Kōseirōdō Hakusho* (White Paper of the Ministry of Health, Welfare and Labour for 2001). Tokyo: Kōseirōdōshō (Ministry of Health, Welfare and Labour).

Kōseirōdōshō. 2001. 'Heisei 14 nendo Kōseirōdōshō Koyōkintō/jidōkateikyoku Gaisan Yōkyū no Gaiyō (Summary of Request for Estimated Expenditures of the MHRW Employment Equality and Child and Family Bureau for 2002).'

Kōseishō, Jidōkateikyoku. 1996, *Enzeru Puran, Kongo no Kosodate Shien no tame no Shisaku no Kihonteki Hōkō ni tsuite* (The Basic Direction of Policies for Childrearing Support in the Future: The Angel Plan). Tokyo: Kōseishō.

——. 1997. *Jidōfukushihō Kaisei no Pointo* (Main Points in the Changes in the Child Welfare Law). Tokyo: Gyōsei.

——. 2000. *Shoshika Taisaku Sokushin Kihon Hōshin to Shin Enzeru Puran* (Basic Policy on the Promotion of Policies for the Low Birthrate and the New Angel Plan). Tokyo: Ministry of Health, Labour and Welfare, Bureau of Children and Families.

Kōseishō. 1998. *Kōseisho Hakusho Heisei 10-nen ban, Shōshika wo Kangaeru* (MHW White Paper for 1998: Thinking about The Low-Birthrate Society). Tokyo: Ministry of Health and Welfare.

Maeda, Nobuhiko. 2000. Shigoto to Katei Seikatsu no Chōwa: Nihon, Oranda, Amerika no Kokusai Hikaku (Harmonisation of Home and Work Life: An International Comparison of Japan, Holland, and the USA). Tokyo: Nihon Rōdō Kenkyōkikō.

Makino, Katsuko. 1999. 'Hahaoya, chichioya no seikatsu to kodomo – kodomo ga sodatsu kankyō toshite no kazoku (Children and the lifestyle of mothers and fathers: family as the environment in which children are raised),' in *Hendōsuru Kazoku: Kodomo – jendā – kōreisha*, ed. Shadanhojin Nihon Kasei Gakkai. Tokyo: Kenpakusha.

Ministry of Justice. 2000. 'Basic plan for immigration control (the 2nd edition).' Website http://www.moj.go.jp/ENGLISH/IB/IB2000/ib.htm.

Morikawa, Mie. 2001. 'Problems and future directions of the long-term care insurance system in Japan: rethinking substitution and compensation for family care.' Unpublished paper given at Problems and Future Issues of Long-term Insurance System in Japan, Seoul, 22 June.

Nikkeiren. 2000. Website: WWW://nikkeiren.or.jp/index.html.

Nolte, Sharon and Sally Ann Hastings. 1991. 'The Meiji state's policy toward women, 1890–1910,' pp. 151–74 in *Recreating Japanese Women, 1600–1945*, ed. Gail Lee Bernstein. Berkeley: University of California Press.

——. 1997a. 'Impact of welfare reform in Japan since 1980: with focus on issue of the ageing society.' *Japanese Journal of Social Services Reprint*, no. 1.

Osawa, Mari. 2000. 'Government approaches to gender equality in the mid-1990s.' *Social Science Japan Journal*, 3(1:) 3–19.

Parkinson, Lorraine. 1989. 'Japan's Equal Opportunity Employment Law: an alternative approach to social change.' *Columbia Law Review*, 89(3): 604–61.

Peng, Ito. 1997a. 'Impacts of welfare restructuring in Japan, 1980–1995: dilemmas of welfare in transition,' pp. 5–35 in *States Markets, Communities: Remapping the Boundaries*, ed. Peter Saunders and Tony Eardley. Proceedings of the National Social Policy Conference, Sydney, 16–18 July, 1997: Volume 2. New South Wales: Social Policy Research Centre.

——. 1997b. 'Impact of welfare reforms in Japan since 1980: with focus on issue of the ageing society.' *Japanese Journal of Social Services*, no. 1.

——. 1998. 'Recent reforms in day care policies in Japan,' Draft manuscript for edited volume by Thomas Boje and Arnlaug Leira. Presented at the International Sociological Association, World Congress, Montreal, July 1998.

Roberts, Glenda S. 1994. *Staying on the Line: Blue-Collar Women in Contemporary Japan*. Honolulu: University of Hawaii Press.

Rōdōshō, Fujinkyoku. 1996a. 'Shigoto to katei no ryōritsu no tame ni: ryōritsu shiengyō no goannai (Making work compatible with family: a guide to support services).' Tokyo: Rōdōshō Fujinkyoku pamphlet no. 86.

——. 1996b. 'Ikuji kyūgyō kyūfu no naiyō oyobi kyūfu shinsei tetsuzuki ni tsuite (The provision of childcare leave: content and procedures for application).' Tokyo: Ministry of Labour.

——. 1996c. *Joshi Koyō Kanri Kihon Chōsa – Ikuji, Kaigokyūgyō Seido nado Jisshi Jōkyō Chōsa Kekka Hōkoku Shō* (Report of Results on Basic Survey of Women's Employment: Survey of Conditions from Implementation of the

Childcare and Eldercare Leave Systems). *Fujinkyoku Chōsa Shiryō* no. 28. Tokyo: Rōdōshō Fujinkyoku.

Rōdōshō, Joseikyoku. 1999. 'Ikujikyūgyō ya kaigokyūgyō wo suru kata wo keizaitekini shien shimasu (We will financially assist those who take childcare leave and familycare leave).' Tokyo: Rōdōshō, Joseikyoku.

Rōdōshō, Joseikyoku, Joseifukushika. 2000. 'Josei no ikujikyūgyo shutokusha ha hansū wo koe, 100 nin ijō jigyōshō de ha nanawari ijō ni (Women who take childcare leave now over half, and over seventy percent in workplaces of over 100 people).' in *Women and Work*, 133(286): 8–11.

Rohlen, Thomas P. 1983. *Japan's High Schools*. Berkeley: University of California Press.

Shibuya Kuyakushō. 2001. *Hoikuen Annai Heisei 13 Nen Ban* (Guide to Daycare Centres, 2001 Edition). Tokyo: Shibuya Ward Office Welfare Section Daycare Department, Daycare Section.

Shigoto to Kosodate no Ryōritsushiensaku ni Kansuru Chōsa Kai. 2001. *Shigoto to Kosodate no Ryōritsushiensaku ni Tsuite* (On Policies for the Harmonisation of Work and Childrearing). Tokyo: Prime Minister's Office, Bureau of Gender Equality, 19 June.

Shōshika e no Taiō wo Kangaeru Yūishikisha Kaigi. 1998. 'Yume aru katei zukuri ya kosodate ga dekiru shakai wo kizuku tame ni [teigen] (Towards building a society where [people can] make households with vision and are able to rear children).'

Shore, Cris and Susan Wright, eds. 1997. *The Anthropology of Social Policy*. London and New York: Routledge.

Smith, Robert J. 1983. *Japanese Society: Tradition, Self and the Social Order*. Cambridge, London, New York, New Rochelle, Melbourne and Sydney: Cambridge University Press.

Suzuki, Yoshiko. 2001. 'Age discrimination law lacks teeth.' *Asahi Shinbun* (19 September): 25.

Takayama, Noriyuki. 2000. 'Dansei no hatarakikata wo kaeyō (Let's change men's workstyle),' pp. 24–27 in *ESP* (*Economy Society Policy*), April, special issue, *Jinkō Genshō Shakai wo Koete* (Overcoming the Low-Birthrate Society). Tokyo: Keizai Kikakushō.

Tobin, Joseph J., Wu, David and Dana Davidson. 1989. *Preschools in Three Cultures*. New Haven: Yale University Press.

Uno, Kathleen. 1999. *Passages to Modernity. Motherhood, Childhood, and Social Reform in Early Twentieth Century Japan*. Honolulu: University of Hawaii Press.

Upham, Frank K. 1987. *Law and Social Change in Postwar Japan*. Cambridge, Mass. and London: Harvard University Press.

Wijers-Hasegawa, Yumi. 2001. 'Single mothers left out in financial cold: more women are in need of support, but welfare pie is not growing.' *Japan Times* (30 October): 3.

Yamada, Masahiro. 1999. *Parasaito Shinguru no Jidai* (The Age of Parasite Singles). Tokyo: Chikumo Shobo.

Yashiro, Naohiro. 1999. *Shōshi Kōreika no Keizaigaku: Shijō Jūshi no Kōzō Kaikaku* (The Economics of the Aging/Low-Birthrate Society: Market-Centred Structural Reform). Tokyo: Tōyō Keizai Shinpōsha.

—— et al., eds. 1982. *Japan's Rapidly Aging Population*. Tokyo: Foreign Press Centre, Japan.

4 Reproducing identity: maternal and child healthcare for foreigners in Japan

Carolyn S. Stevens and Setsuko Lee

One of this volume's goals is to examine the way state policies affect individual lives. Here, we are looking at two sets of public policy: one from the Ministry of Health and Welfare, the other from the Ministry of Justice. We are particularly interested in the way the former provides guidance and funding to public hospitals and health centres, and in the way the latter, amongst other things, determines who is eligible to receive these public health services. This chapter sets out government policies regarding both nationality and maternal and child healthcare amidst a growing foreign population in Japan. Health statistics of foreign mothers and their children in Japan differ from their Japanese counterparts. It is our contention that legal as well as cultural stresses on the foreign mother in Japan make it difficult for her to access the healthcare she needs and this leads to higher risk pregnancies.

The great majority of people involved in research on maternal and child health (hereafter, MCH) care are medical professionals, but this area is also of interest to the anthropologist because it throws into relief notions of the collective and the individual in terms such as the 'family' and 'identity' in a changing society. Kinship has long been anthropological territory but recent developments mean that traditional analyses may no longer apply. The *ie* (extended household, or sometimes called the stem family) and the *koseki* (the household register), two social institutions often used to define individuals in Japan, have always been considered essentially Japanese. In fact, the *koseki* can be seen as a kind of co-requisite to Japanese citizenship. The *koseki* makes the patrilineal family a required ideological structure to which everyone must subscribe. Because most of the foreigners marrying Japanese today are women, they are automatically disadvantaged in two ways: first, because they are foreign (and thus cultural and legal outsiders); and second, because they are women (subordinated to a patriarchal system). Children of these marriages are less easily categorised as many have 'Japanese' blood and a name, which gives them, according to the state, access to Japanese citizenship. Their simultaneous foreignness, however, makes them unlike their 'fully Japanese' peers.

This brings up a second anthropological concern. 'Race,' 'nationality,' and 'ethnicity' are blurry concepts that differ but may overlap in meaning. However, it is important to note that these categories are constructed ones, and are often created to promote specific economic and political agendas. Precisely because boundaries are blurred, issues become clearer in oppositional contexts. The study of foreigners in Japan tells us a little about the immigrants' host culture, but tells us much more about Japan.

The perception of ethnicity does not just change the way foreign individuals are viewed and how they participate in Japanese society. Public health laws, influenced by abstract notions of ethnicity, affect real people's health. We will show that concomitant with increases in the birth rates of foreign women in Japan, we see a rise in problematic statistics for foreign women and their children. Foreigners have higher infant and maternal mortality and foetal death rates than Japanese nationals. To date, no new policies to deal with this emerging public health problem have been established, and this suggests a dual reality of health and welfare for different residents in Japan.

We also include a more reflective section on the experience of carrying, delivering and raising a child in contemporary urban Japan, based on the experience of one of the authors. This discussion, while demonstrating only some of the difficulties that foreign mothers experience in Japan (limited to the author's experience as an American married to a Japanese), illustrates a somewhat unusual application of the participant-observer methodology in traditional anthropology.

Maternal and child healthcare in Japan

Public healthcare in Japan is organised in a multi-layered fashion, where services are delivered and administered by national, prefectural and municipal government offices. The central Ministry of Health and Welfare (hereafter, MHW) subsidises local organisations to carry out national programmes as well as the administration of local health centres. Public maternal and child health activities at local centres include educational programmes, free check-ups for pregnant and puerperal women, infants and preschool children, immunisations and home visits to mothers of premature babies. In the past, a MCH centre was a place where maternal health services were actually delivered by public health nurses and midwives. After 1955, due to the restructuring of the Japanese medical system, there was a rapid increase in the number of women choosing both to receive prenatal healthcare and to deliver their babies in hospitals. Currently, the Japanese obstetricians' 'access to and control over specialized obstetrical technology reflect and legitimate ... authoritative status' (Fiedler 1996: 195). Thus, MCH centres have come to serve a primarily educational function in the community.

The quality of the services available to expecting and new mothers is relatively high. Health officials make this claim based on statistics for Japanese nationals (see row 1 in Table 4.3). Japan's infant mortality rate is the lowest in the world; the perinatal mortality rate is also one of the lowest in the world (Mothers' and Children's Health and Welfare Association 1992: 4–5). In fact, the survival rate of extremely low birth weight infants in Japan is so high that doctors working in this area have been criticised for contributing to an increase in the number of handi-capped children (Nishida 1993: 611). Though the maternal mortality rate has declined sharply in the last 80 years, it is still higher than other industrialised countries (Mothers' and Children's Health and Welfare Association 1992: 7). The subsidisation of perinatal and neonatal inten-sive care units by the national government has also increased Japanese nationals' access to high quality foetal and infant healthcare (ibid.: 8).

A legal structure accompanies this medical system to ensure that Japanese citizens have access to healthcare. Three welfare laws provide specific benefits and services to all pregnant women and their children in Japan: the maternal and child healthcare law (Boshi Hokenhō, ratified in 1965), the child welfare law (Jidō Fukushihō, ratified in 1947) and the childbirth assistance programme (*shussan enjo*) under the livelihood assis-tance law (Seikatsu Hogohō, enacted 1950). All Japanese citizens and legal residents are eligible for these benefits and services. Services provided by these programmes include prenatal and postnatal check-ups for mothers, check-ups and vaccinations for the child, introductions to and support for entry to *josan'in* ('maternal homes' or birthing centres) and daycare centres, and counselling on childcare (for details on programmes and availability, see Lee 1994: 627). In order to receive the services, a preg-nant woman registers with her local public health centre and there she is given a Maternal and Child Healthcare Handbook (*Boshi Techō*). This book contains health information and coupons for check-ups and immunisa-tions, and acts a record for the child's birth. This is extremely important for foreigners, as this book, along with a hospital birth certificate, provides sufficient documentation for establishing foreign citizenship.

In sum, the MCH services available in Japan are among the best in the world. They are offered to the public on a local level, controlled by a central ministry. The onus of responsibility to receive healthcare is on the individual.

Foreigners in Japan since the 1980s: from migration to maternity

The phrase *uchi naru kokusaika*, or 'internal internationalisation,' is a term first used in the late 1980s by resident Korean authors and activists. They wanted to problematise the word *kokusaika*, or Japan's recent attempts at internationalising certain aspects of Japanese life (trade and education, for example). It was thought that *kokusaika* was merely a means to protect and promote Japan's place in the global political economy, not to truly change ethnocentric policies regarding foreigners living in Japan. For some, 'internationalisation' also connotes by extension a new sense of nationalism, as Japan's current relations with other countries for the most part revolve around Japan's role as creditor not only in the third world but also to its former occupier, the United States (Ikeda and Amano 1988: 21). Hashimoto Masaru notes with irony that a practical outcome of 'internationalisation' in Japan has been a loss of sensitivity to the human rights of others, as Japan's place in the global economy has risen to unprecedented heights (1995: 109). The concept of 'internal internationalisation' calls attention to the *domestic* issues that are a result of international demographic changes.

During the 1980s 'bubble economy,' there was an acute labour shortage, mainly in manufacturing and construction, as young Japanese chose to work in other areas such as the service industry. These economic choices are further exacerbated by a decreasing birthrate in Japan; there are fewer and fewer young people able to fill jobs in less desirable industries. This is the major demographic reason given as a cause for the continuance and worsening of Japan's labour shortage in the near future.

In response to labour shortages, the Japanese government made allowances to permit some foreigners to perform unskilled labour, but even these changes in migration patterns are closely influenced by the prevailing social ideology. Japanese legislation allows *Nikkeijin* (foreigners of Japanese descent) to migrate for short periods of time.

If immigrants can prove Japanese ancestry, they can receive a 'trainee' visa that allows for study and employment for a period of time in Japan. Most of these immigrants come from Brazil and Peru. This policy has proved problematic as it attempts to counter the 'internationalisation' of society by bringing in 'Japanese' foreigners. Furthermore, this has led to the 'destruction of the *Nikkei* communities in Latin America' as sudden increases in migration cause the deterioration of these districts' business and social activities (Komai 1995: 203, 205).

Labour was not the only reason for an increase in immigration. A shortage of marriageable women in Japan, especially in rural areas, caused a demographic crisis as women sought better educational and vocational opportunities in urban areas (see Keizai keikaku chō sōgō keikakukyoku 1989; Nihon Seisansei Honbu Rōdōkyōgi seijō iinkai, 1992; Hanami Tadashi and Kuwahara Yasuo 1993 and Sōmuchō gyōsei kansatsu kyoku 1992). The practice of 'international marriage' helped to reconcile this demographic crisis, but we will see this practice is not limited to rural Japan.

Meanwhile, demographic pressures in Japan were augmented by economic conditions abroad. In the Philippines, the internal employment situation has worsened since the mid eighties; in 1987, the official unemployment rate was 14.2% but considering that only 57 percent of the population was working at fulltime jobs, we can consider that 43 percent of the Filipino population is either unemployed or underemployed (Komai 1995: 165). The official unemployment rate in Thailand as of 1993 was 9.1%, but this figure discounts housewives, students and those deemed 'unfit for work' (Ishii and Yoshikawa 1993: 148). In Thai agricultural areas, seasonal unemployment ranges from 16 to 19 percent, depending on the region (ibid.: 149). Asian governments encourage migration to alleviate the situation.

Unemployment is not the only reason for increases in migrant labour. Shortages of foreign currency and trade imbalances in these countries are acute. In the late 1980s, the Philippines' balance of payments worsened considerably, with a 1987 figure of US$28 billion in foreign debt (Komai, 1995: 165). In Thailand, during this time there was an increasing imbalance of trade with Japan: in 1965 it was 2.78 billion baht in Japan's favour; in 1975 it was 8 billion; in 1985 it was 41 billion and in 1991 it was 150 billion (Ishii and Yoshikawa 1993: 402–3). So, a fundamental disparity in the economic relationship between Thailand and Japan provides further reason for workers to migrate temporarily to Japan.

Whatever their reason for coming to Japan, as long as their stay is documented, foreigners' movements and vital statistics are recorded by Japanese civil servants. If it is not, only their departure is recorded. Though the data in this paper are primarily drawn from censuses of registered foreigners (except for infant mortality rates, which include the deaths of children of undocumented foreign mothers), it is important to note these are not the only foreigners in Japan. In 1997, the number of 'overstaying' or undocumented foreigners workers and/or residents was 282,986, including 127,047 females. The number of undocumented foreigners nearly tripled in the years between 1990 and 1992. Numbers of undocumented workers released by government officials vary against other sources. For example, it was estimated in 1995 that there was 600,000 foreign workers in Japan, including those without visas (Komai

Table 4.1 Registered immigrants to Japan from Korea, Brazil and the Philippines, 1999[1]

	Korea	*Brazil*	*Filipino*
Total population	636,548	224,299	115,685
Percentage of this population who are women aged 20–39	18.1%	24.2%	73.2%

1995: 1). This number implies that activists and scholars believe there are more undocumented residents than the government claims.

Records held by the two ministries show how the government prefers to categorise foreigners, especially in the area of MCH statistics. The MHW divided the information from 1955 to 1991 into four groups: Korea, China, US, and 'other countries.' When this classification system was no longer useful, data from 1992 to the present were framed in five further national categories: the Philippines, Thailand, Britain, Brazil and Peru. The change in classification illustrates the impact the immigrants from these 'other countries' made in the late 1980s.

It is often said that 1986 was 'year zero' for foreigners (especially foreign women) travelling to Japan, as it was in the late 1980s that numbers began to increase dramatically. (For a more detailed discussion of the history and cultural understanding of female migrants to Japan, see Mackie, 1998.) Although not all of these women give birth in Japan, this increase in migration will have an impact on MCH, considering the gender and age of the immigrants.

In the ten years between 1986 and 1996, foreign registrations increased by 63.2%. During the 1950s and 1960s, most of the foreigners registered were classified as Koreans. The Emigration, Migration and Refugee Law was changed about the same time as the 'bubble economy' expanded, drawing a cheap labour force from abroad. This resulted in a decrease of the ratio of Koreans registered as foreigners and an aging of the Korean population (as most of the new immigrants were aged 20–40, fit for employment; see line 2 of Table 4.1). Between 1950 and 1988, the country with which most registered foreigners claimed affiliation was Korea; second was China and third was the US. After 1989, the Philippines (and then later Brazil) replaced the US in third place. There were increases in residents from all regions but the most dramatic have been those from South America.

In 1999, 40.9% of all registered foreigners were permanent residents; the largest group in this sector were those 'sponsored by Japanese nationals' (including foreign spouses) at 17.4%. Until 1988, visas in this

Table 4.2 Foreign birthrates in Japan, 1997

Area	Foreign birth rate*
Nationally	1/36 (2.8%)
Tokyo Metropolitan Area	1/18 (5.7%)
Tokyo Municipal Area	1/14 (7.0%)
Shinjuku Ward, Tokyo	1/5 (19.1%)

where at least one of the parents is foreign

category were mostly granted to Chinese, Korean and Filipino spouses of Japanese nationals. Registration records for 1999 show relatively even gender distribution of foreigners in Japan. However, this changes significantly when divided by country of origin. Over 80 percent of all registered foreigners aged over 65 were Korean, again suggesting the aging of the resident Korean population. Brazilians aged under four constitute the largest subset in this age group and Filipina women aged 20–39 make up the vast majority of the total Filipino population in Japan.

Trends in international marriage change public demand for MCH services. Children born to mothers from 'other countries' the category used to describe migrants from countries other than Japan, China, Korea or US in 1999 constituted 52.2% of total foreign births. Births to foreign women from 'other countries' between 1987 and 1999 increased 480.7%. For women aged 15–39 in Japan, Filipina, Thai and Peruvian women make up the most fertile section of the population. Filipinas are the largest group of foreign wives in Japan, have the second highest birth rate, are the third most represented nationality in the resident foreign population aged 15–39, and are the fourth most represented in the registered foreign resident population. Before 1984, about 90 percent of all births to foreign mothers were Korean. This decrease in Korean and Chinese births can be seen as a direct result of changes in the nationality law. After the reform, children of Japanese women married to resident Koreans or other nationalities could also claim Japanese citizenship (hitherto the law only recognised paternity in awarding citizenship). Effectively, that had meant a Japanese woman who married a foreigner lost some of her rights as a Japanese citizen (i.e., transferring citizenship to her child) and became a foreigner herself.

How healthy are foreign children and their mothers? Statistics on maternity, foetal and infant death rates help to determine the success of MCH programmes for foreigners in Japan.

Korean deaths from 1988 to 1992 are the lowest on record and are in line with the statistics of the Japanese population. Infant deaths have

Table 4.3   Statistical index of Japanese and foreign maternal and child healthcare in Japan, 1988–1992[2]

	Total of live births[*]	Maternal death rate[**]	Foetal death rate[***]	Infant mortality rate
Japanese	6,170,242	1.0	41.6	4.6
Korean	42,909	0.5	45.2	5.4
China	11,607	2.6	44.5	4.0
USA	1,994	0.0	48.2	1.1
'Other'	27,539	3.3	82.9	10.0

[*] *divided by mother's country of origin; in the Japanese total, 44.385 children were classified as 'Japanese' but were born to foreign mothers.*
[**] *this and all other rates are per 10,000 births.*
[***] *includes spontaneous miscarriages and terminations.*

greatly decreased for babies born to Japanese, Korean and Chinese mothers. American infant deaths are currently higher than any other nationality.[3] From 1992–96, the foetal death rates for foetuses of Thai, Peruvian and Filipina mothers were much higher than the Japanese rate. In 1996, children born of mothers from 'other countries' died the most frequently. Children from 'other countries' constitute only 38.7% of all registered foreigners but they are more likely to die than foreign children from Korea, China and the US. Taken together, the maternal and child health statistics suggest that foreign mothers and their children, especially those from 'other countries' (the Philippines, Thailand, and Peru, among others), are at risk.

Cultural issues

Statistics give some idea about the pregnancy and birth outcomes but tell little of the qualitative experience of having a child as a foreign woman in Japan. Such women come to Japan after spending their childhood and/or early adulthood in another country where diets, hygiene, education, medical care and lifestyles are quite different. These different contexts contribute to the differences in pregnancy outcomes for foreigners in Japan, but we intend to examine cultural differences that also influence the way a pregnant woman seeks out and receives prenatal care and how a mother cares for her newborn.

Foreigners in Japan have expressed fear about issues such as patients' rights in decision-making and the discouragement of fathers in the delivery room; some even were concerned about the cleanliness and safety of the hospital facilities (Clarkson 1996: 3).[4] Language is thought to be the main culprit; for example, in other migrant countries such as Australia, non-English-speaking mothers are reported to be half as satisfied as their English-speaking counterparts with their childbirth experience (Martin 1997: 4). Language barriers exist for all migrants to Japan, but in the cases of couples where both partners are foreigners or in the case where the woman becomes pregnant or gives birth very soon after arriving in Japan, language poses more serious problems when seeking healthcare. This is especially true for the last group where the mother does not possess a Japanese-sponsored visa as in the case of international marriages. Though certain services are available to overstaying pregnant women (such as registration for the Maternal and Child Healthcare Handbook [Boshi Techō]), many women are unaware of these options. Language hurdles, as well as confusion as to entitlements for foreigners, suggest that there is an under-utilisation of available public health and welfare systems due to poor communication (see Stevens 1998; Stevens, Lee and Sawada 2000).

Clarkson (1996) notes that for most foreigners in Japan, the absence of informal support groups is the most distressing. The authors have field experience in support groups for foreigners: primarily Kalabaw no Kai being the most active group which addresses the needs of all foreign workers in the Kantō area; and the Iryōhan, which offers free medical consultations to foreign and native Japanese labourers. Catholic churches also provide important support but their help in maternal matters is often coloured by theology; Filipina women who want to terminate their pregnancies seek help elsewhere. NGO and other not for profit community groups tend to support primarily concerns of male workers (e.g. injury at the workplace and unpaid wages). This suggests that in Japan as well as the host countries of these women, pregnancy and childbirth are considered private matters. Women married to Japanese men are expected to conform to Japanese home life and seek support from their families.

Despite the medicalisation of birth in Japan, drug-free deliveries and midwife-assisted births are more common in Japan than in other industrial countries (Clarkson 1996), and this can cause anxiety for some expectant mothers who are not accustomed to the idea of natural childbirth. Education and professional counselling (such the services offered by the Committee to Facilitate Maternal and Child Healthcare for non-Japanese Residents in Tokyo) provide some answers, but the Japanese medical community must also recognise the cultural gaps between their practice and the backgrounds of foreign mothers in Japan.

The researchers have direct experience with these cultural issues: Setsuko Lee (a midwife and associate professor in public health) is a third-generation Korean, born, raised and educated in Japan. Carolyn

Stevens (an American anthropologist) is married to a Japanese man and spent part of her first pregnancy in Japan. Together, we found that there were significant differences in the way a foreign woman might view her pregnancy, how her Japanese family viewed it, and how this differed from the Japanese medical professional opinion. Gaps in understanding (and not just language) contribute to stress during pregnancy and make it harder for the foreigner to receive the healthcare she needs.

Despite the linguistic gloss in English, 'morning sickness,' or *tsuwari* in Japanese, is not an illness but merely an inconvenience that does not merit discussion even within the family. Pregnancy, though as medicalised in Japan as in the West, is still not considered an excuse for bowing out of social obligation.[5] A common adage heard was 'in the old days, people weren't so nice to pregnant women' (*mukashi no hito wa sonna ni yasashiku nakatta wa yo*). Interestingly, this was a view held by women as well – not just men – who appeared to think that pregnant women were indulging themselves (*amaeru*) by not continuing with regular activities. One doctor consulted was not concerned about vitamins during the pregnancy and also was not worried at all about alcohol or caffeine intake (Japanese women continue to drink green tea throughout their pregnancy), in contrast to the popular belief in the US and Australia. Japanese pregnant women appear to get on with their lives as normal (or at least they are told they should), while in Australian and American culture, it seems that pregnant women often make significant lifestyle changes.

Another cultural gap is apparent in attitudes to childbirth. Nitrous oxide, spinal blocks, epidurals and other forms of pain relief such as opiate injections are more commonly used in the US and Australia (in 2000, one author was told that in the private section in the Royal Women's Hospital in Melbourne, only 20 percent of mothers used no pain relief). Japanese women are encouraged to forgo these drugs, and the age-old belief that women should not cry out during labour is still noted (though Lee's experience in the delivery room shows that these customs are not always observed). The majority of Japanese mothers do not seem to take politically active stands against increasing rates of Caesarean procedures. It is thought that the doctor (usually male) knows best and that the patient should not interfere with these decisions. *Tachiai*, or the practice of the father being present in the delivery room, is slowly increasing but still not nearly as common in Japan as it is in the West. Despite the preference for 'natural' childbirth, breast-feeding is not considered *de rigeur*; even Japanese mothers who do not work supplement breast milk with formula or bottle feed exclusively, as illustrated by the layout of a baby care room in Takashimaya, a large department store in Japan. A 'breastfeeding room' was embedded within the much larger feeding and changing room and was off limits to men. The room only contained four chairs, implying that very few women needed to use the premises. This is a matter of personal choice and not necessarily one dictated by work schedules or moral grounds.

In sum, pregnancy, childbirth and breastfeeding in Japan are generally considered domestic, private matters that are not part of the public sphere. This makes it even more difficult for a foreign mother to seek out and obtain support and advice during her pregnancy and directly after childbirth.

Ethnicity, identity, and citizenship

The number of marriages between Japanese nationals and foreigners has increased, most markedly since 1986, but actual figures may be higher because de facto marriages are not included in the census. Because the number of marriages and the number of births are approximately equal, we can assume that most of these marriages are not ones of 'convenience'. In 1999, approximately one birth in 36 was a product of an international marriage. This suggests a new multi-cultural element in Japanese society, and an 'internationalisation of children' in Japan.

How is Japanese citizenship obtained? Before the enforcement of the 1899 Nationality law, the *koseki* or family registry was the primary means of determining Japanese citizenship (Hirowatari 1994: 93–4). Technically there are two possible paths to nationality: nationality by origin (*ius sanguinis*) and nationality by place of birth (*ius soli*). In Japan, though the latter form is possible, Hirowatari (1994: 92) says that it is used in only 'exceptional cases'. This is in contrast to policies frequently enacted in the United States, Canada and Australia, where place of birth is either an immediate determinant of citizenship or eventually an acceptable one. Japan, like some European countries such as Germany and until recently France, operates on a nationality by blood policy of citizenship. Hirowatari (1994: 93) suggests that nations that desire to maintain a uniform, homogenous population will rely on nationality by origin rules while multicultural and pluralistic nations accept nationality by place of birth as the standard. Bade writes that:

Jus sanguinis placed the principles of nation and national community above those of civil rights and republic, in strict opposition to the principle of territory (jus soli) embodied in the French Republican idea (1997: 17).

In Japan, as well as in Germany, there are 'native foreigners' and 'foreign natives,' to modify Bade's (1997: 24) terminology. However, we are concerned here not with 'full' Japanese born abroad or at home, but

Table 4.4   Trends in marriages by nationality in Japan, 1999

Foreign bride, *Japanese groom*	*Foreign groom,* *Japanese bride*	*Foreign* *couple*
24,272	7,628	3,240

with children whose parents are not originally from Japan. They don't fall neatly into these categories based on concepts such as blood and place.

Today, any child of a mixed marriage may claim Japanese citizenship (as long as the child's paternity, in the case of a Japanese father, is recognised). However, Table 4.4 above shows that most marriages are between Japanese men and foreign women, femininising the issue of reproducing identity in international marriages. Women are the ones caught between two cultures, legal and medical systems and ideologies.

Figure 4.1 shows that the three most fertile groups of women in Japan are from a non-Japanese background. Legally married or not and regardless of their own visa status, pregnancy and childrearing ties these women closely to the Japanese state. They are producing Japanese citizens who

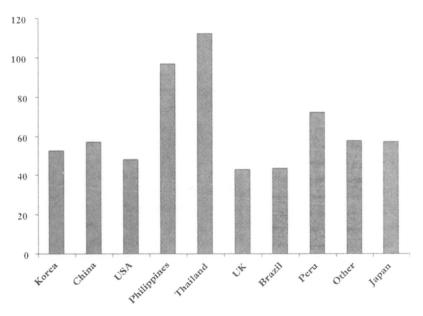

Figure 4.1   Number of births to women aged 15–39 in Japan by mothers' nationality, 1996 (per 1000 people)

are not 100 percent 'Japanese.' They are creating a society where those legally considered Japanese might not necessarily be of the 'pure Yamato race' (see Weiner, 1997). Resistance to this concept is played out in the social and legal ramifications of the various paths an international marriage may take.

Studies of contemporary families show that Japanese women feel pressure from their husbands' families to conform to custom (Hodge and Ogawa 1991: 230–5). One may hypothesise that foreign women married to Japanese men, as new members of an *ie*, are under pressure to support this system. Foreign women who have come to Japan primarily to work under employment training programmes may view pregnancy as an impediment to their goals. For foreigners, the normal stresses of carrying a child to term are compounded by negative aspects of being a foreigner: linguistic barriers, homesickness, discrimination, and so on. In sum, pregnancy in the foreign community entails a multitude of concerns that differ from the experiences of Japanese women. Depending on her own health, language abilities, economic status and the strength of her personal networks, a foreign woman may be at a higher risk for miscarriage, stillbirth, or even dying herself in childbirth.

Once her child is born, a mother needs to adjust to caring for the infant. The birth of a child, however, does not stabilise the foreign mother's status in Japan. A foreign wife receives a sponsor visa that must be renewed every three years; if her husband withdraws his support for her visa, she will lose her residency. She may apply for a 'parental visa' (*oyaken bisa*), but often the single foreign mother has inadequate financial or emotional support in Japan and so returns to her home country. Therefore, her connection to the Japanese state remains tenuous and only valid if she remains in the patriarchal family system. In either case, a foreign mother is not recognised as an individual by the Japanese state. Her livelihood in Japan is legitimated only through connection to either a man or a child, unless she is qualified for and chooses to take Japanese citizenship, renouncing ties to her native country.

For a foreign woman with a foreign partner, a child born in Japan is a happy event, but is a child 'born out of place.' The child needs to be registered with both Japanese and foreign authorities so that the child does not become stateless. These families have access to MCH care and national health insurance (if their stay is longer than one year) but, to utilise these programmes, they sometimes have to pay fees and often need interpreters. Interpreting in languages other than English is, however, commonly not available at welfare offices in Japan.

Pregnancy poses further problems for foreign women without residency papers. In a preliminary study of overstayers' MCH care in central

Yokohama, researchers found that only 13 percent of undocumented women had received prenatal care (Stevens, Lee and Sawada 2000: 58). Specifically, only seven out of 53 overstaying women had clearly received prenatal care. In two of these cases where care was sought, it commenced only in the third trimester. In the interest of protecting the health of children born in Japan, some public health programmes aimed at maternal and child healthcare are being made available to overstayers (see Lee 1994: 627). However, the implementation of these programmes has not been well documented, and further research is necessary to convince the government of volunteers' and NGO workers' claims that the problem is even more severe and widespread that at first thought.

Conclusion

What are the 'paths' for reproducing identity as set out by laws, customs, practices and beliefs in Japan, and are these expectations met in the foreign community? As we often see in the anthropological record, identity is fluid. In Japan, we see individuals making various choices that 'mark' their children. Some children of international marriages are registered as 'Japanese;' others retain their ethnic affiliation as 'registered foreigners.' The Japanese government allows a child to retain dual citizenship until the age of 20; then the individual must choose one nationality and passport. We should, however, be wary of labels parcelled out to individuals by the Ministry of Justice. Just because a child of a Japanese mother and a Korean father is registered as Japanese, this does not mean the child has no consciousness of his or her cultural heritage. Falling rates of Korean registration and similar MCH statistics do not necessarily mean that long-term-resident Koreans and their children are 'turning Japanese' while other foreign groups are not. What it does mean is that younger resident Koreans are responding to social pressures in different ways. This is most probably because they have come to be considered an 'invisible' ethnic group in Japan (no longer marked by race or language). One can make the argument that they are doing so successfully, considering their MCH data.

As is noted in Roberts' chapter, the general trend is that Japanese (and Korean) women are having fewer, healthier babies than their foreign counterparts. Socio-economic pressures are at work. Children are 'expensive' in Japan no matter what the nationality of the mother. Japanese women are opting for smaller families, due to high costs of housing and education and the desire to explore other activities. Foreign women, no doubt, have similar experiences as they live in the same environment and pay the same prices. If economic factors are important when a woman makes a decision regarding childbirth and childcare, this can be seen as a further commodification of people in a post-industrial society. Parents cannot avoid thinking about how much children 'cost' when deciding how to build their families. Women are seen to be 'taking control' of their reproductive lives, but we may well ask if this is truly a result of the liberation of women, or merely the result of economic rationalisation. Foreigners who come from backgrounds where this is not the customary way of thinking find it difficult to adjust, but there is little room for compromise in a society where public services are in great demand and waiting lists for childcare facilities are long. Economic rationalisation is a strategy for many mothers, whether they are Japanese or foreign.

The foreign woman who gives birth to a child with a Japanese father will be drawn more closely to the *ie* system and she will become, ideally, a permanent member of a system that ties all Japanese to the state. When a foreign woman becomes 'Japanese,' in the great majority of cases, the new identity is relational rather than direct: her status is determined by her relationship to a man or to a child, and she must remain within this patrilineal system to maintain her status. Despite recent advances for Japanese women in other areas, patriarchy is still a strong attribute of the kinship system. The enduring divisions between those born 'Japanese' and those who are later brought into the system are complicated by the fluid 'Japanese-ness' of the children born between these two groups.

Increasing rates of international marriage will probably result in a diversification of ethnic identities for those classified as 'Japanese.' What is the ethnic identity of these children? Their passport may say 'Japanese,' but what is their own sense of identity? How should they be educated, at public or private schools (which would meet their special linguistic needs)? What are the costs involved? What is the Japanese government's responsibility for providing these children with free access to their cultural backgrounds? These unresolved questions show that Japanese society is still resistant to multicultural development, illustrating its reluctance to give up a unified image of ethnicity.

The anthropological perspective explores the ideological factors that affect the MCH data. Statistically, foreign mothers are defined as a high-risk group; the anthropologist looks for non-medical reasons why. Language is often cited as the greatest barrier to healthcare and the source of stress to foreigners living in Japan. Discrimination against foreigners (especially those from non-European backgrounds) may cause financial difficulty, and these economic factors may limit their ability to receive proper prenatal care. Limited support from the mothers' natal families due to distance and a tenuous relationship to the Japanese community due to linguistic differences may also cause emotional stress to pregnant foreign women. Finally, we can venture that foreign wives/partners are marginalised in larger Japanese society because of their tenuous positions in the traditional family and in the state, showing continuing conflicts arising from the juxtaposition of an 'international society' and established concepts of Japanese ethnicity and kinship. This research demonstrates that the approach taken by policy makers must broaden. To improve MCH statistics for foreign women in Japan, it is necessary not only to facilitate prenatal and postnatal care but also to restructure the political and social roles of foreign women in Japan. Initiatives are needed from the individual level (such as improving the conditions of visas available to foreign mothers) to the collective (such as establishing an active, supportive foreign community). Until then, foreign women are likely to continue experiencing difficult pregnancies and childbirth.

NOTES

1   Dr Lee personally gathered all data presented in the following tables from records held at the Ministry of Justice (Hōmushō daijinkanbo shihō hōsei chōsabu, including the Hōmushō nyūkanrikyoku) and the Ministry of Health and Welfare (hereafter, MHW, Kōseishō daijinkanbo tōkei jōhōbu no jinkō dōtai tōkei). For more detail, see Lee (1998).
2   For analytical purposes, the following divisions of data for this table, and others in this chapter, were devised:
    Marriages between foreigners and Japanese were divided by nationality of partner and country of origin of the foreign partner. This information was only available from 1965 to 1996.
    Data on foreign births were gathered from 1955 to 1996. This includes the total number of children born after 1987 to couples where either partner is a foreigner, and the latter results were calculated according to the mother's country of origin. Because MHW did not release statistics on the numbers of births of women of different nationalities before 1987, it is impossible to calculate those figures separately.
    Statistics from the 35 years from 1958 to 1992 were divided into seven five-year periods; the total numbers of foetal and maternal deaths were calculated, divided by mother's country of origin, for each five-year period. Furthermore, percentages of infant mortality were calculated based on numbers of live births and infant deaths. Using figures based on mothers' country of origin, foetal and maternal mortality rates were calculated.
    Data from the newly recorded nationality categories (1992 to 1996) were used to calculate foetal and infant mortality rates by mothers' country of origin. Furthermore, a birthrate for foreign women aged 15–39 was calculated by comparing figures on the nationality of registered foreigners, the female population aged 15–39 and the total number of births (where the mother is a foreigner married to a Japanese national).

Data on the numbers of deaths of children under the age of five divided by nationality were calculated by comparing the numbers of deaths in the general population to the numbers of deaths of children of foreigners in Japan.

3   This is thought to be related to higher incidents of SIDS (sudden infant death syndrome) in American babies, although researchers are not quite sure why this is so. It may have to do with the way babies' beds are made and smoking within the US citizens' homes in Japan.

4   Clarkson's analysis is of the legal foreign community in Japan; it is expected that overstaying women will encounter the same fears when facing language barriers and unfamiliar surroundings, but their experience may be more grave if they have not received prenatal care due to a lack of money or information. Overstayers choose to give births in hospitals as the Japanese do. Researchers in central Yokohama found that 90 percent of overstayers' births recorded occurred at public or private hospitals. Fifty-six percent of the mothers chose public hospitals because of the convenience of the location and lower costs (Stevens, Lee and Sawada 2000: 58).

5   Work outside the home is different. Menstruation, breastfeeding and maternity leave are provided under the Labour Standard's Law's Bosei Hogo (protection of motherhood).

PRIMARY DATA COLLECTIONS USED FOR STATISTICS

- Hōmushō daijin kanbō shihō hōsei chōsa honbu (Survey Office of the General Secretary of the Ministry of Justice), 1997.
- Hōmushō Nyūkanrikyoku (Immigration Control Office at the Ministry of Justice), 1997.
- Kōseishō daijin kanbō tōkei jōhōbu no jinkō dōtai tōkei (Vital Statistics from the Ministry of Health and Welfare), 1997.

REFERENCES

Bade, Klaus J. 1997. 'From emigration to immigration: the German experience in the nineteenth and twentieth centuries,' in *Migration Past, Migration Future: Germany and the United States*, ed. Klaus J. Bade and Myron Weiner. Providence, Oxford: Berghahn Books.

Clarkson, Blair. 1996. 'Giving birth in Tokyo: groups help mothers-to-be.' *The Japan Times* (8 December).

Fiedler, D. 1996. 'Authoritative knowledge and birth territories in contemporary Japan.' *Medical Anthropology Quarterly*, 10(2): 195–212.

Hanami T. and Kuwahara Y., eds. 1993. *Anata no Rinjin Gaikokujin Rōdōsha* (Your Neighbour, the Foreign Worker). Tokyo: Tōyōkeizai Shinbunsha.

Hashimoto M., trans. B. Dadswell. 1995. 'Anata mo iranai hito?! Gaikokujingari (Are you too an unneeded person? Alien hunting),' in *Nippon* (Japan) Tokyo: Gendaishokan.

Hirowatari Seigo. 1994. 'Foreigners and the "foreigner question" under Japanese law,' pp. 91–122 in *The Annals of the Institute of Social Science*. Tokyo: University of Tokyo.

Hodge, Robert and Ogawa Naohiro. 1991. *Fertility Change in Contemporary Japan*. Chicago and London: University of Chicago Press.

Ikeda H. and Amano K. 1988. 'Kokusaika to iu fashizumu (The fascism called "internationalisation"),' in *Kokusaika to Iu Fashizumu: Kenshō Shōwa no Shisō* (The Fascism called 'Internationalisation': Inspecting the Ideology of the Shōwa Era). Tokyo: Shakaihyōronsha.

Ishii Yoneo and Toshiharu Yoshikawa, eds. 1993. *Tai no Jiten* (A Thailand Dictionary). Kyoto: Dōbōshashuppan.

Keizai Keikaku Chō Sōgō Keikakukyoku, eds. 1989. *Gaikokujin Rōdōsha to Keizaishakai no Shinro* (The Course of Economic Society and Foreign Workers). Tokyo: Ōkurashō Insatsukyoku.

Komai H., trans. J. Wilkinson. 1995. *Migrant Workers in Japan*. London: Kegan Paul International.

Lee, Setsuko. 1994. '"Uchinaru kokusaika shakai" no genjō to boshi hoken/iryō no kadai (The present state of "internal internationalisation" – maternal and child healthcare and medical treatment).' *Josanpu Zasshi*, 48: 623–34.

——. 1998. 'Zainichi gaikokujin no shūyō shihyō (Principal indices for foreigners in Japan)' and 'Zainichi gaikokujin no boshihoken gairon (An outline of maternal and child healthcare for foreigners in Japan),' in *Zainichi Gaikokujin no Boshi Hoken* (Maternal and Child Healthcare for Foreigners in Japan), ed. Setsuko Lee. Tokyo: Igaku Shoin.

Mackie, Vera. 1998. 'Japayuki Cinderella girl: containing the immigrant other.' *Japanese Studies*, 18(3): 45–64.

Martin, Louise. 1997. 'Women find language barrier adds to the pain of childbirth.' *The Age* (16 October).

Mothers' and Children's Health and Welfare Association. 1992. *Maternal and Child Health in Japan* (a booklet compiled under the supervision of Maternal and Child Health Division, Children's and Families' Bureau, Ministry of Welfare). Tokyo.

Nihon Seisansei Honbu Rōdōkyōgi Seijō Iinkai, eds. 1992. *Rōdōryoku Fusoku Keizaika no Sangyōshakai no Kadai, 21seiki ni Muketa Chūshōkigyō no Kasseika no Tame ni* (Labour Shortages in an Industrial Society: For the Vitalisation of Small and Medium-sized Industries Facing the 21st Century). Tokyo: Nihon Seisansei Honbu.

Nishida, Hiroshi. 1993. 'Outcome of infants born preterm, with special emphasis on extremely low birthweight infants.' *Baillière's Clinical Obstetrics and Gynaecology*, 7(3): 611–31.

Sōmuchō Gyōsei Kansatsu Kyoku (The Office of the Prime Minister of Japan), eds. 1992. '*Kokusaika jidai gaikokujin o meguru gyōsei no genjō to kadai – sōmuchō gyōsei kansatsu kyoku no jittaichōsa kekka* (Conditions and themes of administrating foreigners in an "international" age: the results of the Prime Minister's office's survey).' Tokyo: Ōkurashō insatsukyoku.

Stevens, Carolyn S. 1998. 'Bunkajinruigaku kara mita zainichi gaikokujin no boshi hoken (Anthropological perspectives on maternal and child healthcare for foreigners in Japan),' in *Zainichi Gaikokujin no Boshi Hoken* (Maternal and Child Healthcare for Foreigners in Japan), ed. Setsuko Lee. Tokyo: Igaku Shoin.

——, Setsuko Lee and Takashi Sawada. 2000. 'Unsettled migrant maternal and child healthcare in Yokohama: a case study seen from a volunteer perspective.' *Japanese Studies*, 20(1): 49–65.

Weiner, Michael. 1997. 'The invention of identity: "self" and "other" in pre-war Japan,' in *Japan's Minorities: The Illusion of Homogeneity*, ed. Michael Weiner. London: Routledge.

5   State, standardisation and 'normal' children: an anthropological study of a preschool

Eyal Ben-Ari

In this article, I examine the interrelation between the organisational features of Japanese preschools and the ways by which they are predicated on notions of 'normal' (and normalising) development of children. Based on an in-depth study of one such preschool – Katsura Daycare Centre (*Hoikuen*) in Kyoto – and short visits to a number of other institutions, my article represents an attempt to theorise the organisational character of such preschools. In my earlier work (Ben-Ari 1994; 1995; 1997b) I have suggested that most previous studies of such establishments – kindergartens and daycare centres – tends to see through, rather than look at, the organisational character of such institutions. Consequently, most such studies have tended to focus on the experience of children or on the care proffered them. Thus earlier inquiries such as those carried out by Hendry (1986a; 1986b), Lewis (1989; 1995), Peak (1989; 1991), Tobin (Tobin et al. 1989) – as well as some of my own projects (Ben-Ari 1996; 1997a) – have basically inquired about the kind of socialisation that youngsters undergo in preschools. Here, however, I propose a shift of focus to ask about preschools as institutional structures. This shift allows us to see how patterns of organisation are related to the ways that children are socialised according to a rather uniform set of assumptions and ideas. Yet, an examination of these patterns necessitates problematising these institutions as organisations because the actualisation of cultural concepts in preschools is carried out through the organisational 'logic' – the rules and scale, arrangements and sets of priorities, and mechanisms of social control and coordination – of these establishments. In other words, what I seek to do is to step back from the 'Japaneseness' of child-care institutions to their 'institution-ness.'

How are the main organisational tasks of care and development of children carried out? Preschools such as Katsura Daycare Centre offer a number of what anthropologists call good entry points for the study of organisational issues: teachers' meetings, processes of decision-making, formal training, informal mentoring, or interpersonal dynamics among the teachers. In this article, however, I suggest that another fruitful entry point entails the plethora of documents and documentation found in such establishments. An examination of the profuse array of texts – forms, rosters, records, files, checklists, questionnaires, notices, tables, and reports – found in these institutions may allow us to understand some of their hitherto little explored characteristics. It is in these texts that many of the routine (and not so routine) activities of preschools are recorded, and from which they are retrieved (for action) by caretakers.

The existence and use of these administrative documents allows us to understand that caretaking in such institutions as Katsura Daycare Centre involves 'writing' and 'reading' no less than playing, teaching, and disciplining. This point is important because, reading earlier studies of Japanese early childhood education, one gets the impression that their governing assumption is that caretaking in Japan, as in other indus-trialised societies, is basically like caretaking in oral (i.e. non-literate) societies. In other words, there are very few sustained attempts to examine the relationship between large-scale organised care for children and the literacy that pervades the organisations through which such care is proffered. From an institutional perspective, my contention is that documents are both mediums that incorporate certain notions about organised caretaking, and a major means through which preschools are managed as organisations. In methodological terms, then, I make two concurrent uses of administrative texts in this chapter: first, to help me reveal something about preschools (in this sense they are instruments of my analysis); and second, as examples of the means by which such institutions are organised (in this sense they are objects of my analysis).

Methods; documents; indicators

Between July and September of 1988, and for a short while in 1994, I carried out fieldwork at Katsura Daycare Centre. The centre is located in the south-western part of Kyoto, a city of 1.5 million people (and Japan's ancient capital). Like most of the city's institutions, it is a private preschool, but is recognised and regulated by the city government so that the quality of care it provides is high. Although the centre caters to children from the age of a few months, most of its 110 youngsters belong to the older groups of three-, four-, and five-year-old children. The 24 teachers – including the two cooks – are all registered preschool caretakers and have at least two years of specialised education beyond high school. The children's parents are mostly middle-class and work as salaried employees in (private and public) organisations and as teachers, or run their own small businesses.

The importance and ubiquity of organisational documents in Japanese preschools is remarkable, and, in the course of fieldwork, I gathered a mountain of written material. Doing research at the centre, I often felt that I was being 'bombarded' by written information, and, by the time I left the field, I had accumulated no less than three kilograms of documents. The following is but a partial list of the texts that the highly literate teachers use throughout the year (an extended inventory can be found in Ben-Ari 1997b):

- Yearly, monthly, weekly and daily outlines of curricula.
- Timetables for teachers' assignments.
- Lists of articles the children have to bring with them to the centre.
- The rules of the daycare centre and the parents' association.
- Administrative reports on the centre as a whole, for each group, and for individuals.
- Intake questionnaires for children entering the centre.
- Letters and notices sent home and back.
- Menus and charts for the caloric content of food.
- Minutes of teachers' meetings.

Later, as I reviewed my field-notes, I found other indicators of the centrality of such texts. For example, on a given day, the teachers devote from 30 minutes up to a few hours filling in, reading or preparing documents. Next, the sheer amount of shelf-space devoted to written documents and files is very large and includes not only the centre's office and storerooms but also the shelves in almost all of the classrooms, and small libraries that teachers keep at their tables. Finally, the constant hum of the centre's photocopying machine also attested to the constant reproduction of a variety of texts.

Tabling the curriculum

Let me introduce a number of key texts used at Katsura Hoikuen in greater detail in order to form a basis for the analysis. I begin with one of the most important ordering texts of the centre, the curriculum. I do not focus on the content of the curriculum so much as on its various forms because it is around these forms that much of the organisational order of the daycare centre is constructed. While Katsura Hoikuen has yearly, monthly and weekly sets of curricula for each age group, the infants (because development is thought to be accelerated until the age of three) have individualised curricula. The monthly curriculum for the group of five-year-old children during the month of September when I did fieldwork is typical: it comprises two tables. The top of the first table includes the group's name, yearly theme ('Growing up together'), monthly theme ('Try our best'), monthly objectives (such as 'Try your strength' or 'Listen to others'), and the names of the songs chosen for the month. The table itself comprises three columns: specific objectives, their purpose, and activities to be undertaken to achieve them. The table is arranged so that it can be read at a glance either vertically as lists of goals for the whole month, or horizontally so that a monthly objective, purpose, and activities form a complete unit. Take, for example, the objective of 'Living a healthy lifestyle' that is to be achieved by explaining to the children and involving them in the climactic changes of the end of summer. The recommended activities for 'Moving the body' are building up stamina and stretching and warm-up exercises, and their purpose is preparation for the annual sports day.

The second table making up the monthly curriculum for September includes weekly themes ('Play enjoyably and with everyone' or 'Pay gratitude to old people'); activities to take place (birthday parties, visits by trainee students, or outings); and specific programmes (for example, group games, rhythmic activities, art education, or exercises). Next to the columns giving these details are three lists: the aims to be achieved each day (like learning to follow group rules); the names of the teachers in charge of the day's central programme; and, the material and equipment needed. Here again, the table can be read vertically as ordered lists or horizontally for each day as a unit. In this way a teacher can easily scan the table to get an idea of what will go on at the centre during the coming month and of her duties and tasks.

A number of texts are used to create the curriculum. All programmes at Japanese daycare centres are based on guidelines dictated by the Ministry of Health and Welfare, and are very similar to those set by the Ministry of Education for kindergartens (Schoppa 1991: 181–2). Given this governmental direction, the curriculum varies very little across the country. Other texts used by teachers include professional and semi-professional journals containing articles about play, games, and handling of 'problem' children; handbooks (including specific examples of daily programmes); and volumes devoted to children's songs, diversions, and contests. Most of these documents are written by heads of daycare centres, by experts from teacher training schools or by university lecturers. In this way, a wide body of knowledge about preschool education is integrated into the actual activities at the centre. In addition, teachers are inundated with photocopied excerpts of other books and articles: in one meeting, we were handed pages out of a book entitled *Helping and aiding development*, and an article from a journal called *Music Plaza*. Whenever I asked about how they had prepared specific activities, teachers readily found the relevant texts that they had used.

Creating (bureaucratic) texts

Related sets of documents in which official definitions of child development can be found are charts for appraising development, checklists for identifying 'problem' children, or reports prepared for teachers' meetings. A rather typical incident that I encountered during fieldwork is illuminating in this respect. One morning before lunch, I wandered into the classroom of three-year-old children. One of the teachers was weighing the children and measuring their height. Dealing with each child in turn, she carefully marked the measurements down in a folder in which each child had an individual file, the *jidōhyō* (literally 'child-chart'). She showed me how each file includes data about the children from the time they entered preschool until they left: physical measurements (height, weight, and circumference of chest), linguistic and motor development, social skills, likes and dislikes, and general comments. Each month, information on each child's physical development is recorded on a graph and compared to the norm for that age. In this way, physical 'abnormalities,' she pointed out, can be easily spotted and appropriate action taken if necessary.

Attached to the back of each file are certificates provided by medical experts about the health or development of the child. In this way, external professional opinions are registered in the centre's documentation. The teacher continued:

This section about health is filled out when the children enter preschool. It includes inoculations so that we know when they received them. This part is filled out by the doctor who visits the daycare centre each June and December. He comes here, gives each child a medical check-up, and, if a child is healthy, then he hardly writes anything down, but if the child is unhealthy, then he writes down what is wrong. For example, the doctor discovered that one boy has a head that is bigger than the average for his height and weight and this may develop into a problem of coordination in the future. We have to be aware of this in the future.

In reply to my question, she said that in most cases data on physical attributes are not reported orally from teacher to teacher when a child moves on to the next age group. It is only in cases of deviations from the norm that the document forms the basis for such reports. She then mentioned something about the control teachers exert over parents in regard to medical matters:

Here on the back we stick on the medical certificates confirming that a child can go back to the centre after being sick.

Q. Are there parents who don't provide such documents?

We make it very clear that we will not accept the children if no such certificates are provided. In the five years that I have been at the centre, I don't think there has been any case of parents not sending them in.

Thus, in the name of public health, parents are doubly obligated to seek expert validation of the child's health and to obtain caretakers' permission for re-entry into the centre. I asked her to go back to the child-chart and to review the types of comments the teachers write down:

Here in the section on basic life activities (*kihon tekina seikatsu*), we write about such things as eating habits and things related to the toilet, sleep and neatness. With infants, this section is more important than other sections, so there is much more space on the form for filling these things out. In the section on movement, we report about moving the whole body, or parts of it, like balancing while climbing the horizontal bar ... and how the children use various tricycles and how they engage in free play. In the section on social relations (*shakaisei*), we record how the kids play together in their group, whether they cooperate, whether they keep to the rules and if they can behave like everyone else. In the part about language ability, we write whether they understand what we tell them, and their ability to talk and express themselves.

I then noticed something that was attached to each file:

Yes, these are the intake questionnaires that parents fill in when the children enter the daycare centre. They include information on how the child behaved at home before entry; details about the daily cycle of the child: things like sleeping, eating, likes and dislikes, or strong and weak [body] disposition. All of this information is important so that we know how to care for the child at the centre.

Have you learnt, I questioned further, anything new about the children from reading these files? Invoking one of the most common distinctions found in Japanese preschools – to differentiate between physically, emotionally and cognitively 'healthy' children and others – she answered:

As for 'regular' (*kenjoji*, literally 'healthy') children not very much, but as regards 'disabled' children (*shōgaiji*) quite a lot. Take Emiko-chan, she belongs to a category of children we see more and more of lately: children from single parent families who have very few contacts with the father or generally with other men who are substitutes for their fathers. In addition, they usually don't have much experience of playing with other children. They communicate with their mothers but not much with outsiders. We figured this out from talking to the mother and reading what she had written in the intake questionnaire, and from the report of someone [a municipal official] who went to visit her house. On the basis of this information, we created a programme of gradually bringing her into life at the daycare centre.

I asked then asked whether anyone except the class teachers ever read documents like the *jidōhyō*:

Except for the class teacher, no one. Well, there is the yearly administrative inspection (they come in July) by someone from the [municipal] ward office in charge of welfare. He comes to see if the forms are filled in properly, and the head teacher is the one who submits the forms. Then, for the disabled children, we sometimes prepare material on the basis of these forms for meetings where all the teachers get to see them and help in making special programmes. And then sometime when we meet the mothers of the children we also refer to the documents.

This short exchange, which took no more than 20 minutes, contains many elements that bear upon the questions I have set out to discuss. Let me, then, move on to some of the wider implications of my description of the order and use of these various documents.

Implications

Clearly the administrative texts that are found in preschools such as Katsura Hoikuen aid teachers in managing the flow of people, activities and resources through the times and spaces of the centre. This conclusion involves more than an obvious argument about coordination and integration. My contention is that if we conceptualise preschools in this manner, we begin to understand them not as substantive entities, as objects, but rather, following Pondy (1977: 229; Weick, 2001), as sets of interlocked organising processes that create order.

Timetables: managing efficient organisational flows

If organisations are conceived of as sets of interlocking organising processes, then we must ask about the manner by which these processes are actualised. The most distinctive organisational mechanisms for creating order are timetables, essentially time–space organising devices. Members of an organisation have to know the 'time' most of the time in order for the coordination and synchronisation of people and resources to take place. Because of the sheer amount and complexity of the information involved in such ordering, there is a need for devices that ease the cognitive tasks of managing these flows. Documents such as timetables are such devices because they are publicly distributed storehouses of information that can be retrieved rather easily for organisational purposes. Schedules, through predicating certain priorities, at one and the same time decrease the need for decision-making and help coordinate people and resources. The most obvious example of this role at Katsura Hoikuen, as in all such institutions, is the way timetables allocate different age groups to different spaces at the centre so that they do not impinge one on another.

But a timetable does not just 'describe how events are fixed in relation to one another; it is the medium of their very co-ordination. Timetables organize the day of the individual just as they co-ordinate the activities of potentially large numbers of individuals' (Giddens 1987: 160). The importance of schedules (Zerubavel 1981: 52–3) thus lies not only in the way they describe organisational reality, but also in the way they facilitate the active management of this reality. Their use encourages the development of a sense of priority and through that the systematic (and routine) elimination of all involvements that just 'stand in the way.'

A few examples. From an organisational point of view, the register of attendance is similar to documents allocating educational materials to different classes and activities. It is similar in that both facilitate the efficient use of resources at the centre according to the set of priorities that are at the base of the curriculum. Thus during the summer when many children go on leave, such documents allow the centre to change activities and to conserve resources according to the projected reduction in the number of children. By the same token, such scheduling allows the institution to incorporate the advantages of certain teachers – say their skills and preferences for working with animals, music or rhythmics – into the curriculum. To give another trivial but revealing example, because in one teacher Katsura Hoikuen has a good organ player, she is slotted into a variety of activities so as to make maximal use of her as a resource.

At Katsura Hoikuen, scheduling also makes for the efficient use of such resources as specialist teachers who are not full time staff, and particular rooms (the large hall and the arts and crafts chamber). Because schedules appear in table forms, it is relatively easy for the teachers to visually scan them and to identify 'time wasting,' unnecessary duplication, or relatively unimportant activities. During fieldwork, the centre's deputy head saw that the arts room (normally used by members of the older three groups) was not used during certain periods of the week. She then utilised these time slots to offer members of the younger groups opportunities to participate in arts classes.

Time linkages

Preschool schedules are constructed on the basis of two time-reckoning mechanisms: the state designated calendar and a professional 'folk' theory of childhood development. These two are, in turn, applied to the organisational exigencies (the scale, quality and limits) of specific institutions. In other words, the organisational order of these establishments is created by 'fitting' onto the template of the annual calendar (divided as it is into months and days) certain notions about the developmental trajectory of children. In less abstract terms, the activities regularly carried out at the centre – whether monthly, weekly or daily routines or annual occurrences – are based on their relation to the purported 'normal' development of youngsters. Scheduling allows the allocation of involvements in the various domains of the organisation in a way that is dictated by official definitions of what is desirable or necessary for becoming a 'good' Japanese child (White and LeVine, 1986).

But this kind of scheduling is only the first step. Because care entails very minute activities, it is on the level of the 'microscopic' temporal units of the day (hours and minutes) that the two types of time-reckoning are actualised. It is, in other words, in the daily schedule of activities that the notions of calendrical time and child development are adapted to the organisational circumstances of a specific institution. Because the schedule is not only a classification of reality but also a prescription for a specific organisational context, it guides the teachers in actualising certain activities given the resources (teaching materials or numbers of teachers and trainees, for instance) at the centre. This situation does not imply that the teachers are automatons but rather that the forms that visually set out the priorities of the organisation help them in planning and innovating. Thus for instance, schedules allow the gradual and ordered introduction of group activities (in the pool or small relay races) on the basis of developmental notions about the necessity of group activities from the age of about three.

Take occurrence: all things being equal, the number of times a certain activity is scheduled is an indicator of its importance in organisational terms. In this regard, given the educational goals of fostering group identity and cooperation, it is not surprising to find that the most frequent kind of activities to take place are group activities (Rohlen 1989b; Fuller et al. 1986). Similarly, the 'morning programme period' (see Peak 1991: 89), which is seen as the most important educational event of a given day, appears at the centre of the text of the daily schedule, while periods of 'free play' (*jiyū asobi*) which are not seen as peripheral to preschools' educational programmes appear at the margins – the beginning and the end – of daily schedules. The point I am making is the curriculum as schedule is an embodiment of priorities because 'the arrangement of words (or "things") in a list is itself a mode of classifying, of defining a "semantic field", since it includes some items and excludes others' (Goody 1977: 103).

One further point should be mentioned in this regard. 'Timetables are clearly never purely "internal". Since all organisations involve regular transactions with those in external contexts, such transactions themselves must be time-tabled too' (Giddens 1987: 160). In the case of daycare centres, this 'external' timetabling is crucial because the operating times of these institutions are directly dependent upon those of workplaces. The rhythms of the centre, the opening and closing times and the peak hours during which the children arrive and go home, as well as the occasional special requests of parents to leave their children at the centre for longer

times are all dictated by the rhythms of parents' (usually mothers') workplaces and ultimately by the timetables of Japan's organised work life. In
a similar way, the commuting time of mothers is taken into account in
deciding upon the hours a child may attend a centre. Seen in this manner,
the linkages between preschools and industrial society and the labour
market can be more fully understood.

Uniformity and standardisation

Many scholars have noted the significant homogeneity and standardisation of preschools – in daily routines, behaviour management and
educational goals – throughout Japan (Hendry 1986a: 128; Tobin, Wu
and Davidson 1989: 48). Indeed, on the basis of my experience, I would
concur with Peak (1991: 187) and Kotloff (1988), who note that while
there are differences in philosophy and style in institutions of early
childhood education, these are more variations on a theme than real
differences. But what are the reasons for this relative homogeneity and
standardisation? While phrasing their arguments slightly differently both
Peak (1991: 187–8) and Rohlen (1989a; 1989b) hypothesise that this
remarkable fact is the product of teachers' cultural repertoire, memories
of their own experience as students and as members of society, and the
continuity of certain practices along the life course. According to their
reasoning, certain routinised habits are internalised by the teachers as
children, reinforced along their life course, and then applied to caretaking
situations in preschools.

Along the lines of the argument presented here, however, I would add
that a major, if unexplored, reason for this uniformity in preschool
practices has to do with the simple fact that Japanese society is a literate
one. My contention is that educational standardisation results from the
dissemination of a host of written documents that guide teachers in
childcare. In modern Japan, such a contention is not surprising given the
role of the media and other large-scale organisations in the process of
cultural homogenisation in which a set of national cultural ideals is being
spread and created (Moeran 1984). To cite but two examples, while Ivy
(1989) has shown the importance of the media in creating a mass Japanese
culture, Kelly (1986) illuminated the dissemination of middle-class ideals
in the post-war period. But my argument about the uniformity of childcare
is more complex, and has to do with two levels of standardisation.

On one level, even a cursory review of recent studies of Japanese
preschools reveals the extent to which teachers make active use of a
variety of prescriptive educational texts. Thus for instance, Hendry
(1986a: 98) provides an example of a 'how to' book published by Dr
Matsuda Michio, who is Japan's equivalent of Dr Spock. Peak (1991) for

her part, supplies revealing passages from handbooks and primers in regard to such matters as personal health (pp. 34–5), play and games (p. 84), adaptation to school life (p. 128 and p. 173) or problem children (p. 156). Moreover, as I noted earlier, teachers at Katsura Hoikuen read and make use of an assortment of books and articles as part of care-taking. All of these documents – overwhelmingly written by recognised experts and published in the country's cultural centre of Tokyo – contain practical advice for action. Indeed, many bookstores contain special sections devoted to preschool education that cater to both parents and teachers. It is not surprising then, to put this picturesquely, that if a teacher in Hokkaidō (the country's large northern island) and a caretaker in Kyūshū (the large southern island) constantly read and use the same kind of books that they will tend to offer the same kind of care to the children in their charge.

On another level however, the homogeneity of Japanese preschools is achieved through another role of written documents. The power of such documents as timetables and schedules, I would suggest, lies in coordinating people and activities not only within a specific institution, but also across larger-scale times and spaces. I refer not only to the fact that over the course of a year almost all groups of (say) five-year-old children across the country carry out similar projects, but also that over a number of years groups of such children will undergo basically very similar programmes. The forms governing the curriculum and the operational plans for various activities, by their fixity and their easy use, are utilised time and again in ways that assure a consistent and uniform pattern of care across institutions.

Because an organisation 'orders affiliation between persons and perfor-mances that are too remote for contingent arrangements, by linking them into coherent maps or schedules,' the 'integration transcends what might result from negotiated agreements' (Bittner 1974: 78). In other words, scheduling orders caretaking practices as a set of concerted actions although the people carrying out these activities are not within the sphere of one another's direct manipulative influence. Because of the ability of texts and documents to transcend particular social contexts, there is no need for constant and direct interaction between caretakers to take place so that standardised care is proffered to children. I would hardly deny that there is a large measure of consistency in the socialisation practices found within oral societies, but the very scale of caretaking in literate societies (covering literally millions of lives) can only be achieved via the medium of writing. Thus, the uniformity of care and education in Japan, I would posit, are not only the product of some learnt dispositions, but are very much the outcome of the organisational use of documents that I have been outlining here.

Normalising development: texts in use

The significance of the lists, charts and tables that I have been analysing lies in another aspect of their use for they are an important means through which the official developmental theory is put into effect. At their beginning, various Japanese theories of human development – as such theories in *all* of the industrialised societies – were essentially descriptive and analytical. But through a variety of mechanisms –the work of experts and advisors, therapists and applied social scientists, and the media and popularisers – they have been turned into normative constructs. Once accepted into the prevailing culture, these theories (of either the psychological or sociological varieties) no longer operated simply as descriptions of human nature and its growth. They have become accepted cultural criteria by which social reality is explicated, made sense of, and evaluated (Bruner 1986: 134). As Hacking (1990: 163) observes:

One can, then, use the word 'normal' to say how things are, but also to say how they ought to be. The magic of the word is that we can use it to do both things at once. The norm may be what is usual or typical, yet our most powerful ethical constraints are also called norms.

Indeed, the movement from description to prescription in developmental theories is generated by the state because of the very characteristic of bureaucratic organisation. Bureaucracies – administrative frameworks – are 'universal' forms that are capable of being applied to a variety of goals in an assortment of social and cultural circumstances. The universal applicability is related to two interrelated properties or peculiarities that mark them. Such frameworks are first of all taxonomic organisations: i.e. highly explicit, well-defined arrangements of categories, levels, and relations between them (Handelman 1981: 9). If one thinks about the most basic quality of bureaucratic frameworks, it appears that they are forms that 'await instruction' to name, to place, and to classify virtually any phenomenal domain to which they are applied (Handelman 1981: 9). But administrative frameworks are also systemising organisations: arrangements for the active construction of the world according to their own internal categorical logic. Bureaucracies do more than classify the world in order to know it. Such frameworks are designs for both knowing and manipulating, for both apprehending and for continuously modelling the world on the lines of their own internal order (Handelman 1981: 9).

Administrative texts: classification and prescription

The dual function of administrative texts – of classifying and prescribing how to change reality – is evident in the way a narrative of normality appears in various documents at the centre. Let me give two examples. In the daycare centre our son attended during the early 1980s, parents were handed a stack of ten cards when their sons or daughters entered the centre. The cards were divided according to chronological age and ranged between three months and four years. The cards consisted of lists of questions to be answered (in writing) before periodic consultations with nurses at city health centres (according to my notes all of the parents at the centre took their children to these check-ups) and lists of questions that parents were to use in order to monitor their children's development in between consultations. While the questions covered the children's motor, cognitive and social skills, they were actually very focussed on concrete indicators of these abilities: for instance, number and times of bedwetting, finger sucking, left and right handedness, recurrent illnesses, likes and dislikes in food, clarity of speech, or playing outside of the house with or without accompanying adults. The language used in these cards was rather simple, and I found that there was much use of both *hiragana* (a cursive writing style, like an alphabet) and parenthetical explanations of complex words – *hikitsuke* for *keiren* [convulsions], or *hashika* for *mashin* [measles]. It should be noted here that *hiragana*, a phonetic writing system, is closer to speech and should be considered more concrete and reportive rather than interpretational.

The second example is a large chart (photocopied on a large-sized piece of paper) that was handed out a few days before a teachers' meeting. The teachers were asked to use the chart (drafted by a paediatrician from Kyūshū University) when preparing their case-reports on specific children. The chart is constructed so that at one glance it is possible to scan the main dimensions of development from the age of one month to the age of four years and eight months. It is made up of one column specifying chronological age (broken up into months and years) and three columns each for movement (*undō*), social character (*shakaisei*) and language (*gengo*). For the three-year-old children, for example, the column for movement includes fastening buttons and turning over topsy turvy (on a mat); social skills focus on washing one's face without help and asking for permission using the expression 'is it alright to?' (*kō shite ii?*); and the language column encompasses the ability to talk to peers and to understand the difference between high and low.

The form of theory

The close connection between the practices involved in the use of administrative texts and the theory of normal development embodied in these documents is related to yet other features of care taking at the pre-school. First, take the way the documents are structured as a descriptive narrative of normality. Indeed, the similarity between the linearity of the theory and the linearity of the documents is apparent in all of the texts aimed at monitoring individuals' development. Sato (1991: xv) notes, that movement:

through time and space seems to provide us with a kind of ultimate prototype of purposeful action in which means and ends are commensurate to one another. We can and do build narratives about this prototype and, once we have a narrative, we can appoint to it a moving persona along the landscape or props that mark the persona's passage and give credence to his progress.

What seems to happen is that texts in preschools are constructed by fitting notions of the appropriate characteristics, abilities and behaviour as defined by the developmental theory to very specific chronological ages. In this manner, it is relatively easy to determine a given child's progress when compared to the 'normal' pace of her or his peers. Documents based on current theories of child development thus enable teachers at Katsura Hoikuen to periodically label, define, and name those children who are 'running ahead' or (more seriously) 'running late' (Roth 1963). Thus in the group of two-year-old children, one boy who talked a great deal was labelled by the teachers as 'the fastest.' In the group of young-sters only a year old, a girl who barely crawled while pushing herself with her left leg was marked as 'a bit slow.' In fact, the teachers informally called the form used for monitoring the development of children under the age of three, the 'growth' or 'progress document' (seichō no kiroku).

But the import of labelling does not lie only in giving official sanction to certain definitions of reality. Its more serious significance lies in the way it shapes the manner by which caretakers act back on reality. Along these lines, the second quality of these forms is their prescriptive charac-ter: forms aid teachers in classifying the ongoing behaviours, processes and interactions of the Hoikuen into discrete categories, and then in 'reacting' on the basis of this categorisation. The classification incor-porated in these documents, allows caretakers to create labels and responses to a variety of what are defined as impediments to normal development. At Katsura Hoikuen this point means, as it does in other preschools, reacting differently to what teachers perceive to be motor, perceptual or communicative difficulties. For instance, if a checklist tells you that by the age of one or three years of age a child should be able to skip or jump forwards and backwards and a youngster can not do so, teachers take appropriate measures to deal with the 'deviance' of the child from the purported norm.

The third quality of these texts is that over time they comprise a record of accumulated knowledge. An example of the way a 'disabled' child was treated at the centre illuminates this point. At one meeting, a teacher brought out a set of photographs of a boy suffering from cerebral palsy that she had taken the year before. She had taken pictures of him climbing stairs, walking and balancing, and holding a spoon. At the back of each picture, she had scribbled in the time of day when the photograph was taken. During the meeting, the photographs were used in conjunction with one of the developmental checklists (the one developed at the University of Kyūshū), the results of a physician's examinations, and records of previous years. The aims of juxtaposing these various texts were to ascertain the child's progress and to discuss further types of treatment in the future. I witnessed numerous other instances in the field when individualised programmes for 'problem' children – hyperactive, autistically inclined, and suffering from Down syndrome, for instance – were created on the basis of records. The collection of records of an individual form a corps of texts that (at once) document a child's behaviour, allows systematic comparison with the child's past actions and with those of other children, and facilitates teachers' proper handling of these behaviours. The element of writing in this case is important, for written forms and documents allow for a much more systematic comparison of divergent experiences of individuals or groups than do discussions based purely on memory.

The final point involves the relative rigidity of the texts used at the pre-school. Forms, once institutionalised, channel caretakers to look at certain matters and not at others: at what are defined as developmentally relevant issues. Part of this rigidity relates to the kind of data teachers are asked to provide. It consists mainly of quantifiable and tangible aspects of behaviour: for example, motor skills (walking, running, grasping); linguistic capabilities (vocabulary or sentence construction); social interactions with peers; or eating (amount and types of food eaten) and toilet habits (number and type of excreta). In these bureaucratic texts, it is relatively difficult to report, let alone formulate, explicit statements about intangibles like moods, anxieties, or temperament. Because in filling out forms, teachers, like bureaucrats around the world, simply follow organisational rules, they receive little invitation to reflect upon the notions embodied in the texts. The very fact that observations are placed on lists or in charts, which are abstracted from the context of ordinary speech, gives the resulting texts a generality that they would not otherwise have had.

Controlling teachers: writing and discipline

Being members of organisations, it is not surprising that children are subject to organisational control. Studies (mainly American) of Japan's preschools have furthered our understanding of the social regulation of children (*Journal of Japanese Studies* [15(1) 1989]). Similarly, some scholars have examined how mothers are controlled by teachers (Fujita 1989; Boocock 1989: 59; Ben-Ari 1987). Yet for all of these analyses, little is known about how teachers do not only control, but are themselves also controlled. In other words, there is almost no mention of the manner by which the actions of caretakers are supervised and directed.

Writing, as Goody (1977: 37) points out, makes it possible to scrutinise discourse in a particularly critical way by giving oral communication a semi-permanent form. Criticism is possible because of the manner by which writing lays out discourse before one's eyes. Let me give a few examples from Katsura Hoikuen. First, I often noticed that the head teacher and her deputy simply compared the programme stipulated in documents to what had been carried out by the teachers: whether they had gone through all of the stages of a morning programme or completed the special walking exercises with a disabled child. Second, teachers were often scrutinised by examining how they had filled out documents and forms: the condition of the class register or the preparation of written material for disabled children. In all of these cases, documents figured as a basis for assessing the professional standards and performance of caretakers in terms of their roles vis-à-vis the children.

But time and again in the field, I found that forms were examined in other ways. Bittner (1974: 78) suggests that one criterion for judging the coherence of the order in an organisation is its 'stylistic unity.' What I found was that the deputy head of the centre repeatedly went over the forms the teachers were using in a particular way. While her purpose was to see that they were properly filled out, she often focussed on the aesthetic 'feel' of the texts and not only on the means–ends links between the texts and the organisational reality of the centre. In what is perhaps a very common bureaucratic mode of inspection, the corrections she suggested were things like filling in a missing square in a table, or making sure that all of the columns of a chart were filled up. One time, she told me that a 'messy document is indicative of messy management and messy implementation.' In these cases then, the aesthetics of texts become indicators of organisational action. Probably as a reaction to this situation, teachers often used 'formulas' – groups of words which are regularly employed under the same conditions to express a given essential idea (Goody 1977: 114) – in filling out the forms so that they 'look good' when filled in.

In addition, the overall management of the centre is inspected primarily through written forms. Katsura Hoikuen's head teacher attributed the large amounts of paperwork she had to do to the many directives of the city office in regard to administrative and financial matters, and wearily shrugged it off as part of running a daycare centre. Indeed, the reports of inspectors not only establish an appraisal of what is happening at a particular centre, but also add up – in a manner similar to personal histories of individuals – to a cumulative record of a preschool. This record, in turn, can then be read by someone disconnected from the immediate context of the daycare centre in a way that creates the history of improvement or deterioration of the institution. Accordingly, when one ward official that I interviewed talked of changes at various preschools, he based his opinions on a variety of reports without the need to be physically present in these places.

In a related vein, the variety of documents produced at the level of specific establishments figure in the control of preschools by the Japanese state. It, like all modern states, draws extensively on this documentation in order to formulate policies and to regulate the flow of resources to different areas and institutions. In this sense, the regulation of preschools cannot be understood apart from more general processes of social control in contemporary Japan. As in the case of biomedicine, 'The dissemination of statistics together with the accompanying commentary is, of course, an integral part of the apparatus that has served in Japan during the post war years to promote social order and facilitate control over the future' (Lock 1993: 47–8). At the ward office, for instance, I was shown tables of such data as the number of children, parents' income, the number and type of disabled children, average age of teachers and salaries. All of these documents, ward officials explained to me, figure in the procedures by which municipal government policies are determined.

Conclusion: the organisation of daycare

An ethnographic look at such establishments as Katsura Hoikuen reveals the importance of documents and documentation in discharging and achieving their organisational programmes. It is in these texts that many of the routine (and not so routine) activities of preschools are recorded, and from which they are retrieved (for action) by caretakers. It is through the use of such administrative texts that the problems of coordinating people and resources across the spaces and times of such institutions are dealt with. Such texts are clearly indispensable for scheduling, for they allow life in this complex organisation to be coordinated, synchronised, and planned. The organisational 'advantages' of written texts lie in their being repositories of knowledge (which caretakers can use at their discretion and without the need to commit too much to memory), means for the scrutinising activities and flows so that wasted phenomena can be eliminated, and instruments for the control of children, parents and teachers.

These texts are also central to the manner by which notions of child development are rendered into the organisational arrangements of

Japanese preschools. My study forms part of a wider set of inquiries that
are uncovering what Peak (1991) terms the Japanese 'folk psychology' of
care and guidance proffered to children, or what White and LeVine
(1986: 55) term the 'culture specific understandings' by which Japanese
parents and educators classify the means and ends of child development.
Hence, if we critically examine the 'common-sense' notions (Bittner
1974: 70) on which preschools are based, we may be able to uncover the
practices by which children, parents and teachers are 'framed' (i.e.
defined and understood), and the manner by which care is imparted in
these establishments. My aim, however, was not to add yet another expo-
sition of Japanese cultural understandings, but to take the suggestions
found in recent studies in a new, and what I think is a fruitful, direction.
In this paper, I examined the ways in which Japanese 'folk' psychologies
or cultural models are actualised in the organisational arrangements of
institutions of early childhood education, that is, in powerful bureaucratic
frameworks charged with caring for children. On a more general level, my
argument is that it is through schedules and timetables that the
space–time paths of children are linked to wider notions of proper development and to organisational exigencies: these are the means by which
the routines of daily life at the centre produce and reproduce beliefs and
professional 'folk' theories about proper care.

Next, take the standardisation achieved by the use of written documents in institutions of preschool education. One explanation for this
homogeneity is that there is a continuity of cultural practices in Japanese
society that explains the uniformity of many features of preschools. While
I agree that such continuities along the life course do exist, I would add
that the continuities are also to a great degree organisationally produced
and maintained. These patterns form part of the processes of normalisa-
tion of individuals (and families) that the Japanese state (like any state)
has undertaken in the name of enhancing unity, stability, and economic
progress (Lock 1993: 43; Holloway 2000). In this sense, the coordinated
and efficient use of people and resources, the discipline and control of
teachers and the national standardisation of preschool education
actualise the macro forces of the state's penetration into individuals' lives.

To take off from Goodman's introduction to this volume, an important
role of anthropology is to uncover the kinds of assumptions that lie at the
base of social policies. What my chapter adds, however, is an exemplifica-
tion of how a detailed ethnographic approach can uncover the means at
the disposal of the state to control its population. In other words, if we
wish to understand the (continued) power of states to institute social
policies, we must take into account the authoritative measures at its disposal. Thus, my argument is not based on some sinister conspiracy theory
at the base of state actions. Rather, if we understand the administrative

means that bureaucracies use in both classifying the world and constructing it according to their own internal set of priorities, we may more fruitfully comprehend the power and pervasiveness of states.

REFERENCES

Ben-Ari, Eyal. 1987. 'Disputing about day-care: care-taking roles in a Japanese day nursery.' *International Journal of Sociology of the Family,* 17: 197–216.

——. 1994. 'Caretaking with a pen? documentation, classification and 'normal' development in a Japanese day-care center.' *International Journal of Modern Sociology,* 24(2): 31–48.

——. 1995. 'Forms of quality? Documentation, standardization and discipline in a Japanese day-care center.' *Education and Society,* 12(2): 3–20.

——. 1996. 'From mothering to othering: organization, culture and naptime in a Japanese day-care center.' *Ethos,* 24(1): 136–64.

——. 1997a. *Body projects in Japanese Childcare: Culture, Organization and Emotions in Preschools.* London: Curzon.

——. 1997b. *Japanese Childcare: An Interpretive Study of Culture and Organization.* London: Kegan Paul International.

Bittner, Egon. 1974. 'The concept of organization,' pp. 69–81 in *Ethnomethodology,* ed. Roy Turner. Harmondsworth: Penguin.

Boocock, Saranne S. 1989. 'Controlled diversity: an overview of the Japanese preschool system.' *Journal of Japanese Studies,* 15(1): 41–68.

Bruner, Jerome. 1986. *Actual Minds, Possible Worlds.* Cambridge, Mass.: Harvard University Press.

Fujita, Mariko. 1989. "It's all Mother's fault': childcare and socialization of working mothers in Japan.' *Journal of Japanese Studies,* 15(1): 67–92.

Fuller, Bruce, Susan D. Holloway, Hiroshi Azuma, Robert D. Hess, and Keiko Kashiwagi. 1986. 'Contrasting achievement rules: socialization of Japanese at home and in school.' *Research in Sociology of Education,* 6: 165–201.

Giddens, Anthony. 1987. *Social Theory and Modern Sociology.* London: Polity Press.

Goody, Jack. 1977. *The Domestication of the Savage Mind.* Cambridge: Cambridge University Press.

Hacking, Ian. 1990. *The Taming of Chance.* Cambridge: Cambridge University Press.

Handelman, Don. 1981. 'Introduction: the idea of bureaucratic organization.' *Social Analysis,* 9: 5–23.

Hendry, Joy. 1986a. *Becoming Japanese: The World of the Pre-School Child.* Manchester: Manchester University Press.

——. 1986b. 'Kindergartens and the transition from home to school education.' *Comparative Education,* 22(1): 53–8.

Holloway, Susan D. 2000. *Contested Childhood: Diversity and Change in Japanese Preschools.* New York: Routledge.

Ivy, Marilyn. 1989. 'Critical texts, mass artifacts: the consumption of knowledge in postmodern Japan,' pp. 21–46 in *Postmodernism and Japan,* ed. Masao Miyoshi and H.D. Harootunian. Durham: Duke University Press.

Kelly, William W. 1986. 'Rationalization and nostalgia: cultural dynamics of new middle-class Japan.' *American Ethnologist*, 13(4): 603–18.

Kotloff, Lauren J. 1988. 'Dai-Ichi Preschool: Fostering Individuality and Cooperative Group Life in a Progressive Japanese Preschool.' PhD Thesis. Cornell University.

Lewis, Catherine. 1989. 'From indulgence to internalization: social control in the early school years.' *Journal of Japanese Studies*, 15(1): 139–57.

——. 1995. *Educating Hearts and Minds: Reflections on Japanese Preschool and Elementary Education.* Cambridge: Cambridge University Press.

Lock, Margaret M. 1993. 'Ideology, female midlife, and the greying of Japan.' *Journal of Japanese Studies*, 19(1): 43–78.

Moeran, Brian. 1984. *Lost Innocence: Folk Craft Potters of Onta, Japan.* Berkeley: University of California Press.

Peak, Lois. 1989. 'Learning to become part of the group: the Japanese child's transition to preschool life.' *Journal of Japanese Studies*, 15(1): 93–124.

——. 1991. *Learning to Go to School in Japan: The Transition from Home to Preschool Life.* Berkeley: University of California Press.

Pondy, Louis R. 1977. 'Effectiveness: a thick description,' pp. 226–34 in *New Perspectives on Organizational Effectiveness*, ed. Paul S. Goodman, Johannes M. Pennings and Associates. San Francisco: Jossey-Bass.

Rohlen, Thomas P. 1989a. 'Introduction.' *Journal of Japanese Studies*, 15(1): 1–4.

——. 1989b. 'Order in Japanese society: attachment, authority, and routine.' *Journal of Japanese Studies*, 15(1): 5–40.

Roth, Julius A. 1963. *Timetables.* Indianapolis: Bobbs-Merrill.

Sato, Ikuya 1991. *Kamikaze Biker: Parody and Anomy in Affluent Japan.* Chicago: University of Chicago Press.

Schoppa, Leonard J. 1991. *Education Reform in Japan: A Case of Immobilist Politics.* London: Routledge.

Tobin, Joseph J., David Y.H. Wu, and Dana H. Davidson. 1989. *Preschool in Three Cultures: Japan, China, and the United States.* New Haven: Yale University Press.

Weick, Karl E. 2001. *Making Sense of the Organization.* Oxford: Blackwell.

White, Merry and Robert A. LeVine. 1986. 'What is an *Ii Ko* (Good Child)?' pp. 55–62 in *Child Development and Education in Japan*, ed. Harold Stevenson, Hiroshi Azuma and Kenji Hakuta. New York: W.H. Freeman.

Zerubavel, Eviatar. 1981. *Hidden Rhythms: Schedules and Calendars in Social Life.* Chicago: University of Chicago Press.

6   Child abuse in Japan: 'discovery' and the development of policy

Roger Goodman

As a review of three of Japan's national quality newspapers – *Yomiuri, Asahi* and *Mainichi* – and its Kyōdō newsagency during two separate periods shows, it was unusual for more than a few days to pass in the middle of 2001 without a story appearing in the Japanese media about child abuse.[1]

5 to 18 May 2001

5 May
Mainichi: Girl beaten to death for eating dog food

6 May
Mainichi: Random torture leaves Sayuri a vegetable

7 May
Kyōdō: Officer's wife arrested for fatally injuring colleague's baby

8 May
Yomiuri: Police arrest couple over abandonment of boy's body

9 May
Mainichi: Autopsy of toddler reveals parents' starvation tactics

11 May
Asahi: Total child abuse cases may be over 30,000 per year

14 May
Asahi: Everyone has role in preventing child abuse
Kyōdō: Aichi women pleads guilty to murdering 2-year-old daughter

17 May
Yomiuri: Poll: Babies often target of serious abuse
Mainichi: Child abuse arrests increase by 27%
Kyōdō: Child abuse soars, 16 dead in 3 months. Report

18 May
Yomiuri: National Police Agency: Child abuse cases up 30%

20 June to 10 July 2001

20 June
Kyōdō: Aichi woman gets suspended term for leaving daughter's body in icebox

21 June
Mainichi: Staggering 18,000 child abuse cases reported last year

22 June
Asahi: Reported child abuse cases up 50%
Yomiuri: Child abuse cases grow 17-fold over past decade
Japan Times: Child-killer sent up for 15 years

23 June
Yomiuri: 2 arrested over death at nursery
Mainichi: Woman dumps newborn's body

24 June
Kyōdō: 73% of female inmates in central Japan sexually abused

26 June
Mainichi: Abusive parents jailed over baby bottle bashing

30 June
Kyōdō: Shimane woman nabbed for drowning infant daughter

2 July
Mainichi: 450 kids killed by abuse over 10 years

4 July
Mainichi: Osaka step-dad beats bed-wetting daughter to death

5 July
Mainichi: Woman admits to fatally beating stepson

9 July
Kyōdō: Man gets suspended term for hanging boy upside down

10 July
Mainichi: Man fatally bashes baby for not drinking milk

Few articles on any day could avoid pointing to the one statistic which summed up the sense that child abuse was becoming endemic in Japanese society, that the number of cases of child abuse reported to the local child consultation offices (*jidōsōdanjo*) which have primary statutory responsibility for investigating such cases had increased 17-fold in just ten years. Figure 6.1 was often reproduced to make the point visually. Other reports suggested that the real rate of child abuse was actually much higher still. One widely disseminated survey (*YS* 10 August 1999; *MS* 15 May 1999),

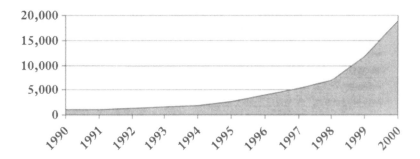

Figure 6.1   Increase in child abuse cases dealt with by *jidōsōdanjo* in Japan, 1990–2000
Sources: KH 1998: 111; *AS* 2 November 2000; *YS* 22 June 2001

carried out by the Centre for Child Abuse Prevention (Kodomo no Gyakutai Bōshi Centre, CCAP) in Tokyo, concluded that as many as 40 percent of mothers actually either abused or mistreated their children and that there were very few overt differences in behaviour between admitted abusers and other mothers.

The philosopher, Ian Hacking (1992: 193), in his well-known article, 'World-making by kind-making,' has pointed out that,

> The selection of child abuse as a vital classification has had enormous conse-quences in the law, in day-to-day social work, in policing the family, in the lives of children, and the way in which children and adults represent their actions, their past, and those of their neighbours.

The widespread public activity and debate at the turn of the millen-nium surrounding the issue of child abuse has certainly had important implications for the relationship between the state, parents and children in Japan as well as suggesting different way of thinking about such appar-ently 'natural' and incontestable categories as 'parent' and 'child.' But perhaps this debate has been all the more shocking in Japan in that just ten years earlier, the majority of Japanese, including many professionals in child welfare, believed that there was no, or virtually no, child abuse in Japan (see, for example, Ikeda 1987: 204). This absence of abuse was confidently explained in terms of the stability of the Japanese family, community and wider society (see Wagatsuma 1981, for a good example in English of this argument).

The general view of child abuse in the 1980s

The structure of the Japanese family, it was maintained in the 1980s, made the likelihood of child abuse much lower than in western societies because 'traditional' family ties remained strong (60 percent of the elderly still lived with someone of a younger generation as opposed to only eight percent in the UK and 14 percent in the US). This meant not only extra hands to help but also extra eyes to detect abuse. Crude divorce rates (the number of divorces per total population) were less than half those of the UK and almost one-quarter those of the USA (*JIC* 1987: 92). Annual illegitimacy rates were still below one per cent (compared to around 30 percent in US and UK and over 50 percent in some European countries). Indeed in recognition of the importance to a Japanese child of having a socially recognised father (*pater*), a husband was sometimes registered as a child's father even if it was known that he was not the biological father (*genitor*) (Shimazu 1994: 83). Teenage mothers were almost non-existent; almost 90 percent of teenagers who became pregnant had abortions (Kojima 1986: 136). Japan had not only one of the highest average ages at first marriage for both men (28) and women (almost 26) but also one of the highest proportions of the population getting married (less than 5 percent of men and women aged 50 had never married) (Ochiai 1996: 55). Few women had followed the path of an increasing number of women in Western Europe and North America of bringing children up by themselves. Single parent families constituted less than 1.5% of all households (Peng 1995).

Both the status and style of motherhood were also seen as playing a major role in preventing child abuse in Japan. Japan had a well-documented and sharply drawn division of labour around gender (male, public sphere; female, domestic sphere) where the two roles were ideologically supposed to complement each other. For women, the dual role of mother and wife was seen as a professional one, and fulfilling it well conferred high status. Non-working women described themselves as *sengyō shufu* (professional housewives) on official forms (Imamura 1987). At the start of the UN Year of the Child (1991), the then Prime Minister Kaifū made a speech in which he declared that the reason Japan had few social problems and a well-educated population was that women stayed at home and looked after their children. With 96 percent of mothers in Japan finishing senior high school and over 40 percent completing some form of tertiary education, Japanese mothers were almost certainly the most highly educated in the world as well as, on average, among the most mature in years at the time they first became mothers.

Other factors that were also seen to make child abuse unlikely included the continuing stability of the community, the high status of community institutions and the acceptance of the authority of the state. The system of local police boxes (*kōban*) meant a much closer relationship between members of the police force and the local community than in most western societies. The *minsei jidōiin* system (see Goodman 1998) meant that any abuse of children within the local community should be picked up very early by voluntary welfare workers, who were members of the same community. Teachers enjoyed high status in society and parents listened to and accepted their advice. Schools gave regular physical check-ups to all children and insisted that parents follow up any concerns by visiting their doctors.

Finally, the stability of post-war society more generally was seen as important in explaining the absence of abuse of children. As sociologists who often argued a link between the two might have put it, the lack of deprivation precluded an increase in deprivation. The fruits of Japan's impressive post-war economic growth had been relatively equally shared throughout the society. Over 90 percent of the population annually declared themselves to be members of a mass middle class and there was a widespread belief in both the cultural homogeneity of the Japanese population and the lack of significant minority groups. Recorded rates for all forms of serious crime were very low compared with all other OECD countries. Murder rates were one-fifth, rates of reported rape one-tenth, rates of robbery one-sixtieth of those in the UK. Arrest rates were remarkably high – 98 percent for murder and rape; almost 80 percent for robbery (*JIC* 1987: 92) – and those arrested were almost always convicted. People in Japan had the sense that they and their children lived in a very safe country. Overall, therefore, it seemed that for a wide variety of reasons Japan diverged from the view of many experts at the time (see Korbin 1987) that child abuse was a concomitant feature of all developed societies.

'Hidden' child abuse

It should be said that even before the 1990s not everyone in Japan accepted that there was no child abuse in the country. Ikeda (1987), for example, suggested that those few cases of abuse that were reported were probably only those instances where it was impossible for the abuse to be ignored any further. Others laid the low rates of reported abuse on factors such as a lack of a well-articulated system of reporting and recording child abuse and a strong reluctance to get involved in the personal business of others in part, according to Kitamura et al. (1999: 24), because of fears of being sued by victims' parents for defamation. Some commentators in the US during the 1980s also described some Japanese cultural practices such as co-sleeping and co-bathing as potentially or even actually abusive, though their writings told us as much about American social values as they did about Japanese society.[2]

Technically, under Article 25 of the 1947 Child Welfare Law, anyone who saw a child who was not being properly cared for was obliged to report it to the *jidōsōdanjo* or the local welfare office. The law, however, was not backed up by any sanction. Very few people reported their concerns about children with whom they had no direct link; in 1990 of the 12,000 child welfare cases referred to the twelve Tokyo *jidōsōdanjo*, only 0.9% were referrals by neighbours (Tokyo-to Fukushiyoku Jidōbu 1990). Even doctors and teachers often appeared unwilling to report suspicions of abuse (Hashimoto 1996: 146). A 1991 survey in the Kinki district of Japan suggested that less than half of the doctors in the area would unconditionally report to *jidōsōdanjo* child abuse cases, which they came across in the course of their work (*JTW* 12 December 1994). Similarly, while teachers at the compulsory school level (up to the age of 15) were obliged to visit students at home at least once a year, it would appear that they very rarely took suspicions of possible child abuse any further than talking directly to the parents and/or guardians involved.

Even when cases were taken further, some critics suggested that the local government workers in the *jidōsōdanjo* were reluctant to seek recourse to the law for fear that a case they brought would be unsuccessful and that this might harm their future careers in local government. As a result, the trend appeared to be to redefine cases of suspected child abuse as '*yōiku kanren*' (general concerns to do with bringing up children) and attempt to advise the parents on correct and acceptable practice, rather than seek to remove the child, even temporarily, to a safer environment.

Further, there was considerable evidence that the police were reluctant – and of course Japan was far from alone in this – to get involved in domestic 'disputes.' The section of the police that dealt with such cases, recently renamed the *seikatsu anzenka* (life safety section), had little or no specialist training in dealing with issues of abuse and tended to be looked down upon by other sections of the force. According to various voluntary civil rights groups, girls who were picked up by the police for teenage prostitution sometimes claimed that they had been abused at home but were often taken back there without their allegations being examined (*JTW* 13 June 1994).

Even if the police did wish to pursue a case, it was widely recognised that the courts were reluctant to become involved in issues of child abuse because of the rights afforded to parents in Japan. According to Kamiide (1990: 8), although there was a provision for removing parental powers under Article 33–6 of the Child Welfare Law, there were only ten instances where this was in force in 1990. In any case, even when courts placed children in *yōgoshisetsu* (children's homes), parents retained the right to remove them when they wanted.

Moreover, as Ikeda (1982: 489 and 1984: 11) noted, once a child was removed from an institution by its parents, the case was considered closed, and there was no follow-up work undertaken with the family or monitoring of the child. Some children's homes were sensitive to this and, as a result, there were examples of children being hidden in homes or moved around between homes as the only means of protecting them from parents or guardians who wanted to claim them back (see Sargeant 1994).

Defining child abuse

Even before the 1990s, therefore, a handful of groups dealing with child welfare issues began to question whether the apparently low level of child abuse in Japan was genuine and some surveys were undertaken to monitor the situation.

Among the most interesting features of the first surveys of child abuse in Japan were the definitions of what constituted child abuse (see Fujimoto 1994). A 1973 survey, the first to be carried out by the government, used the five categories of: abandonment; murder; *oyako shinjū* (discussed below); murder by abandonment; and abuse, which was defined as causing physical injuries by violence, not providing food over a long period and endangering life. The distinction in the survey between 'abandonment' and 'murder by abandonment' referred largely to where the child was found abandoned. In the former case, children were generally left in open public areas such as parks, hospitals and post offices with the intention that they should be found and taken into care; in the latter case, they were found locked in their own homes or coin lockers and had been left to die.

The survey was undertaken in the light of reports of an increase in the number of infants being abandoned by mothers in coin lockers, which had recently been installed in Japanese railway stations. Indeed, over a quarter of all murdered babies that had been abandoned were, according to the survey, found in coin lockers, and while countermeasures were taken in 1981 which dramatically reduced the number, the practice continued, as did other forms of murder by abandonment (see Kouno and Johnson 1995). According to some commentators, however, there was a considerable degree of sympathy towards the mother in such cases. If the mother of the abandoned baby were found, she was rarely given a prison sentence. According to Haley (1998: 88–9), around 40 percent of prosecutions in cases of maternal infanticide were suspended and

> where mothers are sentenced, sentences tend to be light and seldom do the courts actually enforce even a mild sanction ... Japanese generally empathize with the mother and tolerate without condoning the action.

The category of '*oyako shinjū*' perhaps gives the most interesting insight into how ideas about abuse are linked to the relationship between parent and child in Japan. *Oyako shinjū* is also known variously in

Japanese as *boshi shinjū, fushi shinjū* and *ikka shinjū* where the first word in each expression refers respectively to parent–child, mother–child, father–child and whole-family and the word '*shinjū*' connotes a double suicide committed out of love. (It is indeed the word used for a suicide pact made by lovers.) Neither in Japanese – nor in English translation – is the word 'murder' ever used in what is, in practical terms, the murder of the child by the parent followed by the parent's suicide.

The practice of *oyako shinjū* has a long history in Japan but high rates have particularly been recorded in times of economic depression. The expression '*oyako shinjū*' probably dates from the mid-1920s when abortion was made illegal – in a state-driven attempt to increase the fertility rate – and many unwanted babies were born. Indeed, in the 1930s, it became so widespread that it was in response to it that the government enacted the first child welfare legislation in 1933 (Jidō Gyakutai Bōshihō) and 1937 (Boshi Hogohō).

Figures for *oyako shinjū* are clearly difficult to collect and there is wide variation in the numbers given for different years. The crux of the problem is that no official figures are kept and hence researchers have to rely on newspaper reports and many cases either do not reach the newspapers or else are reported only in local editions. From the top end of the scale, Pinguet (1993: 49) cites an unidentified source giving a figure of 494 cases in 1975; Garrison (1984) gives the figure of 400 reported incidents of *oyako shinjū* involving over 1000 deaths in 1983; Takahashi (1977: 66) states that there were 59 cases during the three months of April, May and June of 1974; Tsuji (1982: 2) says there were 80 cases reported in the Tokyo edition of the *Asahi Shinbun* for 1978; CAPNA (1998: 63–4), again working from media reports, suggests that there were 54 incidents leading to the deaths of 76 children in 1996 and 1997 combined. In surveys of *oyako shinjū*, it would appear that 70–80 percent are in fact cases of *boshi shinjū* (mother-and-child suicide); almost all involve married parents generally in their thirties; and it would appear to largely be an urban phenomenon, although this may reflect the rate of reporting as much as of actual practice. The vast majority (over 80 percent) of the children who died were aged seven or less.

Describing what is in effect child-murder as family-suicide is revealing of social attitudes. Even more revealing, though, are accounts of the criticism of those who have committed – or who have attempted to commit – suicide without first killing their children. Takahashi (1977) and Garrison (1984) both describe the case of a mother who unsuccessfully attempted suicide and was severely criticised for not having murdered her children first; she successfully performed *boshi shinjū* at her next attempt. The specifically cultural nature of *oyako shinjū*, however, is best demonstrated when the practice has taken place overseas, a well-documented example of which is the so-called 'Santa Monica *Oyako Shinjū* Case' (see Woo 1989).

In 1985, a Japanese woman in her mid-thirties living in California, on discovering her husband's infidelity and with one failed marriage behind her already, decided to commit suicide and took her two children (aged four years and six months) to the beach with her. She managed to drown the children in the Pacific Ocean but was rescued by people who were on the beach at the time and subsequently found herself facing prosecution for the double murder of her children. The Japanese–American community with support from Japan managed to collect a 25,000-name petition on her behalf appealing that the case should be viewed as an example not of child murder but of *oyako shinjū*. Her supporters argued that there had been no malice towards the children in what she had done: indeed, she had done it out of her love for them and, hence, she should be given a lenient, probationary sentence. According to Woo (1989), her American lawyer was unwilling to pursue this cultural defence, not least because, in arguing that she knew what she was doing in killing the children, she would be seriously prejudicing her own position in terms of American law. Instead, he found a number of American psychologists who were able to diagnose her mental state at the time of the incident as one of 'introjection' – the inability to distinguish her own life from those of her children which in American cultural terms could be termed a form of temporary insanity – and thereby neatly turned a cultural practice (*oyako shinjū*) into a psychological pathology.

The above case goes a long way in demonstrating the different perceptions of the parent–child relationship in Japan and the United States at the time. In Japan, the child has often been described as a *mono* (object) that is an extension of, rather than separate from, the parent (Yamamura 1986: 34). The rights of the family have come before those of the child, and where the child has clearly suffered, this has been explained in terms of the over-zealous actions of an adult who was acting only in the best interests of the family. According to Wagatsuma (1981: 120), writing in the early 1980s, the fact that parents were more likely to kill or abandon their children than keep and abuse them explained the apparently low rate of the forms of child abuse that were practised in other societies. Similarly, Ikeda (1987: 206) made a distinction between what she called Japanese-style (*Nihongata*) forms of abuse (such as abandonment and *oyako shinjū*) and 'Western' (*Ōbeigata*) forms of abuse (such as sexual and physical maltreatment).

In 1988, however, a large survey of child abuse in Japan was undertaken which did not include the category of *oyako shinjū* at all (see Table 6.1). Instead, the definition of abuse used was 'physical violence, abandonment and desertion, neglect or refusal to protect, sexual assault, emotional

Table 6.1 Survey of abuse of children under the age of 17 (1 April–30 September 1988)

	Physical violence	Abandonment/ desertion	Refusal to protect	Sexual assault	Emotional abuse	Forbidden to go to school	Total
Natural father	106	39	111	20	28	13	317
Step-father	29	3	17	10	1	–	60
Live-in father	15	–	3	9	2	2	31
Foster father	–	–	–	1	–	–	1
Natural mother	79	162	235	–	20	10	506
Step-mother	15	–	7	–	12	–	34
Live-in mother	4	1	5	–	3	–	13
Foster mother	1	–	–	–	–	–	1
Other people	26	–	13	8	2	3	52
Unknown	–	24	–	–	–	–	24
Percentage affected	26.5	22.0	37.5	4.6	6.5	2.7	

N=1039
Source: Fujimoto, 1994: 59 (based on a survey by the Association of Heads of Jidōsōdanjo [Jidōsōdanjochōkai])

abuse and prevention from attending school' (Tsuzaki 1996: 112–16). These categories were much closer to definitions of abuse in North America and northern Europe at the time.

The figure for sexual abuse in the survey (less than 5 percent of all abuse cases) reflected a situation in Japan which was different from that in the US and UK where, as Hacking (1991) pointed out, sexual abuse had by itself in the late 1980s become virtually synonymous with the category of child abuse. (According to Pringle [1998: 33], however, within Europe, the focus on sexual abuse is peculiar to the UK.) La Fontaine (1988; 1990) has argued that it was the redefinition of child sexual abuse in terms of an abuse of power that led to a major change in the perception of abuse in general in the UK in the mid-1980s. The redefinition of incest as child abuse was a particularly important step. In Japan, the view of incestuous relationships according to some commentators, has been, as La Fontaine (1988: 6) said the view was in the UK in the mid-1980s, 'oddly muted'. Allison (1996: 7), for example, examines in detail articles that explored the issue of mother–son incestuous relations in the 1970s and 1980s in Japan, the tone of which she describes as ranging 'from condemnatory to sympathetic and almost celebratory'. While it is difficult to measure such things, it would seem that if there is a slightly higher preponderance of mother–son incest cases in Japan than elsewhere (for which the evidence in any case is very weak), it is still the case (despite media and other reports to the contrary – see Kitahara 1989b) that they represent only a small fraction of all incest cases. Allison (1996) ascribes the attention focused in the 1970s and 1980s on such cases to a conservative, probably mainly male, backlash against the increased number of women in the workplace and a perception that women were becoming increasingly selfish in fulfilling their desires to have both children and a career.

Japanese law still does not recognise incest (*kinshin sōkan*) as a crime – though morally it may be abhorred – unless rape or indecent assault has taken place (which may be difficult to prove) and the victim is prepared to press charges (which is very hard for them to do). Child sexual abuse reporting, therefore, has almost always been limited to the sexual abuse of girls over the age of ten (almost always by adult men) or the forcing of children to perform obscene acts with a third party (Ikeda 1987: 70). In Table 6.1, all but one of the cases of sexual abuse were of girls over the age of ten. In all but one case, the perpetrator was a man. Indeed, one interesting feature of the rising rates of reported child abuse during the 1990s was that the relative proportions of different categories of abuse generally remained the same. In almost all years, just over half of all cases involved physical abuse; around 30 percent related to cases of neglect; ten percent involved psychological abuse; and around six percent involved sexual abuse. The idea that young boys and girls can be sexually abused has proved to be the most difficult perception to change. In part, Kitamura et al. (1999: 24) suggest, this is because of the embarrassment in investigating suspicions and fears of stigmatising victims.

The definition of physical abuse in the early 1990s was also unclear in Japan. Indeed, when child abuse hot-lines were set up in Osaka and Tokyo in 1990 and 1991 respectively, they immediately received up to 20 calls a day mainly from mothers, mainly wanting to know whether what they were doing to their children constituted abuse and, if so, what they could do to stop it (Nashima, *JTW* 13 June 1994). By the end of the first year of both hot-lines, some 90 percent of all calls were on the same theme (Katō and Tatsuno 1998: 108–9). Much of the uncertainty reflected by these callers related to the fact that the use of physical force against children was described using a number of different expressions: '*taibatsu*' (corporal punishment), '*chōkai*' (disciplinary punishment), '*gyakutai*' (abuse) and the more general term, '*shitsuke*' (training). Only the third of these terms carries a totally negative connotation, while the others could all be used in a positive sense depending on the context. As Hendry (1986: 11) points out, for example, the Chinese character for '*shitsuke*' is made up of two parts meaning 'body' and 'beauty'. The right of parents to use *chōkai* 'in so far as it is necessary' is indeed enshrined in article 822 (*chōkaiken*) of the revised Civil Code (Oda 1997: 168).

Confusion about the appropriateness of physical punishment was not restricted to domestic situations. While, legally, the position on using force against children in education is very clear, and physical punishment is banned in all Japanese schools (Gakkō Kyōikuhō, Article 11), in reality, the use of physical discipline has often been accepted as an integral part of turning Japanese children into adult members of Japanese society (Field 1995: 59). A 1984 survey, for example, suggested that physical punishment was practised in almost all (97 percent) of Japanese schools (*AS* 30 May 1984). Perhaps more significant, however, were surveys which suggested that the majority of parents (regularly about 70 percent) supported the use of discipline as being good for their children (*kodomo no tame*). In a 1996 survey undertaken by the All Japan Parents and Teachers Association, only 25.6% of respondents said that corporal punishment should never be administered by a teacher (see http://www.indis.co.jp/sugita).

The most extreme example, however, of the apparent social acceptance of physical punishment in the socialisation of children is probably the case of Totsuka Hiroshi. During the 1980s, at the Totsuka Yacht School in Aichi Prefecture, Totsuka, a former Olympic yachtsman, reigned over a regime of extreme discipline that was intended to 'improve' the anti-social behaviour of children with emotional problems who had been placed by their families in his care. Three children died and two went missing presumed dead as a result of treatment received at the home, and Totsuka was arrested and tried for murder. In 1992, the Nagoya District Court acknowledged that the two deaths were the result of injuries inflicted on them but handed down suspended sentences to Totsuka and three instructors in the school on the grounds that they had acted not for profit but in what they believed were the best interests of the children. Soon afterwards, Totsuka re-opened the school and had no problem finding parents willing to entrust children to his care in the belief that his extreme regime of socialisation, which included beating and confining children, was in the best interests of their children. The institution was only closed in 1997 when the Nagoya High Court, on appeal by the prosecution in the original case, overturned the lower court decision (*MDN* 13 March 1997; Yoneyama 1999: 94–5). Totsuka was sentenced to six years in prison, although he did not begin this sentence until March 2002 when his final appeal was turned down almost exactly twenty years after his original arrest (Kyōdō 30 March 2002). The use of physical punishment by staff in children's homes (*yōgoshisetsu*) was banned by law with the revision of the child welfare law in 1998, but a survey carried out almost two years later suggested that only 30 percent of homes had actually instituted rules prohibiting it and only 15 percent instructed their staff about the rights of the children in their care (*AS* 12 April 2000).

The 'discovery' of child abuse in Japan

The 1988 survey seemed to show a sudden 450 percent increase in cases of child abuse dealt with by the *jidōsōdanjo* since a previous survey undertaken only five years earlier. Certain groups immediately declared that the statistics were the 'tip of the iceberg' (*hyōzan no ikkaku*) (see Ueno 1994: 9) and that child abuse was a serious issue that needed to be confronted in Japan. Partly in response to these concerns, in 1990 the government constructed an official definition of child abuse – limited to the four categories of physical abuse, neglect or the refusal to protect, sexual abuse and psychological abuse (see *KH* 1997: 91 for a fuller definition); established the category of 'abuse' (*gyakutai*) among the reasons for a consultation at *jidōsōdanjo*; and began to publish statistics annually. Some subsequent statistics also included the category of *tōkō kinshi* (prevention of children from attending school), but the numbers were so negligible that they were normally excluded. In Tokyo, for example, they amounted to between one and three cases per year (Tokyo-to Fukushikyoku 1998: 23). (For a good account of the debates over the definition of child abuse in Japan in the early 1990s, see Jidō Gyakutai Bōshi Seido Kenkyūkai, ed. 1993.)

As so often in the history of child welfare in Japan, however, the first major initiatives in dealing with the perceived new and growing problems of child abuse were private. These were the establishment of two child-abuse telephone counselling services (*jidō gyakutai sōdan denwa*) in 1990 and 1991 in Osaka and Tokyo respectively. The Osaka Line was set up by a voluntary group that called itself Jidō Gyakutai Bōshi Kyōkai (Association for the Prevention of Child Abuse, APCA). It received 90 percent of its funding from the Kansai Television Company – which screened three one-hour documentaries on child abuse in 1989 – and it was a non-profitmaking, non-governmental organisation staffed by part-time workers. When the line was set up, concerns were expressed over the role of a major television company and the potential for 'commercial exploitation.' As a result, it has been run by a board of 20 members, of whom ten or more must be employees of the local government.

A year later, a voluntary organisation called Kodomo no Gyakutai Bōshi Centre (Centre for Child Abuse Prevention, CCAP) set up a line in Tokyo. In both the Kansai and the Kanto regions, the main actors in constructing the debate about child abuse were lawyers, paediatricians, nurses at the local health centres (*hokenfu*), academics such as Ikeda Yoshiko, and a few well-known and outspoken individuals who worked in family courts, *jidōsōdanjo* and children's homes.

The opening of the Tokyo Line in May 1991 was preceded by a large conference, which brought together a number of different groups to discuss child abuse from a variety of perspectives. This conference, together with the opening of the telephone lines, presaged a sudden growth in awareness of child abuse in Japan and a new vocabulary – specifically the expression *'jidō gyakutai'* – quickly entered the public arena. An analysis by Ueno (1994: 5) of the keyword expression *'Kodomo no Gyakutai'* (Child Abuse) in the *Asahi Shinbun* (Tokyo Edition) showed two uses in the last six months of 1988, nine instances in 1989, 20 in 1990, 22 in 1991, 21 in 1992, and 22 in 1993. During the second half of 1991, articles appeared not only in medical and legal journals but also in popular women's magazines and newspapers. NHK, the national broad-casting company, aired 'specials' on child abuse on three consecutive nights in September. New special interest groups were also formed: the 'WE' group in Yokohama for professionals and victims; and the Stop Child Sexual Abuse (STOPCSA) group for victims only. A number of mothers who had abused or were abusing their children set up their own self-help group to tackle the problem called the *'Kodomo wo gyakutai shite shimau haha oya tachi* (Mothers who cannot stop abusing their children)'.

By the mid-1990s, discussion of child abuse had begun to become a regular part of the world of child welfare specialists. Official figures on child abuse, while apparently still very low by North American and north

European standards, had begun to show the kind of exponential growth that those societies had seen in the 1970s and 1980s (see Figure 6.1). For example, in the United States (with double the population of Japan), the number of reported cases of child abuse rose from 7,000 in 1967 to 60,000 in 1972 to 1.1 million in 1980 to 2.4 million in 1989 (Gilbert 1997: 3; Hacking 1991, 259). The number of children on the child protection register in England (with half the Japanese population) almost quadrupled from 12,388 in 1984 to 45,300 in 1991 (Berridge 1997: 86–7).

The increase in professional awareness of child abuse was made most noticeable by the increasing number of prefectures and major cities (Hokkaidō; Fukushima; Tochigi; Saitama; Gunma; Yokohama; Shizuoka, and Wakayama) that followed the example of Osaka and Tokyo and set up their own organisations to monitor and advise on cases of abuse. These organisations included institutions such as health centres, schools, hospitals and clinics. An association called Nihon Kodomo no Gyakutai Bōshi Kenkyūkai (Japan Society for the Prevention of Child Abuse and Neglect, JaSPCAN) was established as an umbrella organisation to bring together the many regional and local groups. Its third and fourth meetings in 1997 and 1998 in Yokohama and Wakayama were attended by over 1500 professionals from almost all areas of child welfare.

During 1999, the issue of child abuse was forced into the public consciousness even more strongly. In part, this was due to discussion of a new child sex law (introduced in November 1999) in the light of what was perceived to be a growing problem of young girls offering underage sex in exchange for money (a phenomenon known as '*enjo kōsai*') and international criticism of Japan as the source of 80 percent of the commercial child pornography available on the Internet (*DY* 10 December 1998). In part, it was due to a growing awareness of how far Japan was out-of-line with some Western societies in dealing with the issue of domestic violence, following the arrest of the Japanese consul in Canada for abusing his wife; he is alleged to have said that what he had done was acceptable practice in Japan. In part, it was due to the continuing efforts of a number of groups, including doctors, lawyers and those in the child welfare world to continue to raise awareness of the issue. Newspapers mounted a number of investigations into the subject and a survey by the *Mainichi Shinbun* reported that between January 1997 and April 1999, 83 children had been killed as a result of abuse inflicted on them by their parents or other adults (Yamashina, *MS* 26 August 1999). In large part, too, it was due to the increasing vigour of citizen's groups throughout the 1990s, which in turn had become considerably sensitised to the issues of children's rights by the debates which had taken place in Japan during the 1990s in relation to whether the country should, or should not, become a signatory to the UN Convention on the Rights of the Child (see Goodman 1996).

In July 1999, the Ministry of Health and Welfare published the results of its own survey, which revealed that 328 children had died as a result of abuse over the five-year period between 1992 and 1997 (*AS* 28 July 1999). This followed hard on an earlier announcement that 15 children had died in 1997 from abuse that had already been brought to the attention of *jidōsōdanjo* (*AS* 31 March 1999). As a result, the Ministry sent a circular to all *jidōsōdanjo* that greatly broadened the type of cases that they should deal with under the category of abuse. These included cases of neglect where parents left babies alone in prams on the ground floor while they shopped on the second floor, cases of physical abuse even where an 'assault does not leave an external wound' (*gaishō ga nokoranai bōkō*), and cases of psychological abuse where parents discriminated against one child in favour of another (*AS* 5 July 1999).

By the late 1990s, therefore, there had been a major reappraisal of the notion at the beginning of the decade that Japan was immune from the problem of child abuse that afflicted industrial societies in the West. At the end of 1999, it was announced that there was a great increase in the number of reports to *jidōsōdanjo* about suspicions of child abuse from members of the public (*MS* 16 November 1999). Accounts in the media, which had previously been written at the level of discussing the overall levels of abuse reported, began to focus increasingly on individual cases, often in gruesome detail. While most reports focussed on abuse in the family home (and a large proportion of these focussed on the role of step-parents or live-in partners), other reports described horrendous cases of abuse taking place in unregulated kindergartens and private welfare institutions. In many cases, the inactivity of the state authorities was widely criticised. The case of a six-year-old boy, Masato-kun, was particularly widely reported since he was killed despite the fact that no fewer than three *jidōsōdanjo* in two different areas of Japan had been aware that he was being abused. A NHK report (*Close-up Gendai*, 29 June 1999) on the case was particularly critical of the *jidōsōdanjo* in question and, for probably the first time, workers at *jidōsōdanjo* found themselves under pressure for not having actively intervened earlier, as happened in the UK following the growth in awareness of child abuse in the 1980s particularly following the Jasmin Beckford case (see Franklin and Parton 1991). In some reports, the issue of child abuse in Japan took on the aura of a moral panic so that, rather than simply 'discovering' the possibility of child abuse in society, some sections of the media were beginning to suggest that it was endemic, and some experts that the real rates in Japan were no lower than those in Western societies (see, for example, Kitamura et al. 1999: 21).

Under pressure of reports of the dramatic increase in cases of child abuse, the government announced that to tackle the problem it would increase its budget by an unprecedented 90 percent to 900 million yen from April 2000 (*YS* 29 August 1999) and to 2.14 billion yen from April 2001 (Kyōdō 25 August 2000). In fact, the expected expenditure for 2001–2 was almost 40 percent higher, at 2.96 billion yen. This new money was spent on a number of new programmes including the establishment of a hundred committees across the country with members from schools, daycare centres, local government welfare offices and newly established urban child and family support centres. These committees were charged with raising awareness in the community about child abuse, especially among the police, doctors and teachers. In particular, they were to take some of the burden away from the *jidōsōdanjo*, whose workers, already dealing on average with over 50 active cases, were in danger of being swamped by the increase in the number of child abuse referrals. Over one-third of the new money was invested in a national training centre for child abuse prevention and almost a quarter on introducing support – in the form of specialist staff and psychotherapists – for children living in children's homes who had been abused before coming into care. Children in care had previously been thought to be in need of protection (*hogo*) but not treatment (see Goodman 2000).

In May 2000, the Japanese Diet passed legislation (to come into effect in November of the same year) to tackle what was widely accepted to be the growing problem of child abuse in Japanese society. The new law greatly strengthened the powers of the heads of the 157 prefectural child consultation centres (*jidōsōdanjo*) both to take children into care and to prevent parents from removing them or even contacting them once they were in care. It made it mandatory for those working in the educational, welfare and medical fields to report any suspicions of abuse to the appropriate authorities. It obliged the police to provide back-up to officials conducting on-the-spot inspections of the houses of families where officials suspected abuse might be taking place, and it provided that abuse – which was fully defined in law for the first time – was no longer permitted under the guise of discipline or childrearing. In April 2000, the Tokyo metropolitan government became the first local government in the nation to establish a section to deal exclusively with child abuse cases. It took the step because the existing system was no longer able to function due to the sharp increase in abuse cases and the number of people seeking help at the child consultation centres (*YS* 11 August 2000).

The 'discovery' of child abuse was largely as a result of the campaigns of a variety of different groups in Japanese society. Their explanations for the increase in child abuse in the late 1990s focussed largely on the nuclearisation of the Japanese family (see Shinano Mainichi Shinbunsha ed. 2000 and *AS* 17 December 2000 for good summaries of these views). New mothers have had virtually no experience of childcare (as their mothers had had with, for example, nephews and nieces), nor have grandparents been around to advise them or prevent them from abusing their own children. Further, the nuclear family that has developed has never been formed, as in Western societies, around the husband–wife relationship, but instead centres, some have said to an unhealthy degree, on the mother–child one. In post-war sociological works on the Japanese family, the father has often been described as being more firmly 'married' to the company than to his wife.

Fathers have hardly been involved in the rearing of their children at all, and children have often become excessively dependent on their mothers. A survey from the early 1990s suggested that 30 percent of fathers spent under 15 minutes a day on weekdays playing with or talking to their children and only 50 percent spent more than 30 minutes. Even on Sundays, over 40 percent of fathers spent less than an hour interacting with their children (Yuzawa 1994: 66). As a result, the nuclear family has been seen as being particularly stressful for mothers. This stress has been exacerbated, according to Ohinata (1995a; 1995b), by what she has called the 'myth of motherhood', the idea that women are naturally (*sententeki ni*) programmed to be good and caring mothers. This myth, according to Ohinata (2000), has meant that women are unprepared for motherhood when they first face it and often feel inadequate and unable to seek help when they experience problems. To add to their problems, mothers in Japan have been put under intense pressure to perform as perfect parents. Much of this pressure has come from cultural expectations: mothers have been expected to suffer for the sake of their children (Azuma 1986: 7) and expected to consistently work on improving their parenting skills (what Befu 1986: 24–5 calls 'role perfectionism'). Should they fail in any mothering skills, then their inadequacy has been constantly reinforced by images of parenthood presented in the enormous quantity of child-training literature, which emphasises that there is a way to do everything properly (see Dingwall, Tanaka and Minamikata 1991).

The combined effects of lack of support from a husband, extended family or the wider community, plus the myth of motherhood and the idea that women are directly responsible for the success of their children has been recognised in the notion that many women suffer from what is known as *ikuji noirose* (childrearing neurosis) (see Kojima 1986). In the early 1990s, books on the problems of bringing up children became increasingly popular in Japan (see Shiina 1993; Tachibana 1992). Perhaps most revealing of the pressures on mothers have been surveys which have suggested that mothers are the main abusers of children (see Table 6.2), since this has made it easier for the government to implement some of its

Table 6.2   Gender of main abusers in cases of child abuse (1996)

	Non-sexual Abuse	*Sexual Abuse*
Men		
Natural father	416	47
Step-father	63	15
Adoptive father	58	12
Common-law husband	34	4
Grandfather	11	1
Uncle	3	4
Total	585 (37.5%)	83 (87.4%)
Women		
Natural mother	823	3
Step-mother	50	
Adoptive mother	18	
Foster-mother	2	
Common-law wife	1	
Grandmother	16	
Aunt	5	
Total	915 (58.7%)	3 (3.1%)
Gender not given		
Siblings	12	5
Others	19	4
Unknown	28	
Total	59 (3.8%)	9 (9.5%)
Total (all gender categories)	1559	95

N=1559
Source: KSH, *1998: 111*

policies to alleviate the stress on the women in Japan and thereby potentially raise the birthrate.

Conclusion

It is doubtful whether there is more child abuse in Japan at the start of the 2000s than there was at the start of the 1990s. The figures that suggest that this is the case in fact simply demonstrate a dramatic change in people's awareness of what constitutes abusive behaviour and a greater preparedness to pass on concerns about behaviour to the state authorities and for those authorities to investigate those concerns. As can be seen, the 'discovery' of child abuse in the 1990s was due to the pressure of a number of different interest groups including, according to Ueno (1999), child welfare institutions which needed, in order to stay open, more resources and children to be placed in them at a time when the total number of children in the population was declining rapidly. It was the constant bombardment of stories from the media, and particularly the powerful Mainichi group, however, which probably was most important in making the government act with what, in Japanese legislative terms, was considerable haste in defining and implementing policy to tackle the newly discovered problem of child abuse. In doing so, it radically altered the relationship between the state and parents in giving much greater powers to state authorities to intervene in a context that previously had been seen as the exclusive and private domain of the family. Clear comparisons can be drawn here with the UK and the role of the BBC (especially Esther Rantzen's programmes on Child Line) in mid-1985, which led to much greater awareness of, and financial support for, victims of abuse.

Parents were no longer seen as being 'naturally' and unquestionably good and it was no longer unthinkable that they might, in certain circumstances, resort to abusing their children. Families were no longer considered sacrosanct. The stability of the family – seen by many in the 1980s as one of Japan's greatest strengths in comparison with many Western nations – was no longer seen as necessarily superior to the rights of its individual members, particularly women and children. In the case of women, in October 2001, a new law, The Law on Prevention of Spouse Violence and Protection of Victims, that allowed courts to impose restraining orders against perpetrators of domestic violence came into effect covering not only married couples but also couples living together and divorced individuals still in danger of violence from their former spouses. Even those who worked with children – in nurseries and child welfare institutions, for example – who had previously been held to be largely above suspicion, were no longer immune from prosecution. In many ways, the breakdown of the positive image of the Japanese parent and family was yet another example of a growing list of social, cultural, political and economic institutions in Japan which came to be questioned in the light of Japan's long economic recession during the 1990s. In a very short time, institutions (from the company system to the community to the family) previously accepted as being 'good' (and used as part of the explanation for Japan's economic and social miracles) became viewed much less positively and as contributing to Japan's current woes.

The effect on policy of the new view of the relationship between parents and children has been dramatic. The courts, police and government officials at the *jidōsōdanjo* have begun to intervene in family affairs in a manner unimaginable only four years earlier. In 2000, there was a doubling in the number of applications to take children into care from the year before and a 17-fold increase from only seven years earlier (*MS*

2 June 2001). According to a survey by the Mainichi newspaper, workers from *jidōsōdanjo* forcibly entered 90 households suspected of child abuse in the period from January 1999 to November 2000 (when the new Child Abuse Prevention Law came into effect) compared to a total of only 20 such 'raids' during the previous 42 years (*MS* 12 December 2001). Investigations and prosecutions of suspected abuse have proliferated and sentences have rapidly become increasingly severe. At the same time, officials have come under unprecedented criticism for not intervening early enough in cases which have led to injury or even the death of children (see, for example, *MS* 13 April 2001 and 28 July 2001; *YS* 19 August 2001). The public has become increasingly aware of the fact that many officials dealing with child welfare issues are unqualified. According to an Asahi survey in 1999 (*AS* 7 February), less than 45 percent of all staff working in *jidōsōdanjo* (and none in Tokyo) have any specialist welfare qualifications, and there has been increasing pressure on central government to consider the professionalisation of social work (*YS* 28 May 2001) which has hitherto been carried out by a combination of unqualified local government officers, local volunteers in the *minsei jidōiin* system, and children's homes, most of which are private and many of which are family businesses (Goodman 2000).

There has also developed in the media increasing sympathy for delinquent (particularly female) youth – with the idea that many are themselves victims of abuse (see, for example, *JT* 4 November 2001; Kyōdo 24 June 2001 and 19 August 2001; *MS*, 16 August 2001; *AS*, 19 January 2001) – as well as for some abusing mothers who are seen as provided with insufficient support to bring up their children (see *AS*, 14 May 2001; *MS*, 6 June 2001 and 1 November 2001). In general, however, parents, step-parents, grandparents and workers in child welfare institutions who are convicted of abuse (almost always physical and emotional abuse) can increasingly expect to face custodial sentences in cases where a few years earlier their actions would likely have been treated more leniently as being the result of the excessive, but not cruel, discipline of children who needed a firm hand.

The 'discovery' of child abuse is a common experience in many societies. There is little doubt, looking at the experience of other countries, that the number of reported cases in Japan will continue to rise exponentially. There has been a dramatic rise, for example, in the number of notifications of suspicions of abuse from schools (up by 100 percent in Tokyo in 2000 from the year before) and by neighbours (up by 30 percent over the same period) (*AS* 14 January, 2001). Newspapers reported an increase of more than 25 per cent (from 45 to 61) in the number of children who had died at the hands of their guardians between the years 2000 and 2001. Yet, as Hacking (1995: 55, 240) has pointed out, 'Events,

no matter how painful or terrifying, have been experienced or recalled as
child abuse only after consciousness raising,' and, 'As the concept of child
abuse expands, more and more situations fall under the description of
"child abuse." So there is more child abuse to report.' The 'discovery' of
child abuse in Japan has already had profound effects for the relation
between the state and families and for the development of Japanese social
policy towards children and there is little doubt also that it will continue
to exert an influence for several years to come although, as the experience
from other countries also shows, exactly what this influence will be is
hard to predict.

NOTES

1   As far as possible, these lists include stories only once even if they are covered
in other newspapers on the same day, though it is not always clear whether,
for example, certain stories are referring to the same event, survey or report.
2   These articles could be found mainly in the journal edited by the
psychohistorian Lloyd DeMause entitled *The Journal of Psychohistory* (see
DeMause, 1987, 1991, 1998; Kitahara, 1989a, 1989b).

REFERENCES

Newspapers and annual reports cited in the text:
AS: *Asahi Shinbun* (Asahi Newspaper)
DY: *Daily Yomiuri*
JIC: *Japan: An International Comparison,* produced annually by the Keizai Kōhō
    Centre (Japan Institute for Social and Economic Affairs)
JT: *Japan Times*
JTW: *Japan Times Weekly* (changed to fortnightly from 1999)
KH: *Kodomo Hakusho* (White Paper on Children, produced annually by the
    Nihon Kodomo wo Mamorukai).
KSH: *Kōsei Hakusho* (Annual Report on Health and Welfare, produced by the
    Ministry of Health and Welfare)
Kyōdō: *Kyōdō Tsūshin* (Kyōdo News Agency)
MDN: *Mainichi Daily News*
MS: *Mainichi Shinbun* (Mainichi Newspaper)
YS: *Yomiuri Shinbun* (Yomiuri Newspaper)

Allison, Anne. 1996. *Permitted and Prohibited Desires: Mothers, Comics and Censorship
    in Japan.* Boulder, Colorado: Westview Press.
Azuma, Hiroshi. 1986. 'Why study child development in Japan?' in *Child Develop-
    ment and Education in Japan,* ed. Harold Stevenson, Hiroshi Azuma, and
    Kenji Hakuta. New York: W. H. Freeman and Company.

Befu, Harumi. 1986. 'The social and cultural background of child development in Japan and the United States,' in *Child Development and Education in Japan*, ed. Harold Stevenson, Hiroshi Azuma, and Kenji Hakuta. New York: W H Freeman and Company.

Berridge, David. 1997. 'England: child abuse reports, responses and reforms,' in *Combatting Child Abuse: International Perspectives and Trends*, ed. Neil Gilbert. New York: Oxford University Press.

CAPNA (Child Abuse Prevention Network Aichi). 1998. *Mienakata Shi: Kodomo Gyakutai Databook* (Unseen Deaths: Child Abuse Data book). Nagoya: CAPNA Shuppan.

DeMause, Lloyd. 1987. 'The history of childhood in Japan.' *The Journal of Psychohistory*, 15/2: 147–52.

——, 1991. 'The universality of incest.' *The Journal of Psychohistory*, 19/2: 123–64.

——, 1998. 'The history of child abuse.' *The Journal of Psychohistory*, 25/3: 16–36.

Dingwall, Robert, Hiroko Tanaka and Satoshi Minamikata. 1991. 'Images of parenthood in the United Kingdom and Japan.' *Sociology*, 25/3: 423–46.

Field, Norma. 1995. 'The child as laborer and consumer: the disappearance of childhood in contemporary Japan,' in *Children and the Politics of Culture*, ed. Sharon Stephens. Princeton: Princeton University Press.

Franklin, Bob and Nigel Parton, eds. 1991. *Social Work, the Media and Public Relations*. London and New York: Routledge.

Fujimoto Tetsuya. 1994. *Crime Problems in Japan*. Tokyo: Chūō University Press.

Garrison, Lloyd. 1984. 'The puzzle of oyako-shinjū.' *Time* (11 June): 41.

Gilbert, Neil, ed. 1997. *Combatting Child Abuse: International Perspectives and Trends*. Oxford: Oxford University Press.

Goodman, Roger. 1996. 'On introducing the UN Convention of the Rights of the Child into Japan,' pp. 109–40 in *Case Studies on Human Rights in Japan*, ed. Roger Goodman and Ian Neary. Richmond, Surrey: Japan Library (Curzon Press).

——. 1998. 'The delivery of personal social services and the "Japanese-style welfare state,"' pp. 139–58 in *The East Asian Welfare Model: Welfare Orientalism and the State*, ed. Roger Goodman, Gordon White and Huck-Ju Kwon. London and New York: Routledge.

——. 2000. *Children of the Japanese State: The Changing Role of Child Protection Institutions in Contemporary Japan*. Oxford: Oxford University Press.

Hacking, Ian. 1991. 'The making and molding of child abuse.' *Critical Inquiry*, 17 (Winter): 243–88.

——. 1992. 'World-making by kind-making: child abuse for example,' in *How Classification Works: Nelson Goodman among the Social Sciences*, ed. Mary Douglas and David Hull. Edinburgh: Edinburgh University Press.

——. 1995. *Rewriting the Soul: Multiple Personality and the Sciences of Memory*. Princeton, NJ: Princeton University Press.

Haley, John Owen. 1998. *The Spirit of Japanese Law*. Athens and London: The University of Georgia Press.

Hashimoto, Mieko. 1996. 'Becoming aware of child abuse,' *Japan Quarterly*, 43/2: 145–52.

Hendry, Joy. 1986. *Becoming Japanese: The World of the Pre-school Child*. Manchester: Manchester University Press.

Ikeda, Yoshiko. 1982. 'A short introduction to child abuse in Japan.' *Child Abuse and Neglect*, 6: 487–90.

——. 1984. 'Child abuse in Japan.' *Child Welfare: Quarterly News from Japan*, 5/2: 2–12.

——. 1987. *Jidō Gyakutai (Child Abuse)*. Tokyo: Chūō Kōronsha.

Imamura, Anne E. 1987. *Urban Japanese Housewives: At Home and in the Community*. Honolulu: University of Hawaii Press.

Jidō Gyakutai Bōshi Seido Kenkyūkai, ed. 1993. *Kodomo no Gyakutai Bōshi: Saizensen kara no Hōkoku* (The Prevention of Child Abuse: A Report from the Front Line). Osaka: Toki Shobō.

Kamiide, Hiroyuki. 1990. 'Child abuse in Japan: from a survey by the National Association of Child Guidance Centre Directors,' *Child Welfare: Quarterly News from Japan*, 11/1: 2–9.

Kato, Yōko and Tatsuno, Yōko. 1998. 'Denwa sōdan ni okeru gyakutai yobō no tatewari (The role of telephone consultation in child abuse prevention),' in *Dai Yonkai Gakujutsu Shūkai Programme*, ed. Nihon Kodomo no Gyakutai Bōshi Kenkyūkai. Wakayama: Nihon Kodomo no Gyakutai Bōshi Kenkyūkai.

Kitahara, Michio. 1989a. 'Childhood in Japanese culture.' *The Journal of Psychohistory*, 17/1: 43–72.

——. 1989b. 'Incest – Japanese style.' *The Journal of Psychohistory*, 16/4 (Summer): 445–50.

Kitamura, Toshinori, Kijima Nobuhiko, Iwata Noboru, Senda Yukiko, Takahashi Kōji, and Hayashi Ikue. 1999. 'Frequencies of child abuse in Japan: hidden but prevalent crime.' *International Journal of Offender Therapy and Comparative Criminology*, 43/1: 21–33.

Kojima, Hideo. 1986. 'Becoming nurturant in Japan: past and present,' in *Origins of Nurturance: Developmental, Biological and Cultural Perspectives on Caregiving*, ed. Alan Fogel and Gail F. Melson. New Jersey and London: Hillsdale, Lawrence Erlbaum Associates.

Korbin, Jill E. 1987. 'Child sexual abuse: implications for the cross-cultural record,' in *Child Survival*, ed. Nancy Scheper-Hughes. Dordrecht, Lancaster: D. Reidel Publishing Company.

Kouno, A. and J. F. Johnson. 1995. 'Child abuse and neglect in Japan: coin operated locker babies.' *Child Abuse and Neglect*, 19/1: 25–31.

La Fontaine, J. S. 1988. 'Child sexual abuse and the incest taboo: practical problems and theoretical issues.' *Man* (N.S.), 23/1: 1–18.

——. 1990. *Child Sexual Abuse*. London: Polity Press.

Ochiai, Emiko. 1996. *The Japanese Family in Transition: A Sociological Analysis of Family Change in Postwar Japan*. Tokyo: LTCB International Library Foundation.

Oda, Hiroshi. 1997. *Basic Japanese Laws*. Oxford: Clarendon Press.

Ohinata, Masami. 1995a. 'Kindai no kodomo o aisenai hahaoya no kenkyū kara miete kuru mono: omotoshite shinrigaku ni okeru hahasei kenkyū no tachiba kara (Research on the new mothers who cannot love their children: from a psychological perspective).' *Kazoku Kenkyū Nenpō*, 20: 20–31.

——. 1995b. 'The mystique of motherhood: A key to understanding social change and family problems in Japan,' in *Japanese Women: New Feminist Perspectives on the Past, Present and Future*, ed. Kumiko Fujimura Fanselow and Atsuko

Kameda. New York: City University of New York, The Feminist Press.

——. 2000. *Bosei-ai Shinwa no Wana* (The Pitfalls of the Maternal Love Myth). Tokyo: Nihon Hyōronsha.

Peng, Ito. 1995. '*Boshi katei*: a theoretical and case analysis of Japanese lone mothers and their relationships to the state, the labour market, and the family, with reference to Britain and Canada.' Ph.D. thesis. London School of Economics.

Pinguet, Maurice. 1993. *Voluntary Death in Japan*, translated by Rosemary Morris. London: Polity Press.

Pringle, Keith. 1998. *Children and Social Welfare in Europe*. Buckingham and Philadelphia: Open University Press.

Sargeant, Harriet. 1994. 'A child in crime.' *The Independent Magazine*, 325 (10 December): 34–8.

Shiina, Atsuko. 1993. *Oya ni naru hodo muzukashii koto wa nai* (Nothing is more difficult than raising children). Tokyo: Kōdansha.

Shimazu, Yoshiko. 1994. 'Unmarried mothers and their children in Japan,' translated by Miya E. M. Lippit. *US–Japan Women's Journal* (English Supplement), 6: 83–110.

Shinano Mainichi Shinbunsha, ed. 2000. *Hyōryū Kazoku: Kosodate Gyakutai no Shinsō* (Floating Families: An In-depth Look at Child Abuse). Osaka: Kawade Shobō Shinsha.

Tachibana, Yūko. 1992. *Kodomo ni Te o Agetakunaru toki* (Times when You Feel Like Hitting Your Children). Tokyo: Gakuyō Shobō.

Takahashi, Shigehiro. 1977. 'Child-Murder/Mother-Suicides in Japan.' *PHP*, 8/5: 61–76.

Tokyo-to Fukushikyoku. 1998. *Aratana Kodomo no Kenri Hoshō no Shikumi Tsukuri ni Tsuite* (On the Construction of a Fresh Plan to Protect the Rights of Children). Tokyo: Tokyo-to Fukushikyoku.

Tokyo-to Fukushikyoku Jidōbu, ed. 1990. *Jidō Hitorioya Fujin Fukushi Seisaku no Gaiyō* (Outline of Welfare Policy for Children, Single Parents and Women). Tokyo: Tokyo-to Fukushikyoku.

Tsuji, Yohko. 1982. 'Homicide called suicide: mother–child double suicide in Japan.' Unpublished paper.

Tsuzaki Tetsurō. 1996. *Kodomo no Gyakutai: Sono Jittai to Enjo* (Child Abuse: The Situation and Support). Osaka: Toki Shobō.

Ueno, Kayako. 1994. 'Jidō gyakutai no shakaiteki kōsaku (The social construction of child abuse)'. *Sociology*, 39/2: 3–18.

——, 1999. 'Shōshika jidai no sābībaru: jidō gyakutai mondai kara mita "shakai fukushi no byōri" (Survival in a time of declining fertility: social welfare problems from the perspective of child abuse problems).' *Gendai no Shakai Byōri*, 14: 5–23.

Wagatsuma, Hiroshi. 1981. 'Child abandonment and infanticide: A Japanese case,' in *Child Abuse and Neglect: Cross-cultural perspectives*, ed. Jill E. Korbin. Los Angeles and London: University of California Press.

Woo, Deborah. 1989. 'The people *v.* Fumiko Kimura: but which people?' *International Journal of Sociology of Law*, 17: 403–28.

Yamamura, Yoshiaki. 1986. 'The child in Japanese society,' in *Child Development and Education in Japan*, ed. Harold Stevenson, Azuma Hiroshi and Hakuta Kenji. New York: W H Freeman and Company.

Yoneyama, Shoko. 1999. *The Japanese High School: Silence and Resistance*. London and New York: Routledge.

Yuzawa, Yasuhiko. 1994. *Japanese Families*. Tokyo: Foreign Press Center.

7 Touching of the hearts: an overview of programmes to promote interaction between the generations in Japan

Leng Leng Thang

Among the range of social policies in Japan, the 'policy' of *sedaikan kōryū* seems to have the least direct impact on the immediate 'social panic' of the society. This is because intergenerational interaction is commonly expected to have taken place within the family, and thus within the private realm of responsibilities. However, in recent years, as a result of the panic caused by the predicament of an aging society, accentuated by a changing family structure and the distancing of the generations, the term *sedaikan kōryū* has made more frequent appearances, particularly under social policies and programmes related to aging, community development and lifelong education.

This chapter begins with an examination of the needs and significance for 'intergenerational interaction' (*sedaikan kōryū*) programmes in Japan. This is followed by an overview of the types of intergenerational initiatives available. In the course of discussion, the Japanese interpretation of concepts such as 'volunteerism,' 'family' and ideals in elderly care are examined. In the conclusion, the relations between promoting intergenerational interaction and Japanese-style welfare society is discussed.[1]

Needs and significance of intergenerational interaction

Despite the romantic image of the elderly spending their remaining years in the care of the family, surrounded by a throng of bubbly grandchildren, in reality, more and more Japanese elderly are spending their twilight years isolated from the younger generation.

One indication of the yearning for an ideal family complete with grandchildren is depicted in the demand for a paid service called 'service of the heart.' One company which has provided such 'rent-a-family' service since 1990 reported a high demand for the service, so much so that they have to place many elderly couples or individuals on the waiting list for visits from their purchased 'family members.' A typical rent-a-family session simulates a three-generational family setting. The 'daughter' or 'daughter-in-law' – a trained entertainer – would prepare meals where all would eat together, and there would be other 'family' events such as 'family' walks in the park, gift giving, singing, chatting and playing with 'grandchildren.' The 'grandchildren' usually climb on to the 'grand-parents" laps for intimate games with them (Kaplan et al. 1998).

The success of such a business reveals the diminishing capabilities of real families in engaging the generations. Since World War II, the three-generational households – the backbone of intergenerational interaction in the family – have been on the decline. In 1975, three-generational households with an elderly person aged 65 or older made up 54.5% of all households. By 1998, this had fallen to 29.7%. Adding to the decline in three-generational households is the increase in elderly-only house-holds. In 1975, the percentage of one-person elderly households and couple-only elderly households was 8.6% and 13.1% respectively. The proportion increased to 18.4% and 26.7% by 1998 (Kono 2000).

Japanese are showing a remarkable shift in attitudes towards family sup-port in old age. In the periodic surveys conducted by the *Mainichi Shinbun* since 1950 of women who had ever been married, to the question, 'Are you planning to depend on your children in your old age?' the proportion of those replying 'Yes' decreased from 65 percent in 1950 to only 13 percent in 1998. In the same survey, the respondents were also asked: 'What is your opinion about children caring for their elderly parents?' In the response categories provided, 'Good custom' and 'Natural duty' were taken as an indication of support of the values and norms of filial piety. (The other two response categories were 'Unavoidable' and 'Not a good custom.') From 1963 to 1986, the proportion choosing these two categories had been consistent at about 75 to 80 percent. However, this fell dramatically to about 50 percent in 1988 and has been falling continuously since then (Ogawa and Retherford 1993, Retherford et al. 1999). Equally significant is the shift in young people's attitudes towards the care of their parents. In an international comparative survey where young people aged 18–24 were asked about the support of their parents, the proportion of those who answered, 'I will support them by all means,' decreased from 47.5% in 1976 to 22.6% in 1993, ranking Japan the lowest in the ten countries surveyed[2] (Sōmuchō 1993). With fewer children among the Japanese, as seen through the decline in the total fertility rate, and changing attitudes towards elderly care, the trends for a decline in three-generations families will continue well into the future.

Despite the increase in elderly-only households, a 1985 Family Life Course survey by the Institute of Population Problems shows that only 25.2% of the 7707 respondents believed that the nuclear family was a more natural and human way of living, whereas 52.5% felt that one would be happier if one could live in a three-generational household, and 38.4% believed that three-generational co-living was a more natural and human way of living (Kono 2000: 44).

It is inevitable for those living in elderly-only households to have little contact with the younger generations. The same disengagement between the generations is also happening outside the family. With urbanisation and modernisation, there has been a decline in intergenerational contact in both rural and urban areas. This is particularly evident in suburban areas where job opportunities in the cities after 1955 have resulted in the development of *bed towns* to accommodate the influx of working population to the cities. These suburban bed towns are mostly populated by the families of salarymen who have no original roots there. That these salarymen who work in the cities spend few waking hours within the community further contributes to an erosion of community spirit and neighbourly contacts.

A 1998 survey by the Government Office for Policy on the Elderly on the community participation of elderly people shows that among the 2303 people over age 60, 51.2% answered that they had opportunities to interact with the younger generation in their daily life outside the family. The remaining 48.8%, however, answered 'not at all' or 'almost never' (Sagaza, ed. 2001: 77). This is more apparent among those in their late 70s and 80s. The findings mirror an earlier survey by Sōmuchō in 1993 on the participation of elderly in the community, where those who answered they always had and sometimes had interaction with the younger generations decreased with increasing age: from 64.6% in the 60–4 age group, 57.6% in the 65–9 age group, 49.8% in the 70–4 age group, 40.6% in the 75–9 age group to 25.7% for the 80 years and above group (Ishikuro 1994: 64).

What are the negative impacts of a distancing in the generations? In the US, where there has been an effort to re-unite the generations through movements such as Generations United, more and more studies have appeared to support the need for age integration. Kaplan (1993: 71–2) summarises the negative consequences: a reduction in the extent and quality of both the children's and the elders' social support networks; an increase in feelings of loneliness and increased vulnerability to depression experienced by the elderly; an increase in the younger generation's negative perceptions of, and informational inaccuracies about, the process of aging; and, a decrease in people's familiarity with aging as a natural process in the continuum of life.

In Japan, age segregation is believed to have contributed towards young people's negative stereotypes of the elderly. Opportunities for interaction have been shown to help young people to have a more positive and realistic perception (Sagaza, ed. 2001; Thang 2001). Some of the negative perceptions are also attributed to the influence of mass media, which usually portray the elderly in a negative light (Koyano 1993; Sagaza, ed. 2001).

The youth problems characterising Japanese society today are attributed to the lack of grandparents to serve as moral guideposts and transmit desirable social values to the young. Children nowadays are often overprotected by their own parents in a nuclear family, and have little experience of the wider world. As a consequence, they have less self-control, tolerance and ability to communicate well (Sawano 2000: 57). The increase in deviant behaviour and violence among children has caused great concern among educators, parents and social commentators who wonder, among other concerns, if they can rely on these children to be responsible citizens who will support them in the future.

The advent of an age-segregated society thus heralds concerns on different levels, from personal worries about individual well-being to wider social concerns about the survival and proper functioning of Japanese society in the future.

Efforts to link the generations in Japan

Awareness of the need to re-unite the generations has prompted many conscious efforts in planning to link the generations in Japanese society. Although some people were sceptical and commented that it is artificial to *programme* cross-generational interaction, the positive results gained from such interactions – including genuine cross-age friendships fostered through the *programming* – have outweighed the concerns.

Beginning in the mid-1990s, there has been an increase in research and reports on intergenerational interactions between the old and young in Japan (e.g. JARC [Japan Aging Research Center] 1994; Aoi, ed. 1996; Kaplan et al. 1998; Sagaza, ed. 2001; Thang 2001). Kusano Atsuko of Shinshū University established the Japan Intergenerational Network, which disseminates the 'Interchange' newsletter to introduce intergenerational programmes across the country. Many publications document positive results arising from programmes and activities linking the old and the young. For instance, the JARC report[3] on a survey of intergenerational activities (1994) provides an example of intergenerational volunteer activities initiated by a home economics club in a high school in Toyama prefecture. Out of the 150 members in the club, 47 participated in the volunteer activities focussing on elderly people who lived alone in the community. These students interacted with the elderly through home visits, letter correspondence and telephone calls. Responses from the students reveal that although many lived with their grandparents, they often did not talk to their grandparents until they became volunteers.

From the opportunities to interact with other elderly people, they learnt about the life and thinking of the elderly, and this enabled them to understand and communicate better with their own grandparents.

Activities such as the above that bring together people from different generations with the aim of increasing cooperation, interaction or exchange are typically termed *sedaikan kōryu katsudō*' (intergenerational interaction activities). They include funded and unfunded programmes that may run on a periodical, once-only or seasonal basis. Although the *sedaikan* should involve multigenerations, most activities are confined to interactions between the elderly and school-age children and teenagers.

The national government has played a significant role in promoting intergenerational activities, particularly in the context of aging population. The cover of the year 2000 White Paper on Aging Society (Sōmuchō 2000) promotes the concept of intergenerational contact with a colour photograph of an elderly man playing the violin with a young girl. The picture was taken at the United Nations HQ Lobby during the performance of the New Jersey Intergenerational Orchestra (with members ranging from 6 to 87 years old) to commemorate the International Year of the Elderly in October 1999.

To further promote intergenerational programming, Sōmuchō introduced the Intergenerational Exchange Award. In 1999, awards were given to 33 organisations nationwide most actively involved in intergenerational programming (Sawano 2000).

Mention of intergenerational programmes first appeared in the framework of a 'lifelong learning society' in the early 1980s. As part of lifelong learning programmes, the Ministry of Education has since 1983 implemented 'comprehensive projects to promote purpose of life (*ikigai*) of elders' and included intergenerational programmes as one of the six pillars of the policy (see Mathews 1996). Under this initiative, the Ministry provides financial support to groups comprising the old and younger generations in activities such as camping and hiking, gardening and cultivation of agricultural products, environmental activities or cleaning public places such as rivers and parks (Sawano 2000).

In the 1986 'General Principles Concerning Measures for the Longevity Society,'[4] support for intergenerational programmes appeared under the 'measures for learning and social participation.' The 1986 policy adopted by the Cabinet is a result of the government's efforts since the early 1980s to prepare for the rapidly approaching, aging society. Whereas in the past, *ikigai* for the elderly meant recreational and educational programmes confined to only the elderly, such as old-age clubs, community welfare centres for the elderly and senior citizen colleges, the inclusion of intergenerational programmes reflects a recognition of mutual support across the generations in the promotion of well-being for the elderly.

Under such broad policy guidelines, every ministry started to implement measures in the different areas stipulated for the elderly. The Ministry of Agriculture, Forestry and Fisheries, for instance, under the programme called 'Creating *Ikigai*' started in 1987, caters for intergenerational interaction with the youth in rural areas. The Ministry of Health and Welfare has since 1989 implemented under the policy programme on *ikigai* and health promotion for the elderly, pilot studies of programmes that aim to change the image of the elderly through recruiting elderly people as volunteers.

The 1986 Policy Guidelines were replaced in July 1996 by a new Fundamental Law on Policies for an Aging Society. The new law adopted by Prime Minister Hashimoto's Cabinet is established as a result of political and social awakening of the need for fundamental laws by the government to strengthen the policy on the aging society so as to better cope with its needs. The law continues to show an interest in intergenerational programming, as seen from its policy of 'promoting involvement of the elderly in social activities':

In order to build energetic local communities as well as to help the elderly play an active role in them with something to live for, the elder's environment in social activities will be facilitated. To achieve this goal, opportunities will be provided for the elders and young generations to promote mutual exchange, and voluntary activities of the elders will be supported. Moreover, the social involvement of the elderly will be propagated, information and consulting service will be improved and instructors will be trained (Maeda 2000: 161).

With the incorporation of intergenerational programmes in aging policies as a measure to promote 'active social participation,' intergenerational activities are most commonly perceived as relating to the *ikigai* of the elderly. In the recent years, however, with the rise in problems faced by schools, such as *ijime* (bullying) and *futōkō* (school-refusal), the relevance of and urgency for intergenerational programming is also felt among the younger generations. The Ministry of Education, for instance, has expanded the concept of lifelong education to include children, among whom intergenerational activities are promoted from the perspective of the need for the young to stay in touch with the older generations for the well-being of the children.

Within the broad framework of lifelong education for children is the introduction of school–community partnerships conceptualised under various plans such as the Three-Year National Children's Plan, 1999–2001, and the 'Integrated Learning Time' for all schools to be launched in 2002. These plans provide opportunities for students to do volunteer work and interact with the older generations who represent the community (Sagaza, ed. 2001: 35).

At first glance, support from the government in the form of funding and special projects to promote intergenerational programming gives the impression that *sedaikan kōryu* activities are a top-down initiative. However, as Kaplan et al. (1998) have clarified, many intergenerational initiatives described as 'national initiatives' by ministry-level social welfare and education administrators were also those described as 'local initiatives' by municipal and prefectural-level government administrators and non-profit organisations. This is because what have been the 'big directions' conceived at the national level are implemented through collaboration, coordination, initiative, and, occasionally, funding at the prefectural and municipal levels. Quite often, for the purpose of obtaining funding assistance and official recognition, the bottom-up initiatives are cast in a manner consistent with national programme model guidelines. Therefore, as is the case for many of the intergenerational initiatives described below, it is overly simplistic to construe an initiative as top-down because of the government's involvement in funding support. On the contrary, as much of the creativity and administrative support occurs at the local levels, they should be seen more as representing a case of active individual participation and interaction with the government.

The following overview of intergenerational programmes and activities in Japan – divided into school-based, elderly-based, community-based and age-integrated facilities initiatives – provides concrete examples of the individual/private–government interaction and shows the fuzziness encountered if one must define an initiative as either a bottom-up or top-down effort.

School-based initiatives

This category of intergenerational programmes is initiated by youth-related institutions, mainly the schools, kindergartens and nurseries. These programmes are the most common form of intergenerational activities. Even before the Japanese were aware of the aging society, there were infrequent organised visits by school children to welfare institutions in the vicinity, usually as part of social and welfare education. Among these institutions, homes for the elderly and nursing homes are the most commonly visited facilities.

Nurseries and kindergartens, too, initiate intergenerational programmes to promote intergenerational interaction. In 1994, 146 or about 10 percent of the (licensed) nurseries in Tokyo reported that they had some form of intergenerational programme with the elderly. Most were event-based such as concert performances at homes for the elderly and invitations to schools' sports days. A few invited elderly people in the community to play with the children on a regular basis. A nursery in Tama City, Tokyo, for example, has held a designated 'Grandma's day' monthly for 25 years – essentially an open-house day for the elderly in the community to come in and play traditional games with the children (Higashi Shakai Fukushi Kyōkai Hoikubu Tsūshin 1995).

A nursery in Arakawa Ward, Tokyo, has let its three- to six-year-old children interact monthly with elders in a special nursing home nearby for the last eight years. After a year of group interaction, the children pair up with the 'grandparent' of mutual choice and continue with more intimate dyadic relations.

A more structured initiative by the Ministry of Education started in 1977 with the aim of promoting volunteerism, understanding and awareness of social welfare among school children. Called the 'volunteer school' programme (*borantia kyōryoku kō*), this scheme funds selected schools ¥100,000 annually for the period of their participation. Most participating schools are elementary schools. In 1993, 60 percent of the 4,600 participating schools across the nation were elementary schools. Junior and senior high schools constituted 30 and 10 percent respectively. The programme has received positive feedback, and some students are said to have embarked on a career in welfare services influenced by their volunteer experience in school.

The majority of school children in such programmes visit institutions for the elderly or elderly people living alone in the community. The forms of interaction with the elderly include: letter correspondence; playing traditional games together; learning about traditional crafts and history from the elders; and helping with cleaning. Elderly people are invited to attend sports days, musical concerts, Respect the Elderly Day, and 'culture festivals' at the schools. Sometimes the students have joint sports activities with the elderly, such as gateball and ground golf.

Some schools develop a 'foster grandchild system' in which children pair up with elders in a particular nursing home for frequent and intimate interactions. One elementary school in Higashiyama City (Tokyo metropolitan area) allows the children to bring the elders out shopping in their wheelchairs as the children reach sixth grade. Such consistent contact has encouraged the development of long-lasting relationships between them.

During the three-year 'volunteer school' period, one high school in Ibaraki Prefecture introduced new courses in the home economics curriculum: besides lessons such as sewing, cooking and childcare, there were lessons for the students that included practical activities in understanding social welfare. Students in the cooking class also started a monthly meal service which they called 'the heart of grandchildren' service. The boxed lunches were wrapped with 'lunch mats' made by the sewing class, while students from the childcare class delivered the boxed lunches to the elders and ate with them (Japan Aging Research Center 1994).

The scheme, however, suffers from a lack of funding to continue the projects that were started during the 'volunteer schools' scheme. Some schools have been forced to cut back on costly projects, although some managed to secure new funding from local administrative bodies to enable the activities to continue uninterrupted (Saito 1994: 177).

Opportunities to volunteer and interact with the elderly are perceived as one important component of 'education of the heart,' a part of social education and lifelong education in schools. It is hoped that thoughtfulness and kindness cultivated through contact with the elderly will help alleviate problems such as bullying and school phobia faced in the Japanese education system today (Kurauchi and Suzuki, eds 1998).

The 'education of the heart' will further be expanded from the year 2002 when all schools embark upon the five-day school week and weekly time for integrated learning (*sōgōteki gakushū*). Students are expected to gain more experience in activities relating to welfare and volunteering in the community during their Saturdays and integrated learning time. Such community activities will provide opportunities for intergenerational contacts since the elderly are identified as an essential presence in the community.

During the experimental integrated learning time for the fourth graders in an elementary school in Kodaira city (Tokyo metropolitan area), children were encouraged to propose their own projects and request help from their parents and neighbourhood to execute them. Among the various things they could do under the theme 'Let's widen our world!', one group chose to interact with elderly people from homes for elderly people in the community. The children initiated regular visits; besides the integrated study time, they also went during the weekends and after school. As one student expressed it, 'When we make friends, we have to meet a few times to become close. Therefore we want to meet the elderly many times.' (Sagaza, ed. 2001: 145–6).

Frequent interaction between the old and the young in a casual setting has been made increasingly possible as schools are 'opening up' to the community. Ideologically, the 'opening up' of schools to outsiders relates to the 'community school' movement started in the 1930s in the US, (Kurauchi and Suzuki, eds 1998: 121). However, more pragmatic reasons prevail behind the 'opening up.' Among them is to use the extra spaces in schools resulting from a falling birthrate.

In the last decade, the number of public elementary school students has decreased more than 20 percent from 9.26 million in 1990 to 7.24 million in 2000 (Hani 2001). To make full use of these vacant classrooms, the local government has opened these school premises to other social services, such as daycare centres and centres for the elderly. The Takashima Number Sixth Elementary School in Itabashi Ward (Tokyo), for example, in 1996 converted the empty classrooms into a mini day service centre for the elderly in the community. Close proximity to the elderly enables the school to plan various programmes to enhance inter-action between the generations. To further promote intergenerational interaction in a casual setting, since 1999, the school has run an 'in touch lunch' programme (*fureai kyūshoku*) which enables elderly people from the day service centres to attend school lunch with the children (Tokyo Volunteer Action Center 2000: 52–3).

Elderly-based initiatives

Intergenerational programme initiatives by the elderly reflect not only a growing number of elderly people who are living longer and in good health; it also reveals the changing cohort of Japanese elderly who are beginning to see beyond the family in serving and interacting with younger generations. Initiatives from the elderly are often regarded in the light of volunteering.

Among the initiatives by the elderly, old-age clubs are prominent as bases for intergenerational programmes. Most old-age clubs interact with elementary school students (Saito 1994: 166). Many old-age clubs initiate interaction through traditional games, crafts, food and cooking. Some programmes aim at restoring past living experiences, such as teaching children to plant and harvest rice.

Old-age clubs were initiated by the 1963 Welfare Law for the Elderly to promote social participation among the elderly. Although they receive funding from the state and municipalities, their programmes are typically bottom-up initiatives, usually conceived as responses to community needs. Surveys show that intergenerational programmes are organised by 58.6% of the old-age clubs; with old-age clubs in rural areas playing slightly more active roles in organising such activities (Ishikuro 1994: 67).

One example of an intergenerational initiative by old-age clubs in the rural area is found in Miyagi prefecture (Miyagi Prefecture Federation of Old-Age Clubs 1991). Members of an old-age club in the rural Nonodake area volunteered to teach school children how to plant rice in an effort to improve their traditional dance performance. The desire to help was prompted by a rice harvest traditional dance performance by the middle school students during the Sports Day. As the audience, the elderly felt the children's performance – a dance to pray for a good harvest – lacked something since the children had no experience with planting. This caused them to approach the school and PTA to offer their help. Since the first encounter, the elderly have widened their interaction with the young through initiatives to teach them the history of their local district and traditional crafts and games.

Initiatives reflecting the interaction between individual and official efforts are also shown in a programme by the Educational Committee of Shizuoka prefecture. Based on the responses to a 1991 survey on learning opportunities and social participation by the elderly from a 'silver college,' where more than half the respondents expressed the hope to be able to use what they had learnt in the community, the Educational Committee started a programme of sending graduates from the 'silver college' to teach as part-time teachers in elementary and junior high schools. It received positive responses during the experimental period in 1993 and 1994, and has since 1995 expanded to more schools (Yamamoto, 1997). The programme promotes intergenerational interaction via the objective of creating *ikigai* for the elderly through social participation. In elementary schools, the graduates from the 'silver college' teach in subjects such as social studies, art, traditional crafts and agricultural activities. In secondary schools, they teach subjects including Japanese calligraphy, haiku poetry, home economics, physical education and club activities such as arts and craft (Yamamoto 1997: 91).

There are also instances where local initiatives by individual elderly people are noticed and adopted as top-down initiatives on a wide scale. Tochigi Prefecture, for example, now has 'childcare space' (*kosodate hiroba*) established in various public places. The idea, though, was first formulated by one elderly woman who volunteered to offer childcare to parents in the community by setting up a space in the shopping centre for mothers who needed some time for shopping on their own.

Individuals like these are referred to as 'senior volunteers' – a term widely publicised by the Tokyo Volunteer Action Center to attract elderly people to serve as volunteers. The Tokyo Volunteer Action Center, set up in 1981[5], receives funding from the metropolitan government, the state and through donations. With directives from the state to promote volunteer activities among citizens, it facilitates volunteer opportunities by providing advice, venues and information dissemination. Although it receives government funding, the Director (when interviewed on 8 June 2001) emphasised that they facilitate bottom-up activities. Through regular seminars on senior volunteerism organised by the Center, they attract interested participants and provide them with an opportunity to network and initiate volunteer projects among themselves. They also match interested parties with requests from the community for volunteers. In addition, the Center publishes various reports and guidelines to guide the volunteer groups.

Among the activities embarked upon by senior volunteers, many are intergenerational initiatives. They provide interaction between the elderly and the young in productive ways: as volunteers in after-school centres (Suginami Ward, Tokyo); as mentors for elementary school students

(Saitama Prefecture); as consultants and teachers in the Children's Society supervising carpentry and traditional crafts (Higashiyama City, Tokyo); as employed assistants in children's welfare institutions (Shiga Prefecture); as teachers to urban children at a farm experience school (Shinagawa Prefecture); as museum and gallery guides for groups, usually school children's groups (Tokyo Volunteer Center 1993a; Shakai kyōiku shisetsu borantia kenkyū kai 1997).

The word 'senior' in 'senior volunteer' has come into use since 1992. As literature from the Tokyo Volunteer and Action Center shows, 'senior' has replaced 'silver' because 'silver' has a negative image:

> The word 'silver,' such as silver hair or white hair, equals aging. As in 'silver seat,' it implies a passive existence, as the object of needing a helping hand (Tokyo Volunteer Center 1993b: 4).

The word 'senior' is intended to bring a new image to elderly volunteerism, and to encourage participation by those who have hesitated because of the stigma attached to 'silver.' In other words, while 'silver' means frail, passive and unproductive, 'senior' – a relatively new English-Japanese word – depicts the nuances of an emerging group of 'newly-old' in today's aging society: they are healthy, active and productive; and a separate group from the frail elders whom they may volunteer to help.

The use of the term 'volunteer' (borantia) in katakana – instead of its Japanese equivalent of hōshi – also indicates another deliberate effort to emphasise the fresh perspective of serving. Although interchangeable in meaning, however, as emphasised by the director of Tokyo Volunteer Action Center in an interview (in June 2001), 'hōshi has the connotation of self-sacrifice and a not so happy image.' On the contrary, the term 'borantia' emphasises equality, 'not I do something for someone, but more as part of life learning, where in giving, we are also receiving and are benefited. It has to be something you like to do, not are made to do. As ikigai.' Apart from defining volunteerism as 'receiving ikigai', the Center also promotes the concept of 'volunteer therapy', where volunteer activities have the effect of improving the mental and physical health of the persons who do them. For example, in the case of the dakko volunteers (hugging volunteers) – where elderly can volunteer to support childrearing in the community by becoming hugging volunteers in childcare centres, emphasis is placed not only on benefitting the babies, who are put to sleep in the warmth of the 'grannies'' arms, but also benefitting the elderly as the experience of natural 'skinship' with the babies will help them recall the happy childrearing of their younger days (Yamazaki 1995: 12).

The flexible definition of volunteerism is reflected in the definition of 'passive observation' as a volunteer activity. As a video entitled 'A

Volunteer Just by Being Present' produced by the National Old-Age Club Federation (Kihara 1995) shows, elderly people sitting on the benches in the park watching the children play are volunteers too. The producer explains the rationale of this:

As one ages, one gets less obsessed with the importance of blood-connectedness. It does not matter whose child it is; with affectionate eyes, they attend to the children who are there. The children, too, notice these elderly and feel reassured. This is a trivial task, but the elderly are also performing a role this way. It is good to have more active social participation, but to participate simply by watching, anybody can do it; isn't that so?

The video emphasises the volunteer roles the elderly could play with the children. 'Children are the lovers of the elderly,' it asserts, claiming that the elderly and children are natural companions for each other. Therefore, even bedridden persons can play the role of 'volunteers of the heart' (*kokoro no bora*) for the children who are visiting them because 'they bring out the sense of empathetic feeling in the young.' This all encompassing and unconventional interpretation of the concept of volunteerism thus broadens the scope of intergenerational interaction and gives new roles and meaning even to frail elderly receiving visits from children.

Community-based initiatives

Community-based initiatives can be broadly defined to include inter-generational activities and programmes organised by social organisations (such as neighbourhood associations), civic halls, local volunteer groups, self-governing bodies, charity organisations, private business groups and even community individuals. These activities are wide ranging and often enlist the participation of school children and elderly people from old-age clubs.

Some municipalities organise regular intergenerational programmes for the community. Since 1992, Kamou Town in Kagoshima Prefecture designates the third Saturday of the month as the 'Intergenerational Interaction Day' on which all civic halls organise activities such as 'listening to the experience of the elders,' 'learning about local history,' sports, volunteering and crafts to enhance interaction across the generations (Japan Aging Research Center, 1994). Ehime Prefecture started an 'open space for little children and elders' interaction' programme to encourage interaction among the community elders, nursery and kindergarten children and their mothers (Miyazato and Tsushida 1994: 154).

This category also relates to lifelong learning activities. Many 'silver colleges' include interaction with the young as part of their curriculum

(National Federation of Civic Halls 2000:173). For instance, a seminar for the elderly in Saitama prefecture organises a module called *ikigai* class or *fureai* class in the civic hall with intergenerational interaction as the learning objective. In the class, the elderly participants play traditional games with children. They also do *origami* and play ground golf together (Aoi, ed. 1996).

In recent years, there are also municipal efforts to create space for the old and young to interact within the community, such as building 'elders' spaces' in children's playgrounds (Hyōgo Prefecture), establishing a children's library in an old-age home (Saitama Prefecture), and placing swings and slides in the open ground of an old-age home.

Community projects initiated at the grass-roots level to preserve and beautify the environment also often draw on multigenerational efforts and have developed into an intergenerational activity. In 1991, a retiree in Saitama prefecture started a volunteer project to plant cosmos in the footpaths near his residence. Elementary school students were soon invited to help. Finally, the beautiful bloom prompted the idea of a cosmos festival; now the festival has become a community event held every autumn (Kanamaru 1999).

More often, festivals and events like these that enliven and unite the community and the generations within it are organised as municipal initiatives. These activities are often event-based and annual, or 'one-shot deals.' They include festivals and events that promote cultural and religious themes, seasonal events, and activities tied to environmental appreciation and preservation themes (Kaplan 1996). One characteristic of these initiatives is their emphasis on three-generational interactions. Some examples are three-generational family singing performances, three-generational sports meets and walkathons for multigenerations.

Multigenerational participation is seen as important as an ideal manifestation of a community. As a report on the *Fureai* Festival organised by the Civic Hall of Toyama City (Toyama Prefecture) shows, the cultural festival focussing on folk music (*minyō*) used to involve only the elderly. However, people found that the festival lacked the community festive mood, so the organisers re-defined it from 1998 to include in its objective the promotion of intergenerational interaction. This reflects the perception of the involvement of both the old and the young in such gatherings as representing the revival of the community (National Federation of Civic Halls 2000: 37).

Intergenerational activities in the community represent efforts to (re)unite the whole community and the multiple generations within it. Such efforts resonate in the larger on-going project of *furusato-zukuri* ('old village' making) – efforts on the national and local levels to integrate 'present-day activities and interpretations with past events, and to set in motion the construction of an "authentic" image (flavour) of the future' (Robertson 1991: 14).

Initiatives in age-integrated facilities

Perhaps, the closest resemblance to intergenerational interaction in the familial context is found in age-integrated facilities. Defined as the coexistence of services targeting different age groups, age-integrated facilities have a wide scope of combinations, ranging from day service centres for the elderly in elementary school classrooms, to the sharing of premises by nursery and nursing home. They usually choose to coexist with each other because of practical factors such as the effective use of limited land and resources as well as the 'emotional' motivation to provide opportunities for intergenerational interaction.

Although age-integrated facilities enjoy the benefits of having the old and young in close proximity to each other, not all service providers are enthusiastic about formulating programmes and activities to encourage intergenerational interaction. Many find the coordination needed to plan such activities time-consuming and complicated. Several are also discouraged by hindrances from parents who feared that their children may contract disease from the elderly, whom they perceive as sick and senile. In addition, despite policy statements to promote intergenerational exchange, the extra efforts to promote intergenerational activities by the service providers receive little formal concrete support from the bureaucracy, which view age-integrated facilities simply as 'built together' due to 'limited land' (Rōjin Hoken Fukushi Janaru 1993: 8).

Although the age-integrated facilities persist in promoting intergenerational interaction for the elderly and children, they usually refer to themselves as analogous to the ideal traditional family setting of multigenerational living. Kotoen, an age-integrated facility in Tokyo, which combines a special nursing home for the aged, a home for the elderly, day care services for the elderly (including those with dementia) and a nursery for children from age zero to six, has shown itself to be unique in its commitment to the *daikazoku* (big family).[6] It is worth noting that when the idea of putting all generations under one roof was conceived by the Director and proposed to the ward office, the proposal received little support and the proposers were forced to comply with the regulation of separating the services for different generations with a wall (which they constructed as removable and never put up). Thus, unlike some integrated facilities that were constructed as municipal efforts, but whose administrators were reluctant to organise intergenerational activities, Kotoen represents a private initiative by an NPO (*fukushi hōjin*) not only in placing cross-age services together but also in the active promotion of opportunities to integrate them through intergenerational programming. The attempt was novel when it first started in 1987.

Under the framework of the age-integrated facility as a big family – both in terms of size (where it has about 250 members) and multigenerations (with members ranging from age one to 95 years old), Kotoen strives to achieve the goal of a 'happy home' (*ikka danran*) through well-organised intergenerational activities and events. In daily interaction, a family-like atmosphere is created where children are reminded to greet and show respect to their Kotoen 'grandparents.' The elderly residents, too, are expected to perform their roles as 'grandparents' by playing with the 'grandchildren,' helping them to change their attire before and after their afternoon naps, telling them fables and tales, and making them gifts during traditional festive celebrations.

The *daikazoku* concept is well accepted by the children, their parents and the elderly residents in the institution. The parents and children find the multigenerational presence enriching of their lives as members of a nuclear family. Some mothers have even established frequent contact with the elderly through their children. The elderly residents agree that the *daikazoku* emphasis bring warmth and love to institutions for the aged that are usually stigmatised as a dumping ground for the family-less elderly.

Although the residents at Kotoen have come to identify themselves with the social world constructed by the facility, their interpretation and vision of a welfare institution as a *daikazoku* does not necessarily resonate with the wider public. On the one hand, it receives some favourable support, such as from viewers who were moved to tears by scenes of intergenerational contacts at Kotoen when it was shown on TV. (Kotoen has appeared on several TV programmes since it started in 1987. In 1989, it was featured in a 45-minute documentary by NHK entitled, 'A Big Family with 80 Grandchildren.') On the other hand, there is scepticism expressed at such a 'too-good-to-be true' setting. One officer at a city welfare office called it a 'drama-family' (*engeki kazoku*) when he learnt of Kotoen. Two Japanese who were invited to Golden Fair – an annual event to celebrate Respect the Elders' Day at Kotoen – were disturbed by the cheerful atmosphere not conforming to the stereotypical negative image they had of a welfare institution. They were particularly critical of the performances that, incidentally, were a 55-minute synopsis of a decade at Kotoen through dance, song and drama. While the performances, which emphasised the achievements of the facility in realising the *daikazoku* ideal, had moved many in the audience to tears (including the elderly, the staff and even the administrative director), they commented that it felt unnatural and 'the whole thing looks like some kind of new religious movement.'

Their metaphor of a new religion is interesting. The age-integrated facility does share various positive aspects in common with new religious movements; like the new religions, which have provided meaning to many people who are distressed by a lack of human fellowship in the modern mass society, Kotoen, too, attempts to reinforce the intergenerational ties in contemporary society by dramatising its vision through the *daikazoku* setting.

In general, even when the Japanese may be sceptical about the spontaneity of intergenerational interaction outside the familial context, the nostalgic image and longing for *daikazoku* (defined as multigenerational family) still remains. Most elderly people interviewed chose multigenerational living as the ideal living arrangement. Even when they claimed that they prefer to live alone, most still hoped to live with a child when they became frail. The *daikazoku* setting of an age-integrated facility thus addresses the dream of Japanese (especially the older Japanese) to be cared for by, and well connected with, the younger generation in a multigenerational family.

Intergenerational interaction and the Japanese-style welfare society

An overview of the intergenerational programmes shows a diversity of activities and programmes framed under 'intergenerational interaction.' Their connection with senior volunteerism shows the functional relationship between activities to promote intergenerational interaction and *'ikigai'* of the elderly as they provide an opportunity for the elderly to play an active role through contact with the young.

Regardless of who or which agency initiated an activity, one dominant feature of intergenerational programming in Japan is its emphasis on the past. Many intergenerational activities hinge on the traditional, cultural and historical knowledge of the elders[7]. During these intergenerational meetings, children gain knowledge about the past from activities ranging from learning about agriculture; more 'conventional' Japanese traditional crafts such as *origami*, bamboo crafts, rope crafts and traditional childhood games; to activities with *furusato* (old community, hometown) flavour. Elders also visit schools or children's clubs to talk about the past, such as war experiences and the community during their childhood, contributing to the young people's understanding of local history. Even contact between the frail elderly and the young reveals connections with past ideas and the desire to revive diminishing filial traditions. One report on intergenerational activities claims that these activities 'provide the opportunity for the young to learn how to take care of their own aging parents in the future.' (JARC 1994: 31). They impart the idea that one's place is with the family. As a child comments on his visits to a nursing home, 'The building is so grand, but I think they may be lonely not to be staying with their family' (Tokyo Volunteer Action Center 2000: 86). The age-integrated facilities further imply nostalgia for the traditional ideal of three-generational living. Underlying these practices is the sentimental belief that the past is ideal; maybe, it offers some answers to the dilemma we are facing in an aging society today.

Such emphasis on past images and traditions places programmes and activities for intergenerational interaction within the rhetoric of the Japanese-style welfare society – an idea first developed in the mid-1970s as the 1974 oil crisis forced the state to retract from the earlier development of a Western-style welfare state to one relying more on the family and individuals.[8] The Japanese-style welfare society rhetoric represents an 'invention of tradition' as it draws 'on idealised visions of a Japanese society where communities had always lived co-operatively and harmoniously, caring for each other, and especially for their aged and their sick.' It also emphasises 'Confucian values of filial piety, loyalty, obligation, respect for seniority' (Goodman 1998: 150).

Such ideology has invited debates that criticise the rhetoric as the state's intention to deny its responsibility to provide for the welfare of its people, particular in the care for the elderly. The recent introduction of the Long-Term Care Insurance Law in April 1999, indeed, shows a changing tendency in the direction of the government with the realisation that changes in the society and family have made it difficult for the family to provide care to the elderly. As observed by Koyano (1999: 166), today's intergenerational relationships between elderly parents and their adult children are more affection-based, convenience-oriented, and free from the Confucian norms of filial piety than they used to be.

Despite the criticisms and the reaction (in terms of the introduction of care insurance), paradoxically, the *daikazoku* invention in intergenerational interaction and the various instances of using the *kokoro* (heart) to symbolise intergenerational activities express the continuing wide acceptance of a Japanese-style welfare model among the Japanese. The activities to promote intergenerational interaction not only hope to inculcate in the young a sense of empathy towards the old, but more importantly, they reveal hopes that such contacts serve as lessons to teach the young filial piety and that they should provide care for their own parents in the future.

Given the potential of intergenerational programmes and activities in realising the ultimate goodness in interpersonal relations where harmony and mutual help are stressed across the generations, we can expect further interest in promoting them from advocates of the Japanese-style welfare society. In the face of drastic social, demographic as well as recent economic changes, the challenge remains, however, as to the effective allocation of financial, administrative and training resources to touch the hearts of both generations without having to purchase them through family-rental services.

NOTES

1   Data for this paper is derived from materials collected in the field in 1995–6
    (see Thang, 2001) and 2001. The author is grateful to grants from the Japan
    Foundation and Hitachi Foundation (Komai Fellowship) respectively for
    making the field research in 1995–6 and 2001 possible.
2   Responses from youth in some other countries included in the survey are as
    follows: America, 62.7%; United Kingdom, 45.9%; Sweden, 36.8%; Korea,
    66.7%; Thailand, 59.3%.
3   The study represents one of the several research initiatives funded by
    Sōmuchō to survey intergenerational initiatives across the country and
    develop some guidelines for planning and implementation.
4   The other measures under the policy include 1) securing employment and
    income, 2) health and welfare 3) housing and living environment and 4)
    research and development.
5   Tokyo Volunteer Action Center was previously known as Tokyo Volunteer
    Center until 1998.
6   I studied Kotoen and similar facilities in Tokyo area in 1995–1996 and
    revisited Kotoen in June 2001. See Thang (2001) for an ethnographic work
    on Kotoen.
7   A survey of the children and elderly, however, shows that they do not think
    that traditional games are the only means of interaction. Among the children,
    70.8% want to have activities which both can enjoy and 23% activities
    relating to traditions. The responses are similar among the elderly (Sagaza,
    ed. 2001:26).
8   See Goodman (1998) for a concise description and evaluation of the debates
    on the Japanese-style welfare society.

REFERENCES

Aoi, Kazuo, ed. 1996. *Sedaikan Kōryū no Riron to Jitsugen* (The Theories and
    Practices of Intergenerational Interaction). Tokyo: Chōju Shakai Kaihatsu
    Centre (Centre for Exploring the Long-lived Society).
Goodman, Roger. 1998. 'The "Japanese-style welfare state" and the delivery of
    personal social services,' pp. 120–39 in *The East Asian Welfare Model: Welfare
    Orientalism and the State*, ed. R. Goodman, G. White and H. Kwon. London:
    Routledge.
Hani, Yoko. 2001. 'Empty classrooms renovated for public use.' *The Japan Times
    Online* (11 March).
Higashi Shakai Fukushi Kyōkai Hoikubu Tsūshin (The East [Division] Social
    Welfare Association Child Care Department Correspondence). 1995.
    October 20.
Ishikuro, Chiiko. 1994. 'Shakai fukushi ni okeru borantia katsudō ni tsuite (About
    volunteer activities in social welfare),' pp. 43–72 in *Sedaikan Kōryū Kenkyūkai
    ni Okeru Hiaringu Kōenshū* (Compilation of Talks held by Research Group
    on Intergenerational Interaction). Tokyo: Chōju Shakai Kaihatsu Centre
    (Centre for Exploring the Long-lived Society).

Japan Aging Research Center (JARC). 1994. *Sedaikan Kōryū ni kansuru Chōsa Kenkyū Hōkokusho* (Survey Report on Intergenerational Interaction). Tokyo: Japan Aging Research Center.

Japan Intergenerational Network. http://cert.shinshu-u.ac.jp/project/jigen/top.html

Kanamaru, Hiromi. 1999. *Jibun no Tame no Ikigai Tsukuri* (The Creation of Ikigai for the Self). Tokyo: Ichimansha.

Kaplan, Matthew. 1993. 'Recruiting senior adult volunteers for intergenerational programs: working to create a "jump on the bandwagon" effect.' *Journal of Applied Gerontology* 12(1): 71–82.

——. 1996. 'A look at intergenerational program initiatives in Japan: A preliminary comparison with the US.' *Southwest Journal on Aging,* 12(1–2): 73–9.

Kaplan, Matthew, Atusko Kusano, Ichiro Tsuji and Shigeru Hisamichi. 1998. *Intergenerational Programs: Support for Children, Youth and Elders in Japan.* New York: SUNY Press.

Kihara, K. 1995. *Iru Dake de Borantia* (A Volunteer just by being Present). Tokyo Shine Video: Zenkoku Rōjin Kurabu Rengokai (Federation of National Old-age Clubs).

Kono, Shigemi. 2000. 'Demographic aspects of population aging in Japan,' pp. 7–52 in *Aging in Japan* ed. Shigeyoshi Yoshida. Tokyo: Japan Aging Research Center.

Koyano, Wataru. 1993. 'Age-old stereotypes.' *Japan Views Quarterly,* 2(Winter): 41–2.

——. 1999. 'Population aging, changes in living arrangement, and the new long-term care system in Japan.' *Journal of Sociology and Social Welfare,* 26(March): 155–67.

Kurauchi, Shiro and Mari Suzuki, eds. 1998. *Shōgai Gakkushū Kiso* (The Basics of Lifelong Learning). Tokyo: Gakubunsha.

Maeda, Daisaku. 2000. 'Social security, health care, and social services for the elderly in Japan,' pp. 105–42 in *Aging in Japan*, ed. Shigyoshi Yoshida. Japan Aging Research Center. Tokyo: Japan Aging Research Center.

Mathews, Gordon. 1996. *What Makes Life Worth Living? – How Japanese and Americans Make Sense of their Worlds.* Berkeley: University of California Press.

Miyagi Prefecture Federation of Old-age Clubs. 1991. *Chiiki ni Ikitsuku Shiruba Borantia* (Silver Volunteers who Liven Up the Community). Tokyo: Tōei Company Educational Filming Department.

Miyazato, I. and Tsushida Yūko. 1994. 'Sedaikan kōryū no borantia katsudō (Volunteer activities with intergenerational interaction?),' pp.142–59 in *Kōreika Shakai no Sedaikan Kōryū* (Intergenerational Interaction in Aging Society), ed. K. Aoi. Tokyo: Chōju Shakai Kaihatsu Centre (Centre for Exploring the Long-lived Society).

National Federation of Civic Halls. 2000. *Atarashii Kōminkan Katsudō no arikata ni kansuru Chōsa Kenkyū Hōkokushō* (Report on Survey of New Activities at Civic Halls).

NHK (Japan Broadcasting Corporation). 1989. *Mago Hachijūnin no Daikazoku: Rōjin to Hoikuenji no Fureaiki* (A Big Family with Eighty Grandchildren: Elderly in touch with Children at Child Care Center). April 27.

Ogawa, Naohiro and Robert Retherford. 1993. 'Care of the elderly in Japan: changing norms and expectations.' *Journal of Marriage and the Family.* 55(3): 585–97.

Retherford, Robert D., Ogawa Naohiro and Sakamoto Satomi. 1999. 'Values and fertility change in Japan,' pp. 121–47 in *Dynamics of Values in Fertility Change*, ed. R. Leete. Oxford: Oxford University Press.

Robertson, Jennifer. 1991. *Native and Newcomer: Making and Remaking a Japanese City*. Berkeley: University of California Press.

Rōjin Hoken Fukushi Janaru (Journal of Elderly Healthcare and Welfare). 1993. *Hitotsu Yane no Shita ni Atsumareba* (As we Gather under one Roof), October: 4–17.

Sagaza, Haruo, ed. 2001. *Shōshi Kōreishakai to Kodomotachi* (Aging and Falling Birthrate Society and Children). Tokyo: Chūō Hōki Publisher.

Saito, Sadao. 1994. 'Shakai fukushi bunya ni okeru sedaikan kōryū no genjō – fukushi kyōiku o tōshite (Present conditions of intergenerational interaction in social welfare sphere – through welfare education),' pp. 160–205 in *Kōreika Shakai no Sedaikan Kōryū* (Intergenerational Interaction in Aging Society), ed. K. Aoi. Tokyo: Chōju Shakai Kaihatsu Centre (Centre for Exploring the Long-lived Society).

Sawano, Yukiko. 2000. 'Intergenerational exchange programme for lifelong learning: Japanese experiences,' pp. 56–61 in *Report of the 1st International Conference on Intergenerational Programmes, 13–14 October 1999*. Netherlands.

Shakai Kyōiku Shisetsu Borantia Kenkyū Kai (Study Group of Volunteers in Social Educational Facilities). 1997. *Shakai Kyōiku Shisetsu Borantia no Jiko Keisei II* (The Self-Formation of Volunteers in Social Educational Facilities II).

Sōmuchō (Ministry of Public Management, Home Affairs, Post and Telecommunications). 1990. *Rōjin no Seikatsu to Ishiki ni Kansuru Kokusai Hikaku Chōsa* (International Comparative Survey on the Lives and Consciousness of Elders). Tokyo.

Sōmuchō (Ministry of Public Management, Home Affairs, Post and Telecommunications). 1993. *Daigokai Sekai Seinen Ishiki Chōsa* (Fifth Survey on Youth Consciousness).

——, ed. 2000. *Kōreishakai Hakusho* (White Paper on Aging Society).

Thang, Leng Leng. 2001. *Generations in Touch: Linking the Old and Young in a Tokyo Neighborhood*. Ithaca: Cornell University Press.

Tokyo Volunteer Center. 1993a. *Senior Volunteer Activity Manual*. Tokyo: Tokyo Volunteer Center.

——. 1993b. *Senior Volunteers' Coordinators' Manual*. Tokyo: Tokyo Volunteer Center.

Tokyo Volunteer Action Center. 2000. *San Nen Kan no Takara Sagashi* (Three Years of Treasure Hunting) Volume 4. Tokyo: Tokyo Volunteer and Citizens Center.

Yamamoto, Yoshihiro. 1997. *Shichōson ni okeru Shōgai Gakushū Borantia Banku no Katsuseika ni Kansuru Jisshōteki Kenkyū* (Case Research of the Activation of Lifelong Learning Volunteer Bank in Cities, Wards, Towns and Villages). Tokyo: National Education Research Center.

Yamazaki, Mikiko. 1995. 'Atarashii bunka wo sōzō shi, fukamete iku katsudō no kaikaku wo (Creating new culture, exploring intensifying activities),' pp. 8–15 in *Senior Volunteer Book*, ed. Tokyo Volunteer Center. Tokyo: Tokyo Volunteer Center.

8   Death policies in Japan: the state, the family, and the individual

Yohko Tsuji[1]

The inscription on Stendhal's tombstone, 'He lived, wrote, and loved,' sums up his life in one short sentence. By contrast, the inscription on the typical Japanese tombstone reads 'Ancestral grave of X family' and contains no reference at all to the lives of the individuals buried in it. Today, most Japanese assume incorrectly that the practice is an age-old tradition, whereas in fact it became widespread only during the Meiji period (1868–1912) as a result of the government's attempt to 'modernise' the nation.

In this paper, I examine death-related policies in Japan over the last 130 years to reveal the complex and dynamic process of policy implementation. First, I review death policies in the early Meiji period and demonstrate how the state's control of death was tied to its drive to modernise the country and how death policies, especially those relating to household-based ancestor worship, facilitated the new regime's control over the family and the individual. Next, I deal with death-related policies that developed after World War II in the period of democratisation. I am particularly concerned with the lingering effects of the household principle on the new policies, and the extent to which these new policies have failed to keep up with the rapid pace of change in contemporary Japan. Finally, I explore the impact of death policies on people's lives and their responses to policy change. I conclude that mortuary practice is shaped by an intricate interplay among policies, individual actors, and traditions, as well as various other situational factors.

Death policies of the Meiji government

The Meiji regime began to build a modern nation-state with two opposing objectives: '"renovation" that implied rejection of the past and "restoration" that implied the preservation of and return to the past' (Kitagawa 1966: 210). Policies on death constituted an integral part of this contradictory 'modernisation' process.

The state's control of death occurred at the onset of the new era. In 1872 (Meiji 5), the government banned the existing custom of burying a corpse at the edge of a cultivated field (Mori 1993: 151) as well as *jisō*, the self-conducted funeral by the bereaved family, requiring that the funeral be officiated by either Shinto priests or Buddhist monks (Mori 1993: 139; Oguchi and Takagi 1956: 336). It also opened some Shinto cemeteries (Mori 1993: 140–1; Haga 1996: 243). At this stage, the Meiji government treated death as a religious issue. The major reason behind the ban on self-conducted funerals was to exclude Christianity from people's religious experiences (Mori 1993: 143). The inclusion of Buddhist priests was a pragmatic compromise (ibid.: 139).

The following two years witnessed the issuing of additional death-related policies. In 1873 (Meiji 6), cremation or *kasō* was prohibited together with the construction of a new cemetery without the government's permission. In 1874 (Meiji 7), official cemetery rules were announced, defining the cemetery as a place not only for burial, but also for worship, and demanding each one be approved and registered by the government (Mori 1993: 153–4). In addition, the official model of the Shinto funeral was put into effect (ibid.: 140).

One remarkable fact about these policies was the involvement of Shinto in the realm of death. Shinto, idealising purity, detested the pollution of death (Mori 1993: 134; Hardacre 1997: 1). Besides, death had been so closely tied to Buddhism in Japan that Japanese Buddhism was often called 'funeral Buddhism' (LaFleur 1992: 80). Thus, until early Meiji, Shinto funerals had been virtually unknown (Smith 1974: 29).

The Meiji government tried to change this tradition in order to 'restore' the indigenous Japanese way. In its first year of power, it ordered the separation of Shinto, a native religion, and Buddhism, a religion of foreign origin, and an anti-Buddhism movement (*haibutsu kishaku*) ensued.

The ban on cremation (*kasō*) reflected this anti-Buddhist ideology. Cremation had been practiced in Japan for over a thousand years. It was brought to Japan with Buddhism and became widespread in the sixth and seventh centuries. It is mentioned in some classic literature, the *Man'yōshū*, a poetry anthology of the seventh and eighth centuries, for instance (Inoue 1990: 117–8; Yasuda 1991: 44–6). But Confucian and Nativist scholars[2] in the Edo period maintained that the practice violated the indigenous Japanese way (Mori 1993: 147). The opportunity to amend the situation came in 1873 (Meiji 6) when the Tokyo Police Department contacted the Ministry of Justice regarding the problems caused by cremation. Concerned that the smoke and the odour from the city's crematoriums would jeopardise people's health, the Police recommended crematoriums be moved to the outskirts.

The issue was brought to the office of the Administrative Council (*Dajōkan*), which promptly decided to outlaw cremation. Labelling cremation as 'a barbarian custom of Buddhist origin that was too brutal for any human being to bear,' the Council was afraid that permitting the relocation of crematoriums might be interpreted as de facto approval of cremation (Mori 1993: 145, my translation).

This policy did not last very long, however. Only two years after banning it, the government reinstated cremation. Beside this, it openly began to withdraw Shinto from funerary rites. In 1880 (Meiji 13), the construction of new Shinto cemeteries was no longer approved (Mori 1993: 156). Two years later, Shinto priests were forbidden to officiate at funerals. Do these policy changes indicate that the government's attempt to restore the indigenous Japanese way failed?

After cremation was outlawed, strong protest movements erupted nationwide, involving not only Buddhist priests and crematorium operators, but also many private citizens (Hashizume 1990: 44). Reversal of the new death policies might appear to be a surrender to these protestors' pro-cremation, pro-Buddhist arguments. It might also reflect the government's failing efforts to establish Shinto as a national religion.

We must note, however, that lifting the ban on cremation was not to restore the old folkway. The reinstatement of *kasō* came with strict regulations. The government allowed it only at properly equipped crematoriums that were located a good distance away from residential areas. For instance, the decree announced by the Ministry of Home Affairs in 1873 (Meiji 6) required the chimney be at least 24 *shaku* (approximately 24 feet) tall and people, not the government, bear the construction costs (Aoki 1993:2). In addition, I maintain that the policy reversal was a pragmatic compromise by the Meiji oligarchy to 'modernise' the nation while maintaining tight 'feudal' control.[3] How did cremation serve to achieve these seemingly contradictory goals?

The ban on cremation caused many problems. When urban dwellers coming from a distant area died, their bodies could not be cremated and began to decay before the next of kin came to bury them (Hashizume 1990: 44). Imagine how horrendous the smell was! Though I did not find any documented evidence, the fact that burial was more costly than cremation may have forced some people to abandon the corpse, aggravating the problem of decaying bodies. The prevalence of infectious diseases also made cremation more advantageous in maintaining public health.[4] Lack of burial space caused another problem.[5] Besides, having precious land occupied for the dead might prove an obstacle to city planning.

As the capital of a modern nation, Tokyo had many deficiencies. Its streets were narrow. Numerous densely built wooden structures crowded it even further. It lacked city water as well as sewage and had no public parks. Moreover, there was no railway service. Nor was its port equipped to meet the demands of the new era (Koshizawa 1991: 2).

Re-building Tokyo was one of the most urgent requirements to 'modernise' the nation.[6] In the process, many existing structures had to be removed. Moving burial grounds presented special problems, because it involved exhuming the corpses and reburying them.[7] Cremating the dead made this job less cumbersome. Furthermore, as cemeteries were not taxable properties, encouraging cremation and limiting the space for cemeteries promised more revenue for the government.

Thus, reinstating cremation contributed to building the infrastructure of the modern nation and city. At the same time, it helped establish an 'immanental theocracy' (Kitagawa 1966: 204) by facilitating the institution of the family grave as the locus of ancestor worship.

The *ie* system played a significant role in this theocracy (Itō 1982) because the conception of the household was intimately connected to that of ancestors (Smith 1974: vii), and '[n]otions of the strong family became bound up with those of the strong nation' (LaFleur 1992: 121). The Meiji Civil Code of 1898 established the *ie* as a legal entity to which every subject must belong. Though as early as in 1870 (Meiji 3) the new regime allowed everyone to bear a surname, a privilege not available to most commoners until then, this seemingly 'modernising' action contributed to organising all individuals into families, which, in turn, became part of the 'national' family. The Household Register Law of 1871 also served to achieve this end, together with the 1872 decree of the Administrative Council (*Dajōkan*) that denied the freedom to change one's family name and Article 746 of the Civil Code that stipulated '[t]he head of a house and its members bear the (family) name of such house' (Sebald 1934: 169). The state also used the *ie* as a shrewd tactic to control every single citizen by granting its head authority over other members and imposing on him the responsibility for their maintenance and behaviour (Kano 1983: 59). In addition, the institution of *kōban*, the police-box, helped the state's 'policing' of its subjects (LaFleur 1992: 121).

Hence, the *ie* continuity became an important national concern. The Meiji Civil Code specified male primogeniture as the rule, but it was also explicit on the *ie* succession in case this ideal was not achieved. To legitimate the *ie* as a perpetual entity, ancestor worship was demanded and the family grave became its locus. Article 987 of the Meiji Civil Code stressed the significance of graves for the *ie* by declaring their ownership as 'a special right pertaining to succession to [the *ie*]' (Sebald 1934: 232).

This legal provision defined the family as the unit of burial, terminating the existing custom of separate graves for individuals or married couples (Mori 1993: 183). Cremation promoted the spread of the *ie*-based grave because, without cremation, placing all the dead in the family in one grave might have been difficult. Cremation also made ancestor worship possible for an increasing number of people who moved to urban areas and lived and died away from home.

Ancestor worship during the Meiji period was more than a religious practice. It was an ideology essential to implement the 'immanental theocracy' (Kitagawa 1966: 204) by 'promoting the emperor cult as the most important ingredient of Shinto' (Kitagawa 1966: 203). In this scheme, the emperor was 'both the sovereign and the father of his people' (Smith 1974: 31), and all his subjects were his *sekishi* or children (Itō 1982: 2). As children must show *kō* or filial piety to parents, people owed *chū* or loyalty to the emperor. In short, both the head of the state and the head of the *ie*, as well as their ancestors, were to be venerated, although loyalty to the emperor always took precedence over filial piety. The *Kyōiku Chokugo* (Imperial Rescript on Education), promulgated in 1890, indoctrinated '[e]mperor worship combined with the Confucian ideology of loyalty, filial piety, and obedience to superiors' (Anderson 1975: 29). By legally sanctioning these requirements and enforcing them through moral education, the Meiji regime linked Shinto emperor worship to Buddhist ancestor worship with 'dazzling success' (Smith 1974: 4).

Thus, Shinto's withdrawal from mortuary rites did not mean its defeat to Buddhism, but rather indicated two significant, interrelated shifts in the government's policies. First, after failing to establish Shinto as a national religion, the government politicised it. This *Kokka Shintō* or 'State Shinto' elevated the emperor to 'the exalted status of a "living kami"' (Kitagawa 1966: 203). Despite its basis in the Shinto tradition, '[it] was essentially a newly concocted religion of ethnocentric nationalism' (Kitagawa 1966: 213). The government's decision to remove Shinto priests from the realm of death was to engage them in this 'national cult.' By so doing, it distinguished Shinto from other religions (Hardacre 1989: 33), declaring it was the 'national cult' transcending any ordinary religion (Mori 1993: 166).

Secondly, realising that death would affect taxation, public health, and city planning, the Meiji government removed death from the religious domain and made it part of the administrative dominion. To endorse this change, the Administrative Council (*Dajōkan*) issued the Regulations Concerning Burials and Graves in 1884.

New regulations required a burial permit and, to obtain it, a doctor's certificate of death. Before then, it was Buddhist priests who acknowledged death although village officials were involved if death was accidental or its cause questionable (Mori 1993: 168–70). The new regulations also restricted the place of burial to the cemetery and allowed only cremation (*kasō*) or burial of the corpse (*dosō*). Thus, the state came to control both the authorisation of death and the disposal of the remains. More importantly, the new law redefined the cemetery as a clean and sacred place where the dead rested eternally and were worshipped with respect. Since death was customarily viewed as polluting and hence to be avoided, such purification of the cemetery became essential to support the 'national cult' in which the emperor and his ancestors were revered as 'gods.'

With this new ideology of graves and the restrictions on burial methods and places, the Regulations Concerning Burials and Graves limited individual freedom concerning death (Inoue 1993: 209). As a result, the variety of existing customs diminished, leading to the standardisation of mortuary practice. In addition, the policy reversal firmly incorporated death into the Meiji regime's grand plan of ruling the country with the Shinto 'national cult.'

Before Meiji, a surprising range of variations was observed in burial customs in terms of where the dead were buried, who was buried in the grave, and how the dead were memorialised. For instance, the ban on burying the corpse at the edge of a cultivated field indicates this was a common practice. So was *yashikibaka*, home graves. Some graves were for the individual while others were for the married couple, the lineage, or even for the entire village. Some graves had no tombstone for a memorial (*muboseki-sei*). On the other hand, *ryōbo-sei* involved separate graves for burial and memorial. In some of the *muboseki-sei* cases, a portion of bones was brought to the temple to be memorialised there with the remainder abandoned at the place of cremation. (See Mori 1993: chapter 3.)

The Yasukuni shrine provided another example of deaths controlled by 'State Shinto' (Kitagawa 1966: 203; Haga 1996: 267). An important apparatus of the 'national cult,' it was built to enshrine and worship as gods the spirits of those who had died in war (Mori 1993: 10). Under the jurisdiction of the Ministry of the Army and the Navy rather than the Shrine Office of the Ministry of Internal Affairs, the Yasukuni shrine maintained ceremonial styles distinctively different from other shrines (Haga 1996: 267). The families of *eirei* or '"glorious" military dead' (Nelson 1998: 14) enshrined there received honours and privileges, being granted government money to build their graves, for instance. However, the spirits of *eirei* were no longer 'the property of individual families' but 'became ... a valuable political commodity for the state' (ibid.).

Though the 'modernisation' policies of the Meiji regime inevitably involved rejecting the past and adopting Western ideas and systems, they also '[followed] the ancient Japanese model of "unity of religion and government" (*saisei-itchi*)' (Kitagawa 1966: 201) to establish a new 'theocracy' with the emperor as a living god. The family served as an effective state agent in controlling the individual through the authority invested in its head. By submerging individuals and regulating families, the Meiji oligarchy governed the nation. The death policies of the early Meiji period were intimately connected to this 'theocracy,' helping to produce loyal subjects and filial children rather than developing each individual as a unique person.

Death policies after World War II

Japan's defeat in World War II drastically changed relationships between the state, the family, and the individual. The emperor renounced his divinity, and the New Constitution declared that sovereign power resided in the people. The democratic constitution also guaranteed equal rights to every citizen and freedom of religion.[8] In addition, the New Civil Code abolished the *ie* system. When the family and ancestor worship ceased to be a political tool, 'a fundamental change' occurred in death policies (Smith 1974: 4).

Nevertheless, ancestor worship continued to be practiced (Smith 1974; Plath 1964), and the *ie*-based ideology of death survives in the New Civil Code of 1948. Its Article 897 states, '… the ownership of … tombs and burial grounds is succeeded to by the person who, according to custom, [should] hold … the worship to the memory of the ancestors' (Ministry of Justice 1972: 187–8). Though the new law does not specify who is to inherit the family grave, the 'according to custom' clause implicitly requires the *ie*-based burial practice and patrilineal succession of the family grave.

Similarly, Article 769 of the New Civil Code suggests the *ie*-based right to inherit tombs and burial grounds. It stipulates that those who had changed their surnames after marriage and inherited tombs and burial grounds belonging to their spouse's family are to lose the ownership of such property in case of divorce (Ministry of Justice 1972: 161; Inoue 1990: 76–7; Ishikawa 1988: 127–8). Behind this provision is the persistent idea that an individual owns the grave only as representative of his or her family and sharing the same surname is an important criterion in determining family membership. The same idea is manifested in the current controversy over granting separate surnames to a married couple.

Such lingering *ie* principles are apparent in some of the cemetery regulations. For instance, Tokyo Prefecture demands the eldest son's consent if he is not designated as the heir when a grave is purchased (Inoue 1990: 71–2; Takeuchi 1993: 110). Another common rule is that only one family name should be inscribed on the tomb and it should match that of the heir (Yasuda 1991: 185). This makes it practically impossible for a married-out daughter to inherit the grave of her natal family, though Article 897 of the New Civil Code does not explicitly ban women's succession to the grave. A patrilineal bias is also manifested in that some cemeteries will not sell a grave to anyone without male descendants.

Post-World-War-II death-related policies include specific rules regarding the treatment of remains and burials. According to Article 190 of the Criminal Code,[9] it is a punishable act to destroy, abandon, or steal human remains and bones. Laws Concerning Graves and Burials, promulgated in 1948, replaced the similar Meiji legislation discussed earlier. But, like the old law, its Article 4 prohibits the burial of human corpses and bones except at a cemetery (Yasuda 1991: 215).

In contemporary Japan, these death-related policies may create some serious problems. For one thing, while the *ie* concept continues to govern death policies and practices, the Japanese family has become very different from the *ie* in the past. Traditional three-generation stem families have drastically decreased. Nuclear families are also on the decline with the steady increase of couple-only and single-person households.[10] The birthrate is alarmingly low.[11] The divorce rate grows constantly.[12] Correspondingly, the number of remarriages is on the rise.

All these changes undermine the idea of the family as a perpetual entity, producing a growing number of people without 'proper' descendants to take care of their graves. The shortage of graves and their exorbitant cost, on average ¥3 million (Inoue 1990: 220), aggravate the problem. But current death policies do not adequately respond to this new situation. Consequently, various unconventional mortuary practices have appeared. I will discuss these practices in the second half of the next section.

Policies and people's lives

This section considers the impact of various death policies on people's lives and their reactions to the state's control of death. It explores the intricacy and dynamics of policy enforcement, first for the early Meiji period, and then, since World War II.

Meiji policies

Death regulations by the Meiji government brought many changes in mortuary customs. Most importantly, they standardised the practice, requiring the family grave as the locus of ancestor worship and restricting burial to a cemetery. Official regulations governing death sometimes created complications in people's lives. Smith and Wiswell report one such case that involved the death of one of newborn twins in Suyemura in the 1930s (1982: 242–8). The twins' family found that they could not hold a funeral until death was registered at the village office. But, to register the baby's death, his birth had to be recorded.[13] To record his birth, the dead boy needed to have a name. Thus, the family, in the chaos of simultaneously dealing with birth and death, held the naming ceremony for both the surviving twin and his dead brother (Smith and Wiswell 1982: 242–8).

In Nishi-Monobe, a village in Shiga Prefecture, even the short-lived ban on cremation had some enduring influence. When cremation was prohibited in early Meiji, people in this village had switched from *kasō* (cremation) to *dosō* (the burial of the remains) and, despite the swift reinstatement of cremation, continued *dosō* until 1983 (Aoki 1993: 5–6 and 11).

Though the Meiji regime imposed tight, monolithic control over its subjects, people did not always obey its death policies. As mentioned in the first section of this chapter, the ban on cremation was met with strong protest movements that swept the nation. The difficulty of terminating cremation was also indicated by decrees that some local governments issued to reinforce the ban. Even after the ban was lifted, an edict was proclaimed in Ishikawa Prefecture to stop the exhumation of a buried corpse for cremation (Aoki 1993: 3).

Similarly, the tightening state control of death in subsequent years was not totally successful in changing traditional mortuary practices. For instance, *yashikibaka*, the grave in the yard of a private home, continued in some areas by burying the body at the cemetery during the day and secretly moving it to a home grave at night (Mori 1993: 80–1).

Also perpetuated were varied forms of ancestor worship that did not conform to the *ie* principle. One such case stressed parent–child relationships, distributing parents' tablets among all the children who were equally responsible for worshipping the parents' spirits. This was a departure from the official rule of male primogeniture. In another case, the *ie* head and his wife were worshipped at two separate households: the husband by the eldest son, the heir, and the wife by the second son who established a branch family. This custom made a woman the founding ancestor of the branch family. Needless to say, it violated the patrilineal *ie* principle (Mori 1993: 201–2).

While these cases may indicate that the power of tradition overrode the authority of the state, another case involves non-conformity by starting a totally new mortuary practice. In 1916, the leader of Oshiage, a hamlet in Niigata Prefecture, initiated such a practice by unifying the family graves of all of the region's 103 households into one newly built collective grave. The bones of approximately 3,000 residents were exhumed and placed in the new grave. The hamlet leader had two aims: to solve the problem of *muenbo* or graves without descendants/caretakers and to use scarce land more effectively for enhancing the local economy based on fishing and agriculture. Today, this collective grave is still being used, and, since its establishment, the bones of an additional 700 residents have been entombed (*AS* 24 May 2000).

In addition to these cases of deviation, it is important to remember that following the state's regulations does not necessarily mean individuals' passivity. Motivations for compliance are manifold. Sometimes, people choose to conform, not because they are coerced, but because they find it advantageous. Let us look at the case of Nishi-Monobe, a village in Shiga Prefecture mentioned earlier.

People in Nishi-Monobe practiced cremation (*kasō*) until it was outlawed in 1873 when, responding to the new policy, they switched to *dosō* (the burial of the remains). What is unusual in this case is that even after cremation was reinstated, they continued to practice *dosō*. *Kasō* was such a well-established custom that, once the ban was lifted, some people elsewhere even dug up buried corpses to cremate them. Why did villagers in Nishi-Monobe stick to *dosō*? Did their persistent practice of *dosō* reflect their strong desire to observe the indigenous Japanese way that the Meiji regime so eagerly tried to restore?

The reason for Nishi-Monobe villagers' adherence to *dosō* was pragmatic, not at all political or religious. In reversing its policy on the ban of cremation, the Meiji government allowed *kasō* only if it was held at a properly equipped crematorium that met official standards. The traditional *kasō* in Nishi-Monobe failed to satisfy these requirements. It involved digging a hole in the cemetery ground, crisscrossing the top with wood to place a coffin, and setting a fire. When cremation was completed, the hole was filled with dirt, covering bones dropped at the bottom (Aoki, 1993: 6). Switching back to *kasō* required the construction of a new crematorium, a costly venture. It also meant picking out bones after cremation and burying them at a different location. In addition, the indigenous *kasō* in Nishi-Monobe shared one important characteristic with *dosō*; both disposal and burial of the remains occurred at the same site though what was interred was different: the bones in the former and the corpse in the latter. This fact might have eased the villager's initial acceptance of *dosō* and contributed to its continuous practice until 1983 (Aoki 1993: 11 and 18).

Though death policies of the early Meiji caused a major change in Nishi-Monobe's funerary practice, some traditional customs survived, reflecting the village's past practice of *kasō*. One such example is their unique coffin. Before re-adopting *kasō* in 1983, people in Nishi-Monobe used *zakan*, a coffin in which the dead person was placed in a sitting position. While *zakan* was not uncommon in Japan's past, this one was unusual in that its bottom was open except for two bars. Originally, the open bottom was designed to clear the passage for the flames of cremation, but people kept using *zakan* long after *dosō* became a well-established custom. Another residue of *kasō* was the three bunches of straw that played an important ceremonial role in Nishi-Monobe funerals. In the traditional *kasō*, these bundles of straw had been used to start the fire (Aoki 1993: 10–11).

The complex interplay between the state's policies and local traditions is also observed in a notable change in Nishi-Monobe's graves under the Meiji regime. Before the Meiji government regulated death, no gravestones existed in the village cemetery to memorialise the dead. Wooden posts were erected to mark where the dead were cremated and buried in the manner mentioned above. But some years after Nishi-Monobe switched from *kasō* to *dosō*, this tradition of *muboseki-sei*, having no gravestones, began to change to *ryōbo-sei*, having separate graves for burial and memorial (Aoki 1993: 12–18). The village cemetery was divided into two sections. While the area with wooden posts, the former site for *kasō*, became that for *dosō*, a new area was built with stone tombs for worship.[14]

The wooden post and the stone tomb had quite different meanings; the former was a marker of the individual's burial site, but the latter was for the *ie* and the inscription on the majority of them said '*Senzo daidai no haka*,' literally a grave of generations of ancestors (Aoki 1993: 14–17). The *ie*-based ideology of death, an important state policy, was reflected in this change.

However, ancestor worship in Nishi-Monobe deviated from the convention in that its family grave was purely for memorialisation and no bones were placed in it. Furthermore, the shift to the family grave came only slowly despite that the Meiji Civil Code instituted the *ie* system in 1898 (Meiji 31). Out of 36 tombstones whose year of construction was known,[15] only seven were built in Meiji and five in Taishō. Though 23 were added in the Shōwa period, 11 were erected between 1959 and 1982, after the legal demise of the *ie*. None was constructed between 1945 and 1958, the difficult post-war era (Aoki 1993: 17). These statistics indicate that more than state policies – economic considerations, for instance – were at work in people's decision to have a family grave.

I have shown varied responses to the state's control of death under the Meiji regime. I turn next to the impact of post-World-War-II death policies on contemporary Japan.

Post-World-War-II policies

Though the 'democratic' Civil Code of 1948 contains the lingering *ie*-principle, one year after the new law went into effect, the Osaka High Court made a judicial decision that challenged the *ie* concept. In a dispute over the succession to a grave, the Court nominated the deceased's common-law wife of 20 years as the successor to the grave instead of his brother and sister, the legal heirs. This case established a legal precedent for similar cases thereafter (Takeuchi 1993: 109).

The court's decision derived from two premises: Article 897 does not stipulate the successor to a grave be a relative or have the same family name as the deceased; and the 'custom' in Article 897 does not refer to any old custom under the Meiji Civil Code but to a custom newly created according to the New Civil Code (Takeuchi 1993: 109). This case, which granted the grave and the rest of the estate to two separate parties (i.e., common-law wife and siblings), clearly declares that the ownership of tombs and burial grounds is no longer 'a special right pertaining to succession to [the *ie*]' (Sebald 1934: 232).

Despite its legal demise, however, the *ie* continues to play an essential role in dealing with death and afterlife today (Tsuji, forthcoming a). This creates serious problems for a growing number of people because, as discussed in the middle section of this chapter, the contemporary Japanese family has been drastically transformed from the traditional *ie* and many have become incapable of supporting the *ie*-bound mortuary tradition. Besides, the existing death policies do not adequately address this issue. Yet, under these circumstances, the Japanese people's preoccupation with death and afterlife remains as strong as ever, and they spend much time and money on funerals, memorial services, and graves (Suzuki 2000; Tsuji, forthcoming a and b). How do they negotiate the widening gap between the 'ought' and the 'is' of death?

One common strategy is to adopt unconventional burial practices. For instance, *eitai kuyōbo* or eternally worshipped graves depart from tradition in that their maintenance and worship of the dead are not carried out by the family but are paid for by their buyers. The builders of the graves – temples and other religious or non-religious organisations – assume these responsibilities. Thus, eternally worshipped graves make posthumous care possible without patrilineal descendants.

In some *eitai kuyōbo*, individuals are buried alone while in others bones are consolidated in one grave, not with family ancestors, but with non-relatives. Though having no descendants prompted many to buy these graves,[16] there are people who purchase them even though they have both a grave and descendants. For instance, a married woman might acquire her own grave to avoid being buried with her mother-in-law with whom she did not get along. Those who have discord with their husband attain posthumous 'divorce' by buying *eitai kuyōbo*. *Eitai kuyōbo* also enables posthumous 'marriage' for homosexual couples and heterosexual couples who, for various reasons, could not marry legally.

The increasing popularity of *eitai kuyōbo*, regardless of the existence of descendants, indicates that graves are being transformed from the *ie* symbol to an individual's eternal resting place. *Jumokusō*, burying bones in the woods and substituting a flowering shrub for a tombstone, also follows this trend (*AS* 24 May 2000).

Such a shift from collectivity to individuality is more pronounced in case of *shizensō*, scattering bones in the sea or mountains. It requires neither a grave nor ancestor worship, effectively solving the problems of obtaining graves and their caretakers. However, the most significant aim of *shizensō* is to obtain individuals' control over their own deaths, and it is clearly reflected in the name of the organisation that initiated *shizensō:*

Sōsō no Jiyū o Susumeru Kai (Association for Promoting Freedom in Mortuary Rituals). 'My' death belongs to me, not to the *ie* nor to my descendants who may or may not feel the *ie*-bound obligation to take care of it. In other words, *shizensō* reshapes the *ie*-individual relationship as well as the intergenerational relationship in the family.

How do these new mortuary rites suit death policies? As mentioned earlier, Article 4 of Laws Concerning Graves and Burials (1948) prohibits the burial of human corpses or bones at any other place but an area approved as a cemetery. The only exception is the placement of bones in a charnel house that is approved by the governor of the prefecture where it is located (Inoue 1990: 137). *Eitai kuyōbo*, eternally worshipped graves built at the cemetery, have no problems with this provision. Despite its novelty, *jumokusō* also complies because bones are buried in woods that are registered as a cemetery.

On the other hand, *shizensō* had long been regarded as violating both the Criminal Code and Laws Concerning Graves and Burials. According to Article 190 of the former, it is a punishable act to destroy, abandon, or steal human remains and bones. Scattering bones in the sea or mountains may fall under the ban on abandoning them. It also conflicts with Article 4 of the latter that restricts the burial of human bones to a cemetery (Yasuda 1991: 215).

Thus, it was due to legal concerns that Nakano Yoshio, an authority on English Literature, gave up having his bones scattered. When he died in 1985, his bones were buried in his family grave. The view of *shizensō* as illegal became widespread in 1987 when Ishihara Yūjirō, a very popular actor/musician, died. Because he had loved the ocean off Shōnan Coast, his brother, a well-known writer/politician, planned to scatter Yūjirō's bones there but cancelled the plan after receiving legal advice against it (Yasuda 1991: 144). A government statement in 1988 reinforced such a prevailing belief in the unlawfulness of *shizensō*. In its report, the Tokyo Prefectural Committee to Investigate Cemetery Problems pronounced that scattering bones violated existing laws and could not be performed at present (Yasuda 1991: 144).

Such legal barriers did not deter the advocates of *shizensō* who were deeply concerned about various problems of death in contemporary Japan, in particular, serious environmental disruption caused by the construction of many cemeteries. To help ease the problems and regain individuals' control over their own deaths, *shizensō* promoters re-examined relevant laws as well as the actual burial practice and cast doubts on the widely accepted interpretation of government policies.

They questioned, for example, whether Article 4 of Laws Concerning Burials and Graves was applicable to the *scattering* of bones because it only mentions the *burial* of human remains and bones (Yasuda 1991:

85–6). They also directed attention to the fact that some people keep bones at home rather than entombing them in the cemetery but no legal action has ever been taken against this violation of the law.

To deal with Article 190 of the Criminal Code, *shizensō* advocates pointed out legal contradictions as well as discrepancies between the law and its application regarding cremated bones. Though the Article is clear on the criminality of destroying and abandoning *ikotsu* or human bones, some cremated human bones are normally disposed of as industrial waste because customarily the deceased's relatives pick up only a part of them for interment.[17] Strange as it may seem, this is a perfectly legitimate practice because *zanpai*, leftover bones and ashes in the crematorium, are legally defined as industrial waste (Yasuda 1991: 87–8).[18]

A judicial precedent from the Meiji period also supported *shizensō* advocates' argument over Article 190 of the Criminal Code.[19] In 1910 (Meiji 43), two years after the Law went into effect, the Supreme Court acquitted a defendant who paid to obtain *zanpai*. The premise behind the verdict was that *zanpai* was not a part of *ikotsu* but something more appropriately viewed as dust. The court also made reference to the existing custom of using *zanpai* as fertiliser and proclaimed that the local tradition and the bereaved family's wish determined what constituted *ikotsu* (Yasuda 1991: 141–3).

With the help of mass media and strong support from the populace, a movement to legitimise *shizensō* culminated in February 1991 in the formation of the Association for Promoting Freedom in Mortuary Rituals (Sōsō no Jiyū o Susumeru Kai) (Yasuda 1991: 160). In October of the same year, the Association held its first *shizensō* for a young woman who had died three decades earlier. This unconventional funeral received massive, generally positive responses (Inoue 1993: 209).

The government's reactions also favoured their cause. Unable to ignore the tide of change, two ministries announced their reinterpretations of relevant laws. The Ministry of Justice made public its view that scattering bones does not violate the Criminal Code as long as it is carried out as a funeral rite at a reasonable place and using reasonable means. The Ministry of Health and Welfare declared that Article 4 of Laws Concerning Burials and Graves is applicable only to the burial of human remains and bones and does not restrict the scattering of bones (Inoue 1993: 210; Yasuda 1991: 85–89).

Legitimised this way, *shizensō* is gaining in popularity. Since its inception in 1991, the Association for Promoting Freedom in Mortuary Rituals has conducted 366 *shizensō* ceremonies: 272 in the sea (scattering bones of 533 people), 80 in the mountains, ten in the sky, one in a river, and three in the garden of the deceased's home. Its membership expanded rapidly from the initial 200 to over 8,000, with 13 branch units throughout the nation. Among other things, the low cost of *shizensō* contributes to its growing popularity. Both the prices of individual *shizensō* (¥150,000–¥250,000) and of collective *shizensō* (¥10,000) are mere fractions of the going rate of several million yen for a conventional funeral (*AS* 17 Feb. 2000).

The government's concession to the changing social milieu is also apparent in the 1999 revision of Laws Concerning Burials and Graves in the treatment of *muenbo*, graves without caretakers (*AS* 24 May 2000). As families without 'proper' descendants increased, more and more graves became *muenbo*, causing various problems. Cemetery operators suffered financial loss, as they could not collect maintenance fees for them.[20] But making the place available for a new user took both time and money, because prior to the 1999 revision disposal of *muenbo* was subject to tight governmental regulations. Consequently, many neglected *muenbo* occupied precious cemetery space and became an eyesore. *Muenbo* also created problems for people who sought their graves. It contributed to the shortage and high cost of graves. It prevented some people from obtaining graves because, to avoid the problem of *muenbo*, some cemeteries did not sell graves to those without 'proper' descendants. By loosening regulations concerning the disposal of *muenbo*, the government has tried to ease these multiple problems.

New forms of burial practice and legal changes and reinterpretations enable people to continue mortuary rituals in a situation where both death-related policies and tradition have become inadequate. The rapid expansion of the funeral industry, though criticised for its commodification of death, also offers professional assistance in the observation of traditional intricacies and the creation of new mortuary customs. As is most evident in *eitai kuyōbo* and *shizensō*, current Japanese mortuary rites differ from those of yesteryear in two major areas. First, death is becoming less of the family's duty and more of the individual's concern. Second, the meaning of the grave is changing from an *ie* symbol to the individual's eternal resting place.

This shift from collectivity to individuality[21] may correspond to the Western discourse that associates the subjugation to the former with old times and the assertion of the latter with modernity (Shorter 1975: 18 and 259). The actual picture, however, is more complex, for increasing individuals' rights, freedom, and choices coexists with the continuing emphasis on collectivity. For example, people often attend funerals, not because of their personal ties to the deceased, but because of *giri* or obligations deriving from their membership of groups, most importantly in the family, the community, and the work place.[22] While neighbours' assistance has diminished today, work-related people and organisations play an increasingly significant role in dealing with death. Many Japanese companies build collective graves for their deceased employees and worship the spirits of corporate 'ancestors' and corporate 'warriors' (Nakamaki 1992: 35–46). This role of the company parallels the *ie*'s role in ancestor worship and the state's role in worshipping '"glorious" military dead' (Nelson 1998: 14) at the Yasukuni shrine.

Collectivity is not always imposed upon individuals but sometimes sought after voluntarily. At some *eitai kuyōbo*, people who will be entombed together meet regularly, creating a new community to compensate for the lack of kin or locality-based support.

Individuality is not necessarily in opposition to collectivity, either. As discussed earlier, *shizensō* rejects the collectivity represented in grave and ancestor worship. But the very idea of *shizensō* was born out of its initiators' desire to enhance collective interests. Alarmed by an impending development plan in a remote wooded area near Tokyo's source of water supply, they proposed an alternative project to turn the area into a natural park for *shizensō*. This plan would save forests from destruction, secure a safe water supply for the metropolis, provide urban dwellers with a place for recreation as well as for postmortem 'residence,' and revitalise the foundering local economy (Yasuda 1991).

Individuality might be expressed while conforming to the collective demands. One of my informants vividly remembered his grandfather's funeral in the 1960s. The family held a traditional funeral proper to his status as a patriarch. However, unlike the normally solemn Japanese funeral, this one was unusually merry. A tyrannical man, the deceased was disliked, and everyone found his death warranted celebration. Such sentiment was also reflected in the way the family treated his spirit in the subsequent years. Following tradition, they dutifully held his memorial services,[23] but he was not remembered in their daily worship.

Just as collectivity and individuality coexist, so do tradition and innovation. First, some new customs reflect long-standing traditions. For instance, *shizensō* echoes *sutebaka*, the burial grave for *ryōbo-sei* (the double graves of burial and memorial for the same individual) in the past (Jan Van Bremen: personal communication). In both cases, bones or corpse are forsaken though they normally have a significant meaning in Japanese mortuary rituals (Yamaori 1990). Similarly, the two options of *eitai kuyōbo* – individual graves and collective graves – are not entirely a modern invention, either. Individual graves had existed before graves for married couples that preceded the *ie* graves (Mori 1993: 113). Past customs also include burying together those who belong to the same lineage, temple, or village. What is new today is the consolidation in one grave of the unrelated dead who voluntarily chose such a grave as their eternal resting place.

Second, adopting a new custom does not necessarily mean abandoning an old one. In some cases of *shizensō*, the bereaved family held a conventional funeral afterwards and observed subsequent memorial services according to the tradition. At *shizensō* for some individuals, only a portion of bones are scattered in the sea or mountains and the rest are entombed (Yamaori Tetsuo: personal communication).

Even though the Japanese today may have gained more freedom, rights, and choices in dealing with death than their forebears in the Meiji period, they are not totally free from the hegemony of the state. Controversies surrounding the Yasukuni shrine (Hardacre 1989; Nelson 1998) demonstrate that the war dead belong to the state, not to the family, nor to the individual.[24] Recent legislation on brain death also limits individuals' control over their own deaths, requiring the family's consent for organ donation. In the face of the increasing assertion of individuality, the view of the family – rather than the individual – as a basic social unit lingers on in contemporary Japan.

Conclusion

Policies may symbolise the hegemony of the state, and their strong imposition on its subjects may be compared to internal colonialism (Goodman introduction to this volume, page 6). The first section of this chapter endorses this statement, illustrating how the Meiji regime used death policies to exercise tight control over the family and the individual.

Yet, as the third section of this chapter demonstrates, mortuary practice is not a product of government policies alone, but of a complex interplay among policies, people, traditions, and other situational factors (e.g., economy and natural environment). In other words, the implementation of policies comprises a dynamic process rather than a linear flow of orders from the top to the bottom, validating Goodman's statement, '… even the most essentialised of symbols are not immune from challenge and change' (Goodman introduction to this volume, page 9).

One contributing factor to this complexity is that policies always contain some contradictions. The *ie* system provides a good example. Despite being at the core of Meiji theocracy and essential to building a modern nation, the *ie* was negatively affected by some modernisation policies. For instance, compulsory education drained from the *ie* the cost of education and children's labour while conscription stole adult labour (Kano 1983: 27). Capitalism led to *iegoroshi* or 'domicide' (Irokawa 1985: 287), for it not only hired the *ie* members away from home, but also created poverty-stricken masses and 'forced them to flee to the cities, breaking up their families in order to survive' (Irokawa 1985: 289). Mobility, a major cause of 'domicide,' was accelerated by the state-granted authority of the *ie* head, including his right to dispose of the *ie* property (Muta 1996: 17).

Another contradiction concerns *ihai* or memorial tablets. Though they are an important part of the *ie*-based ancestor worship (Smith 1974: 84–5), the state's death policies ignored them, leaving the practice entirely in the hands of temples and households (Robert J. Smith: personal communication). Earlier, I have noted two cases of *ihai* practice that deviated from the *ie*-based ideology of death (see page 185). The contradiction with the *ie* principle is also manifested in that, unlike graves, memorial tablets are normally for the individual dead and are not silent about the deceased they represent (Robert J. Smith: personal communication). Not only does each *ihai* carry the deceased's posthumous name and the age at death, but it also shows his/her status by the ranking of the posthumous name and the type of the tablet that the bereaved family are willing to spend money on (Smith 1974: 82–4).

Beside their contradictory nature, the viability of policies is also reduced by the gap between the situation under which policies are 'produced' and the situation in which they are 'consumed' (Goodman introduction to this volume, pages 11–12). Thus, even under the totalitarian Meiji regime, there were cases where people did not comply with state's death policies. Rapid social change further widens this gap, undermining policies' efficacy. Contemporary Japan illuminates this point.

These two aspects of policies – contradictions within them and the breach between their 'production' and 'consumption' – generate ambiguity and leeway for individual negotiation, making it difficult to thoroughly enforce the law. At the same time, they also allow some flexibility in applying the law to specific situations or even trigger policy change. The complexity of policy implementation is further compounded by mortuary traditions that mediate people's 'consumption' of policies and, reflecting many regional variations, create non-uniform responses to them.

The state is often viewed not only as the embodiment of hegemonic power, but also '... as a more or less autonomous actor, separate from society and individuals upon which it operates' (McVeigh 1998: 134). In my opinion, however, the state and its citizens maintain a symbiotic relationship. The former cannot exist without the latter. The latter's lives are so much '... state-related that it is hard to imagine any form of modern consciousness that is not somehow contoured by state interests' (ibid.: 135). But, this symbiosis is not always in peace nor in equilibrium. The relationship is dynamic, as much characterised by hierarchy, imposition, resistance, and compromise as by order and conformity. Death in Japan since early Meiji is the product of such symbiotic relationships in which both policies and individual actors play a significant role, together with long-standing traditions.

NOTES

1 I would like to express my deep appreciation to the following people: Roger Goodman, whose interest in social policy gave me the first inspiration to study death policies in Japan; Robert J. Smith, Jan van Bremen, and the late A. Thomas Kirsch, whose comments deepened my understanding of Japan as well as of anthropology.
2 Among them were Kumazawa Banzan, Ōtsuki Risai, Nakamura Ranrin, and Kani Yōsai. It is also well known that Nonaka Kenzan in Kōchi and Hoshina Masayuki in Aizu were opposed to cremation and encouraged burial even among commoners (Mori 1993: 146–7).
3 On their shrewdness, Sansom says, 'It would be difficult to find in the Far East a more pragmatic, and utilitarian group than the ruling elite of [the early Meiji] in Japan' (1950: 466).
4 The threat of such diseases was frequent then. For instance, cholera epidemics occurred occasionally throughout the nineteenth century, including 1877 (Meiji 10) and 1879 (Meiji 12) (Mori 1993: 149).
5 Citing Tokyo's annual death rate of 30,000 per 1,000,000 residents at that time, one crematorium operator warned that if everyone was buried in his own grave, in several decades graves would be ubiquitous (Hashizume 1990: 44–5). Some measures were taken to deal with this problem. For instance, in the year after outlawing cremation, the Administrative Council (*Dajōkan*) announced nine new locations for cemeteries (Mori 1993: 141).
6 One of the important motivations behind 'modernising' the nation was to revise unfair treaties with Western countries by establishing an equal standing with them.
7 Considering the grave as an eternal place for burial and worship, the Meiji regime regarded exhumation as an extremely inhumane act, more cruel than the cremation it detested (Mori 1993: 157).
8 Though the Meiji Constitution of 1889 accorded freedom of religion as long as religion did not interfere with people's duties to the state (Hardacre 1989: 39), it aimed at restoring 'the ancient Japanese model of "unity of religion and government" (*saisei-itchi*)' (Kitagawa 1966: 201) with the emperor as a living god. By contrast, Article 20 of the new Constitution proclaimed the separation of church and state, prohibiting religious organisations from receiving any privileges from the state or exercising any political authority, and the state and its organs from engaging in religious education or any other religious activity (Grover 1964: 153).
9 The current Criminal Code was promulgated in 1907 (Meiji 40), enforced in the following year, and partially revised in 1947 to meet the spirit of the new constitution.

10 According to the 1995 census, nuclear families account for 34.2% of the total households in Japan, families consisting of a couple alone 17.4%, and single-person households 25.6% (*AS* 27 June 1997).

11 The average number of children a Japanese woman reproduces has gone down to 1.39 (*AS* 27 August 1998). Such a low birthrate is caused not only by *shōshika* or a decrease in the number of children couples have, but also by an increase in three other phenomena: *bankon* or later marriage; *hikon* or no marriage; and childless marriage either by choice or due to infertility.

12 The 1998 record shows an all-time high of over 240,000 divorces. It also shows the steady increase of *jukunen rikon*, divorce among couples married more than 20 years (*AS* 1 January 1999).

13 In 1871 (Meiji 4), the new regime promulgated *Koseki-hō*, the Household Register Law.

14 Having the burial grave and memorial grave side by side was not very common. Normally, the former was located away from the place of residence. Hence, one predominant explanation for *ryōbo-sei* is to avoid the pollution of death, though various other theories have also been proposed. (See, for instance, Mori 1993: 90–5 and Part II of Mogami 1979.)

15 One of the 40 tombstones was built in Kyōho 17 (1732).

16 At one such cemetery, 94.5% reported they purchased graves due to the absence of descendants. Buyers included many childless couples, but couples having only daughters accounted for 19.5%. A patrilineal bias is also seen in that while single or divorced women constituted 17.5% of buyers, there was no purchase by bachelors or male divorcees (*AS* 17 September 1996).

17 The bone-picking ceremony is held at the crematorium – usually right after the cremation and the day after until the recent past – and attended by the deceased's next of kin. There is a regional difference in the quantity of bones taken for entombment. Hence, the urn used in the Kantō area (the area around Tokyo) is four or five times as big as that used in the Kansai area (the area around Osaka, Kyoto, and Kobe). But even in the former case, not all the bones and ashes are taken for burial.

18 It is most likely that not all the leftover bones and ashes were thrown away as industrial waste. When I was at the bone-picking ceremony for my grand-father in the 1960s, a crematorium attendant told me that before antibiotics became readily available, *zanpai* were in demand as a remedy for tuberculosis.

19 See note 9.

20 Even as early as in 1984, 7,068 cemetery plots (3% of the total) at Tokyo's eight municipal cemeteries were not paid for. A specialist predicted that in ten years ten percent would become *muenbo* and in three generations (100 years) two thirds of them would follow the same fate (Mori 1993: 236).

21 Tombstones of unusual design also assert the deceased's individuality. For instance, a tailor's tombstone is shaped like a man's suit and a skier's grave represents a mountain slope. More common is a tombstone made of a natural stone with an engraved Chinese character of one's choice (e.g., peace, love, serenity). Cemetery operators, who rejected these unusual tombstones until recently, are accepting them now.

22 *Giri* often obliges the Japanese to attend the funeral of someone whom they have never met, the wife or the parent of their colleague or business associate, for example.

23 The 49th-day and 100th-day memorial services during the first year of bereavement are followed by a series of additional services: the first, third, seventh, 13th, 17th, 23rd, 27th, 33rd, and 50th-year memorial services. Except for the first year, the year is counted including the one in which the deceased died. Thus, for example, the third-year service is actually held two years after death.

24 In June 2001, 252 Koreans – those who had fought in the Japanese military during World War II and the descendants of those who had been killed – filed a lawsuit against the Japanese government to demand reparations and to annul the enshrinement of their deceased kin in the Yasukuni Shrine. Since Korea and Taiwan had been Japanese colonies until 1945 and many residents were drafted to military service, the '"glorious" military dead' (Nelson 1998: 14) at the Yasukuni Shrine include the spirits of nearly 50,000 war dead from these two nations. According to one of the plaintiffs, her father was enshrined in the Yasukuni Shrine in 1959, though the family was not even informed of his war death in China until 1973 and of his Yasukuni enshrinement until the mid-1990s. To her request for annulment, the Shrine officials replied, 'We can't change the status of those who have already become gods' (*AS* 30 June 2001).

REFERENCES

Newspaper cited in the text:
AS: *Asahi Shinbun* (Asahi Newspaper)
——. 1996 (17 September). *'Jibun no haka motome'* (Searching for one's own graves).
——. 1997 (27 June). *'Shasetsu: kazokuzō ni otehon wa nai'* (Editorial: there is no model Japanese family).
——. 1998 (27 August). *'Kekkon ni yume motenai josei-tachi: aratana "oya"-zō no sōshutsu ga kagi'* (No dream in marriage for women: the creation for a new parental model essential).
——. 1999 (1 January). *'Sakunen no rikon kako saikō'* (The divorce rate highest last year).
——. 2000 (17 February). *'Sōsō no jiyū o susumeru kai jūnenme'* (The tenth anniversary of the association for promoting freedom in mortuary rituals).
——. 2000 (24 May). *'Tayō ni "shigo no ie"'* (The diversification of 'the post-mortem residence').
——. 2001 (30 June). *'Yasukuni gōshi yamete'* (Please annul the enshrinement at the Yasukuni shrine).

Anderson, Ronald S. 1975. *Education in Japan: A Century of Modern Development*. Washington, D.C.: United States Department of Health, Education & Welfare.
Aoki, Toshiya. 1993. *'Kasō kinshirei to sōbo shūzoku: kasō kara dosō e* (The ban on cremation and mortuary customs: from cremation to the burial of the corpse),' pp.1–21 in *Minzoku Shūkyō 4: Haka to Yama to Seichi* (Folk Religion Volume 4: Graves, Mountains, and Sacred Places), eds. Noboru Miyata et al. Tokyo: Tōkyōdō Shuppan.
Grover, V. 1964. *The Constitution of Japan*. Delhi, India: Atma Ram & Sons.

Haga, Noboru. 1996. *Sōgi no Rekishi* (History of Funerals). Tokyo: Yūzankaku.

Hardacre, Helen. 1989. *Shinto and the State, 1868–1988*. Princeton: Princeton University Press.

——.1997. *Marketing the Menacing Fetus in Japan*. Berkeley: University of California Press.

Hashizume, Shinya. 1990. '*Shishatachi no yūtopia* (A utopia for the dead),' pp. 35–59 in *Meiji no Meikyū Toshi* (Labyrinthine City in the Meiji Period). Tokyo: Heibonsha.

Inoue, Haruyo. 1990. *Gendai Ohaka Jijō:Yureru Kazoku no Nakade* (The Circumstances Surrounding Graves Today: In the Midst of Changing Families). Tokyo: Sanseidō.

——. 1993. *Ima Sōgi Ohaka ga Kawaru* (Funerals and Graves in Transition). Tokyo: Sanseidō.

Irokawa, Daikichi, trans. and ed. Marius B. Jansen. 1985. *The Culture of the Meiji Period*. Princeton: Princeton University Press.

Ishikawa, Toshio. 1988. '*Kazoku kōzō no henkaku to minpōjō no saishi jōkō* (Changes in the structure of the family and articles on ceremonials in the Civil Code),' pp. 113–41 in *Shōja to Shisha: Sosen Saishi* (The Living and the Dead: Ancestral Ceremonies), eds. Toshio Ishikawa, Masao Fujii and Kiyomi Morioka. Tokyo: Sanseidō.

Itō, Mikiharu. 1982. *Kazoku Kokkakan no Jinruigaku* (The Anthropology of the Family State). Kyoto: Mineruba Shobō.

Kano, Masanao. 1983. *Senzen 'Ie' no Shisō* (Ideology of the *Ie* Before the War). Tokyo: Sōbunsha.

Kitagawa, Joseph. M. 1966. *Religion in Japanese History*. New York: Columbia University Press.

Koshizawa, Akira. 1991. *Tōkyō no Toshikeikaku* (City Planning of Tokyo). Tokyo: Iwanami Shoten.

LaFleur, William R. 1992. *Liquid Life: Abortion and Buddhism in Japan*. Princeton: Princeton University Press.

McVeigh, Brian. 1998. 'Linking state and self: how the Japanese state bureaucratizes subjectivity through moral education.' *Anthropological Quarterly*, 71(3): 125–37.

Ministry of Justice. 1972. *The Civil Code of Japan* (English translation). Tokyo.

Mogami, Takayoshi, ed. 1979. *Sōsō Bosei Kenkyū Shūsei 4: Haka no Shūzoku* (Collected Works on Funerals and Graves No. 4: The Custom of Graves). Tokyo: Meicho Shuppan.

Mori, Kenji. 1993. *Haka to Sōsō no Shakaishi* (Social History of Graves and Funerals). Tokyo: Kōdansha.

Muta, Kazue. 1996. *Senryaku to Shiteno Kazoku: Kindai Nihon no Kokumin Kokka Keisei to Josei* (The Family as a Strategy: Women and the Establishment of Nationalist State in Modern Japan). Tokyo: Tankōsha.

Nakamaki, Hirochika. 1992. *Mukashi Daimyō, Ima Kaisha: Kigyō to Shūkyō* (Daimyos in the Past, Companies Today: Corporations and Religion). Kyoto: Tankōsha.

Nelson, John K. 1998. 'Shifting paradigms of religion and the state: implications of the 1997 Supreme Court decision for social, religious, and political change.' Paper presented at the Association for Asian Studies Meetings, Washington, DC.

Oguchi, Iichi and Hiroo Takagi. 1956. 'Religion and social development,' pp. 313–57 in *Japanese Religion in the Meiji Era*, ed. Hideo Kishimoto and trans. John F. Howes. Tokyo: Ōbunsha.

Plath, David W. 1964. 'Where the family of God is the family: the role of the dead in Japanese households.' *American Anthropologist*, 66(2): 300–317.

Sansom, G. B. 1950. *The Western World And Japan: A Study in the Interaction of European and Asiatic Cultures*. New York: Alfred A. Knopf.

Sebald, W. J., trans. 1934. *The Civil Code of Japan*. Kobe, Japan: J. L. Thompson Co.

Shorter, Edward. 1975. *The Making of the Modern Family*. New York: Basic Books.

Smith, Robert J. 1974. *Ancestor Worship in Contemporary Japan*. Stanford: Stanford University Press.

Smith, Robert J. and Ella Lury Wiswell. 1982. *The Women of Suye Mura*. Chicago: University of Chicago Press.

Suzuki, Hikaru. 2000. *The Price of Death: The Funeral Industry in Contemporary Japan*. Stanford: Stanford University Press.

Takeuchi, Yasuhiro. 1993. '*Saishi shōkei ni okeru haka to hōritsu mondai* (The succession to graves and legal problems),' pp. 107–128 in *Kazoku to Haka* (Families and Graves), eds. Masao Fujii, Akio Yoshie, and Kōmoto Mitsugi. Tokyo: Waseda Daigaku Shuppanbu.

Tsuji, Yohko. Forthcoming a. 'Japanese funerals and *kōden* or incense money exchange: social and personal dimensions,' in *Death in Japan*, eds. John Breen and Brian Bocking. London: Routledge.

——. Forthcoming b. '*Raise* as a mirror of *gense*: from legally sanctioned ancestor worship to modern mortuary rituals in Japan,' in *Practicing the Afterlife: Perspectives from Japan*, eds. Susanne Formanek and William LaFleur. Vienna: Austrian Academy of Sciences.

Yamaori, Tetsuo. 1990. '*Shi to minzoku: ikotsu sūhai no genryū* (Death and folkways: the origin of worshipping human bones),' pp. 15–98 in *Shi no Minzokugaku* (The Folklore of Death). Tokyo: Iwanami Shoten.

Yasuda, Mutsuhiko. 1991. *Haka Nanka Iranai: Ai Arebakoso Shizensō* (Who Needs a Grave: *Shizensō* For Love). Tokyo: Yūhisha.

9 Embodiment, citizenship and social policy in contemporary Japan

Vera Mackie

Citizenship and national belonging

The Japanese citizen, the male citizen, the heterosexual citizen, the white-collar citizen, the fertile citizen, the able-bodied citizen: perhaps these phrases seem tautological, too obvious even to mention.[1] What if we were to look at the obverse of these obvious and tautological phrases? What of the alien citizen, the female citizen, the homosexual citizen, the lesbian citizen, the trans-sexual citizen, the prostitute citizen, the infertile citizen, the disabled citizen? Are these phrases also tautological, or rather oxymoronic and contradictory? To what extent are these diverse kinds of citizens thinkable in modern Japan? What can we learn about citizenship in modern Japan by attempting to think through the gaps between the obviousness of the first group of phrases and the strangeness of the second group? The difference between the pairs of phrases above rests on the concept of embodiment. In this chapter, I will focus on how our understanding of citizenship might be transformed if we were to focus on citizens as embodied individuals.[2]

Citizenship may be discussed in the context of the legal and institutional structures which determine who has the right to participate in the political systems of voting and elected governments and the duties which are linked with these rights: the liability for taxation, or in some countries the requirement that men perform military service. From this point of view, Japan apparently has one of the most liberal constitutions in the post-war world,[3] guaranteeing rights to work, choice of domicile, choice of religion, freedom of assembly and association, and freedom from discrimination on the grounds of sex, race, status, religion or family origin to those who belong to the category of Japanese citizen (Article 14, Constitution of Japan, in Tanaka and Smith 1976). These legal structures do not, however, exhaust the discourse on citizenship. More recent ways of looking at citizenship have considered less tangible aspects of political participation: the familial structures which mediate relationships between individual and state; the ideologies which relegate women to a putative domestic sphere; the sexual division of labour in the home which determines the different ways in which women and men participate in waged labour; the privileging of the heterosexual nuclear family in work practices and social policy; and what I will refer to below as the 'sexual subtext' of citizenship. Another aspect of citizenship in this broader sense involves the possibility of participating in public discourse on political issues. Ghassan Hage (1998) has made the useful distinction between 'national belonging' (those who are part of the national community), and 'governmental belonging' (those who are seen to have a 'natural' role in the management of the nation). Like Hage, I will argue that citizenship is not a simple matter of a binary distinction between citizens and non-citizens, but rather a constellation of features which determine one's position on a spectrum of citizenship.

One of the most sociologically unhelpful aspects of the usage of the formal conception of citizenship to refer to national belonging is that the either (a national)/or (not) logic it embodies, and which is uncritically taken on board by so many analysts, does not allow us to capture all the subtleties of the *differential modalities of national belonging* as they are experienced within society [emphasis in original]. (Hage 1998: 51)[4]

Elizabeth Grosz and other feminist commentators have argued that women and other subordinate groups 'embody' all of those elements which are marginalised from masculine models of citizenship, that women 'take on the function of being *the* body for men while men are left free to soar to the heights of theoretical reflection and cultural production'. Grosz (1994: 22) argues that 'blacks, slaves, immigrants, indigenous peoples ... function as the working body for white "citizens", leaving them free to create values, morality, knowledges.' Although Grosz was referring to those who are marginalised from the ideal model of citizenship in Eurocentric societies, we could argue that Japanese males inhabit a similar structural position with respect to various marginalised 'others' in contemporary Japan. Such processes of marginalisation are common to many industrialised liberal democracies, although the specific details and dimensions of marginalisation vary from country to country.

The undocumented immigrant woman worker from Southeast Asia, in a marginalised and sexualised occupation in Japan, may be seen as the antithesis of the archetypal male besuited citizen: female rather than male, non-Japanese rather than Japanese, engaged in physical labour rather than mental labour, engaging in sexualised labour rather than non-sexualised labour. One way to consider citizenship is through a focus on the archetypical male citizens. Another way to consider citizenship is through a focus on the marginalised others – their marginality highlighting the limits of discourses of citizenship, and the exclusions built into the model of the citizen as a male, heterosexual, white-collar worker.

This male, heterosexual white-collar worker is also the figure who is interpellated as the desiring customer of the sexualised entertainment industry (Allison 1994; Allison 1996; Mackie 1998). This sphere may seem to be a long way from discourses of citizenship, but it could be argued that aspects of contemporary Japanese social policy work to ensure the access of the male citizen to the objects of sexual attachment. By considering his relationship with various marginalised and sexualised others in contemporary Japan, we can also see the sexual subtext of his claims to citizenship. The features derived from this analysis (such as: Japanese/non-Japanese; male/female; heterosexual/non-heterosexual; fertile/infertile; white-collar worker/non-white-collar worker; 'chaste' labour/sexual labour) may be deployed to consider the positioning of other figures at different points on the discursive spectrum of citizenship.

In recent discussions of citizenship and social policy, it has been argued that the workings of social policy can only be fully understood if we recognise that apparently impartial policies may impact differently on those in different social locations, and may impact differently according to the embodied differences that are given social meaning. Moira Gatens (1998: 5–6) has commented:

Gender norms construct specific forms of human embodiment as socially meaningful. Hence, it is possible to 'impartially' apply norms which nevertheless impact differentially on embodied men and women (for example, laws prohibiting *any person* to procure an abortion; the normative expectation that child care is a private, rather than a corporate matter; the laws of provocation and self-defence). When social inequality is associated with *embodied* differences – for example, sexual and racial differences – norms may be 'universally' applied without such 'universality' affecting all classes, or types of person. These particular cases of norms of partiality are precisely of the kind ... that offer the 'ideal means of domination and coercion' [emphasis in original].

In this chapter, I will discuss some of the ways in which social policy in Japan impacts differently on embodied men and women, including those whose differences are coded in ethnicised or racialised terms. Much of this discussion will focus on attempting to uncover the cultural meanings implicit in particular social policies and their implementation. Any attempts at social change will need to come to terms with these conventionalised social meanings, which must be transformed along with the policies under question. Elsewhere, I have argued that political campaigns often need to be accompanied by a form of 'discursive social change' that pays attention to meaning and discourse (Mackie

2000a). In a similar vein, Linder and Peters (1995: 145) have pointed out that:

institutions can become synonymous with cultural meanings and practices and thus beyond the reach of designers intent on reengineering an institution's organizational features. In these instances, the focus for design shifts to the broader canvas of cultural change as the medium of institutional reformation.

To provide my conclusion first, I will be arguing that the archetypal citizen in the modern Japanese political system is a male, heterosexual, able-bodied, fertile, white-collar worker (other features will be added as necessary). In order to justify these features, however, I need to show the ways in which supposedly neutral aspects of social policy impact differently on people who do not share all of these features. Other features, such as 'cultural competence,' 'linguistic competence,' 'mental competence,' 'being law-abiding,' would also be necessary for a full description, but this chapter will focus on features which include an element of embodiment. To avoid misunderstanding, I should also comment that these features are not intended to be used in a banal search for the 'most oppressed.' Rather, I am attempting to demonstrate the complexity of discourses of citizenship. I also wish to move away from the discussion of 'majorities' and 'minorities.' Typicality and marginality are matters of discursive construction rather than numbers.

Japanese blood

The feature [+Japanese blood] is perhaps the most obvious.[5] It may first of all be derived from the Nationality Law (Kokuseki Hō), which operates according to the principle of bloodline (*jus sanguinis*), unlike some systems that operate according to the principle of place of birth (*jus soli*).[6] This is further reinforced by those legal provisions that regulate who may enter Japan in order to work. There are various groups of immigrants in contemporary Japan, whose degree of 'national belonging' varies according to the number of features they share with the archetypal citizen. In 1990, the Immigration Control Act was modified to allow third generation descendants of Japanese emigrants to enter Japan for up to three years, in a long-term resident category with no restriction on engaging in employment. This policy also demonstrates the primacy of the feature [+Japanese blood] in deciding who may participate in the community to the extent of engaging in paid labour. Although the Japanese heritage of such immigrants was probably expected to cut down on problems generated by perceptions of difference, local communities must now deal with contact between groups with different social and cultural expectations, while schools need to address the necessity of multilingual and

multicultural education for the children of these families. The co-existence
of the descendants of Japanese emigrants reinforces the primacy of the
category of [+Japanese blood], but has the potential to undermine the
naturalised assumption that bloodline equates with cultural competence.
This assumption is a feature of many national cultures, as pointed out by
Barry Hindess (1992: 22):

Notions of descent (and the apparently more respectable surrogate notion of a
distinctive national culture that cannot readily be acquired by persons who are
not born into it) have always played an important part in the way citizenship has
been understood within particular communities.

The institutional dynamics of the interaction between culture, bloodline
and nationality work differently in countries that follow the principle of
jus soli, where nationality depends on the place of birth. In the administration of immigration legislation in the United States, for example, there
is a perceived need to prevent foreign nationals from giving birth to
children on United States soil who could later make claims to United
States citizenship. Most systems, however, including the Japanese, also
have procedures for acquiring nationality, regardless of bloodline. Criticism of the Japanese system of naturalisation (*kika*) has focussed on
expectations of cultural assimilation, such as the expectation of adopting
a Japanised name.

The feature [+Japanese blood] also operates in a dynamic relationship
with gender. Until 1985, the Nationality Law was based on patriarchal
principles. It was assumed in Japan, as in many other countries, that
fathers had the right to determine the nationality and domicile of family
members. Only men had the right to pass on Japanese nationality to their
children, and the provisions for naturalisation of foreign spouses were
different for men and women. This became an issue after several cases of
stateless children (with Japanese mothers and non-Japanese fathers)
appeared. These provisions were modified in the mid-1980s, as the
Nationality Law was overhauled in preparation for Japan's ratification of
the Convention on the Elimination of All Forms of Discrimination Against
Women (CEDAW). Although the most blatantly sexist provisions of the
Nationality Law were modified in 1985, the implementation of this law
may still have gendered implications. Both men and women have the
capacity to pass on nationality to their children, but the child of a
Japanese father and non-Japanese mother may only have the 'right' to
Japanese nationality if the father provides official recognition (*ninchi*) of
the child. This was demonstrated in a court case in the early 1990s that
attempted to determine the nationality of 'Baby André,' allegedly the
child of a Filipino mother and a Japanese father (Taylor 1995: 110–29).

James Valentine (1990: 40–1) has also identified the importance of the feature [+Japanese blood], and points out the particular marginality of those of mixed parentage. This, too, becomes a matter of embodiment where such individuals are not immediately assignable to one category or the other on the basis of physical appearance.[7]

The gendered citizen

There is, of course, no legislation that prevents women from exercising the full rights of citizenship. Indeed, the Constitution, as outlined above, specifically prohibits discrimination on the grounds of sex, and this is reinforced by the Equal Employment Opportunity Law (Danjo Koyō Byōdō Kikai Kintō Hō) of 1985 (effective 1986, amended 1997) and the Basic Law for a Gender-Equal Society (effective 1999). Women have exercised the right to vote and stand for office since the first post-war national election of April 1946, after the amendment of the Electoral Law at the end of 1945. Why, then, would we argue that the male citizen is archetypal?

While women participate in the political system as voters and as the members of various grass-roots pressure groups, they form a numerical minority in the political parties and in parliamentary politics, despite the visibility of several high-profile female parliamentarians. The sexual division of labour in the home, the gendered patterns of labour force participation, and the production of competing constructions of masculinity and femininity in the mass media and alternative media determine the gendered patterns of political participation. In interviews with female Diet members after the 1989 election, it was found that women who have responsibility for children have difficulty in meeting the travel requirements of politicians and cannot expect the kind of support from their spouses that male politicians can expect of their wives (Iwai 1993: 112). Less tangible is the masculinism of parliamentary culture, an issue that received public attention when Tokyo Metropolitan Assembly member Mitsui Mariko resigned in 1993, accusing her Socialist Party colleagues of sexual harassment (Mitsui 1994).

Assumptions about women's place in the private sphere and men's place in the public sphere are reinforced by state institutions, policies, and practices which are implicated in the shaping of gender and class relations. Industry policy is generally seen to be 'gender-blind,' but the lack of policies to redress labour market inequalities relegates women to the most vulnerable positions. Women who are in marginal positions in the labour market are less likely to receive the social prestige which goes with participation in a fulltime, white-collar career position, will have correspondingly restricted networks, and may thus be marginalised in political discussions.

Legislation which deals with labour conditions, such as the Rōdō Kijun Hō (Labour Standards Law, 1947), generally assumes the pattern of fulltime permanent work, and may only be applied with difficulty to the kinds of part-time, casual, and seconded labour often engaged in by women who have responsibility for childcare. Separate legislation has been necessary for part-time and seconded labour (Labour Dispatch Law/Rōdōsha Haken Hō, 1985; Law Concerning the Improvement of Working Conditions for Part-Time Workers, 1993), while domestic labour and sexual labour are relatively unregulated.

Welfare policies and the taxation system are also organised around the assumption that most people will live in heterosexual nuclear families with a male breadwinner and female primary caregiver. Taxation concessions are provided for the wife of a fulltime worker if her earnings stay under a threshold income; and wives may be covered by their husband's national health insurance contributions. These policies have the effect of making the choice of part-time work seem like a rational alternative for married women with children, once again denying them the legitimacy which goes with fulltime permanent employment. Fujita (1987: 590) argues that in the 1970s 'the labour shortage pulled women into the labour market, [while] the inadequacy of welfare programmes tended to pull them away again to take care of children and the aged'. Although the Ikuji Kyūgyō Hō (Childcare Leave Law, effective 1992) theoretically allows for either partner to take up to one year of unpaid leave for the purposes of childcare, it is more likely to be the female partner who takes such leave if she has the lower salary (as is likely). Women also provide the mainstay of care for the disabled, the invalid, and the aged, either in their own families, as volunteers, or sometimes as paid helpers on a casual basis. Women's ability to participate in the spheres of waged work, political discussion, and political activism is thus affected by their being delegated the responsibility of caring for the bodily needs of others. Recent policies which provide insurance for the costs associated with the care of the aged attempt to come to terms with the social requirements of a population where the aged compose an ever-increasing proportion of the population (Kaigo Hoken Hō/Law Concerning Insurance for Nursing Care, 1997, amended 2000).

While the gendered assumptions behind labour policy, welfare and taxation may be more implicit than explicit, other policies are directly concerned with the female body as reproductive body. For example, those provisions of the Labour Standards Law directed at women are popularly known under the generic phrase 'bosei hogo' (protection of motherhood), suggesting that women are primarily viewed as mothers and that the state attitude to women is a protective one. Women are seen as weak and in need of protection, rather than as citizens who actively demand their rights.

Similar language is apparent in the 1948 Eugenic Protection Law (Yūsei Hogo Hō), once again concerned with 'the protection of motherhood' and the production of healthy children, rather than the needs of individual women for control over reproduction.[8] In its original form, the Eugenic Protection Law allowed the state to have ultimate control over the reproductive capacity of citizens' bodies. Surgical abortion is illegal except under certain conditions, including the 'economic reasons' clause added in 1949. Abortions can be carried out only by certified physicians who are members of the 'Maternal Protection Association' (Bosei Hogo Kyōkai). There have been regular attempts to remove the 'economic reasons' clause from the Law, which would have had the effect of making access to abortion more difficult. So far, these attempts have been unsuccessful, perhaps as much due to the interests of the medical profession as to the interests of women. In the 1970s and 1980s, attempts to restrict access to abortion were a major stimulus to women's public activism.

The original Eugenic Protection Law also provided for conditions whereby sterilisation could be implemented: where the person or their spouse has a hereditary psychopathological condition, hereditary bodily disease, hereditary malformation or mental disease, or has leprosy; or if the life of the mother would be endangered by conception or delivery (Article 3).[9] Under amendments that became effective in 1996, Article 3 has been amended so that only those conditions that concern the mother's health are retained as justification for sterilisation. Although the explicit eugenic philosophy of the earlier law has been submerged, the title of the amended law 'The Law for the Protection of the Maternal Body' (Botai Hogo Hō) makes state attitudes to the maternal body more explicit.[10]

Citizenship and physical difference

The workings of the former Eugenic Protection Law, which was devoted to ensuring the production of healthy citizens, suggest that for much of recent history being able-bodied was a necessary condition even for the right to be born as a Japanese citizen, as pointed out by groups advocating the rights of disabled citizens (*Agora* 1983). The modification of the Eugenic Protection Law has been an important step in changing the eugenic assumptions which until recently shaped the regulation of reproductive control. Feminists who have addressed these issues have been careful to avoid some of the confrontations that have been a feature of debates on reproductive control in Anglophone and Christian countries. Commentators on reproductive control have retained the concept of a woman's right to make an ethical choice of when to bear children and when not to, but have also actively forged alliances with groups advocating the right to be born and the right to quality of life of those who are born with differences in mental and physical capacities (Buckley and Mackie 1986; Buckley 1988; *Agora* 1983).

For those who are born with physical disabilities, how does this affect the possibility of their participation in the governance of communities and the nation? In this section, I will demonstrate that [+able bodied] is one of the features of the archetypal citizen, and that differently-able individuals are also likely to suffer from marginalisation from career occupations and the associated social prestige.[11]

Attitudes to the disabled are revealed in several sections of Ototake Hirotada's autobiography, *Gotai Fumanzoku*.[12] The title of Ototake's book is a variation on the phrase, '*gotai manzoku*,' which refers to the ideal or normal body, which has all organs and all limbs. Ototake (2000: 294–5) explains:

We don't mind what kind of child we have, as long as there are no physical problems [*gotai manzoku sae ite kurereba*]'. Parents probably have various expectations while waiting for the birth of a baby, but we often hear words like the above used to refer to their minimum expectations. I, however, was born as a baby who was 'not physically complete' [*gotai fumanzoku*]. Not just incomplete – four of the five requisite body parts were missing. So that might mean that I was a child who failed to meet the expectations of parents. But actually that's not correct. My parents never lamented my birth as a child with a disability, and never indicated that they had any more worries than any other parents do in raising their children. I have enjoyed every day of my life. I have no dissatisfaction with my life: I am surrounded by friends and rush around from place to place in my wheelchair ... I want to proclaim in a loud voice: 'Even though I have a disability, I enjoy every day of my life.' ... This is why I dared to give [my autobiography] the rather shocking title of '*Gotai Fumanzoku*'.

When Ototake was born, his mother was apparently prevented from seeing him for several weeks. Here, he reconstructs their first meeting:

It was the 6th of April 1976. Cherry blossoms were in full bloom, and soft sunlight filtered through. It was a gentle day. 'Wah! Wah!' The quiet was broken by the cry of a newborn baby. It was a baby boy – full of life. An ordinary birth to an ordinary couple. Except for one thing: this baby boy had no arms and no legs ... Usually the first event after birth is the emotional '*boshi gotaimen*' (the first meeting of mother and child)... They let [my mother] learn the whole truth about my disability when she actually saw me. In the hospital, they made some preparations for the first meeting. They prepared a spare bed for my mother just in case. The hospital staff, my father, and my mother became more tense. However, my mother's reaction went against everyone's expectations. When she saw me, she simply said '*kawaii*!' [He's so adorable!] ... Rather than worrying about my physical condition, she was simply delighted at finally being able to embrace her baby. ... My mother's feeling on seeing me for the first time was not a feeling of shock or sadness, but of happiness. I was finally 'born', at the age of one month (Ototake 2000: 6–7).

Ototake's parents displayed an ability to create a life for Ototake whereby he grew up feeling that he was very distinctive, but in no way inferior to others. He was also blessed with a series of teachers and class-mates who simply dealt with his presence, finding ways for him to participate in schoolyard games and classroom activities in his own way. His autobiography illustrates several points about living with disability. He had to adapt to the limitations of the physical environment, because the physical environment had been designed with 'able' individuals in mind. What is most instructive, however, are the ways in which Ototake achieved a sense of belonging in successive school and university com-munities, including a measure of governmental belonging, as a valued member of sporting clubs, a committee member of the school festival, the winner of a speech contest in his early days as a student at Waseda University, and more recently as an advocate for the modification of the physical environment of cities. Such advocacy is part of a change in social attitudes to physical difference, whereby it is the inflexibility of the urban environment that is seen to cause problems for people with different physical needs, rather than their own physical distinctiveness. This shift in attitude has led to the concept of 'universal design,' which can deal with diverse needs, rather than attempting to deal with the 'special' needs of those with different physical needs after the fact.

Further perspectives on citizenship and physical difference are pro-vided by Murata Minoru (1994). Murata was born in 1937, some four decades before Ototake, and suffered from infantile paralysis at the age of 18 months, leaving him without the use of his legs. Nevertheless, he was able to complete compulsory education, eventually passed the bar exam-ination, and currently practices as a lawyer. Murata's book illustrates the difficulties for a citizen who moves through the city in a wheelchair. At times his ability to practice his profession is compromised because of the design of streets, buildings, public transport systems and public facilities which fail to fully take into account those with different physical needs. His ability to exercise the basic act of citizenship in a parliamentary democracy – voting in secret – is compromised. Most voters take secluded voting booths for granted, but a voter in a wheelchair may have to vote without the seclusion provided to most other voters because of inadequate facilities (1994: 164–6). Murata also finds that his ability to carry out various social obligations – attending weddings, funerals and other formal ceremonies – is compromised by temples, shrines and reception halls which are inhospitable to someone moving around on a wheelchair (1994: 148–50). Murata's book includes photographs that document the obstacles he must overcome in every day of his life as a worker, a member of a community, and a citizen. When we see a photograph of the sign leading to the Citizen's Plaza outside the new Tokyo Metropolitan Government

Buildings, it is a relief to see the wheelchair icon, which shows that this public space is accessible to citizens like Murata (1994: 63).

Ototake and Murata's stories demonstrate that the ability to exercise active citizenship is intimately related to access to public space, reminding us of the etymological connection between 'cities' and 'citizens', a connection that is preserved in the Japanese word for citizen (*shimin*). Others with distinctive physical needs, such as pregnant women, nursing women, parents who move around with children in prams or strollers, and the elderly, also find regular obstacles to their usage of public space.

In some other countries, women's access to public space at night is restricted through fears for their physical safety, but the high population density in Japanese urban areas seems to provide a measure of surveillance which means that most citizens can move around without undue fears of assault or robbery.

If we examine social policies, we move from the language of difference to the language of disability, although there have been significant shifts in recent years. Social policy to deal with the disabled is a product of the period after the Second World War. Legislation for welfare provisions for the disabled was enacted in 1949, in the form of the Law on the Welfare of the Physically Disabled (Shintai Shōgaisha Fukushi Hō), apparently originally designed to deal with the needs of those with war injuries. The Basic Law on the Disabled (Shōgaisha Kihon Hō) was passed in 1970, and amended as the Basic Law on Policies for the Mentally and Physically Disabled (Shinshin Shōgaisha Taisaku Kihon Hō) in 1993. The amended Law is based on the principle of promoting the full participation in society of individuals with disabilities. We can thus see a shift in official policy from seeing physical difference as a matter of welfare policy, to a recognition of those with disabilities as citizens who participate in the community and society. The visibility of such individuals as Ototake and Murata has also been important in naturalising the presence of differently able individuals in public space: both physical space and the discursive space of the media.

Citizenship and sexual preference

There is no legal prohibition of homosexuality in modern Japan, but neither is there any specific protection of the right to exercise different sexual preferences, as there is in the new Constitution of South Africa. Lesbians and male homosexuals are marginal to the degree that they do not meet the expectations of participating in the monogamous heterosexual nuclear family system. They may also be prevented from accessing the taxation and welfare benefits available to heterosexual couples, although some have circumvented this by using the adoption system to ensure that their relationships are treated as familial relationships (Chalmers 1995: 88–97). Same-sex marriages and partnerships are given no legal status. Few countries do recognise same-sex marriages, but some, such as Australia, give same-sex partnerships a similar status to common-law marriages for such purposes as immigration law or industrial agreements where special compassionate leave is available to care for a sick spouse, partner or family member, and there have been some significant policy changes in some jurisdictions in the United States (*West Australian* 2000).

It is argued here that lesbians are more marginal than male homosexuals because they share two 'marked' features [-male, -heterosexual], or in other words, because men and women have differential access to the privileges of citizenship, as discussed above. Cultural representations reinforce the marginality of non-heterosexuals, with male homosexuals often being portrayed as effeminate figures of fun in popular culture. Lesbians are most often invisible, except in some genres of pornography produced for the voyeuristic attention of heterosexual males, as argued by Chalmers. Their marginality may be lessened, however, to the degree to which they meet the other criteria for citizenship, or conversely, will be increased to the extent to which they are seen to share other 'marked' features (Chalmers 1998: forthcoming).

The question of visibility in public space is relevant to those who do not meet the expectations of the heterosexual nuclear family system. As mentioned above, male homosexuals often appear in public discourse as figures of fun, while lesbians may be the object of voyeuristic masculine sexual fantasies. Both of these modes of representation affect the legitimacy of gay and lesbian individuals as actors in the public sphere. Of even more concern is the issue of violence against those who do not meet the expectations of heterosexuality. Several languages have words that encode the concept of violence against non-heterosexuals: 'gay bashing', the even more offensive Australian equivalent 'poofter bashing' and the Japanese phrase *homo-gari* ('gay hunting') (Kazama 2000: 254). The fact that diverse languages have the need for a word to express systematic violence against homosexuals suggests that there is a certain cultural logic to such violence. Those who do not meet the expectations of heterosexuality are a threat to a social system based on the heterosexual nuclear family, but also provoke a more visceral and emotional response in heterocentric systems, a response which is sometimes translated into physical violence.

In some parts of the world, gay, lesbian or transgender individuals have been successful in gaining election to public office. Such cases highlight questions of the notion of 'representativeness'. Why is it worthy of mention that a trans-sexual, a hermaphrodite or a eunuch should be elected to represent a group of citizens in a particular region? Perhaps it is because their visibility highlights the partiality of any individual who claims to represent a group of citizens. Where the middle-class, heterosexual male is seen as archetypal, much analytical work is necessary to expose the fragility of his claims to representativeness. Where the representative departs from the archetype in their class position, gendered difference, ethnicised difference, or other forms of embodied difference, their partiality is immediately apparent, and this opens up the question of how any individual can claim to represent a group made up of diverse citizens (Mackie, 2001). As far as I know, no openly gay or lesbian individuals have yet been elected to any parliaments in Japan, although at least one openly gay male has unsuccessfully stood for public office (Mark McLelland, personal communication). The last years have, however, seen the creation of groups performing advocacy for the rights of those who do not fit the heterosexual norm, and there is a flourishing 'counter-public' of gay, lesbian and queer media and communications (McLelland 2000).

White-collar work and citizenship

The privileging of white-collar work over other kinds of work is not immediately apparent from mainstream social policy, although it has been argued that more social prestige is attached to white-collar work:

So, despite the fact that the majority of Japanese consider themselves to be middle-class, it is clear that there is a polarity of occupational status in society which can be said to be divided along the lines of blue-collar/low status workers, and the salaryman/white collar/high status workers ...[13] (Standish 1998: 58–9).

While agreeing with Standish's comments, I would argue that the antithesis of the white-collar worker is not the skilled blue-collar worker, but rather the day labourer who engages in physical work and has none of the security and privileges of the middle-class salaried worker. In English-language writing on Japan, the adjective 'blue-collar' has been used to refer to a relatively privileged sector of usually male workers with technical skills (Koike 1996). The Japanese working-class male may in many cases share the patriarchal privileges of the middle-class, white-collar worker. Although the working-class male may be celebrated in some cultural forms, it is the besuited white-collar worker who is seen as archetypal (Dasgupta 2000; Kondo 1997; Mackie 1999; Mackie 2000b).

The regulation of labour conditions generally assumes a worker in a fulltime permanent occupation, with casual workers or day labourers tending to be seen as special cases. Similarly, welfare policies tend to assume a permanent worker in a stable occupation, part of a heterosexual nuclear family, and with a permanent fixed address (Stevens 1995: 371–6). Despite the celebration of this archetype, the elite workers who enjoy the benefits of lifetime employment and seniority promotion and the protection of company unionism have generally been less than a third of the total workforce, and the vast majority of these have been males between the ages of 25 and 55.

The feature [+white collar worker] becomes more apparent in an examination of immigration policy. There is an implicit privileging of mental labour over physical labour encoded in immigration policy – a mind/body split whereby intellectual, white-collar work is given recognition, but not manual and physical labour, and certainly not sexual labour. Some elite white-collar workers enter Japan temporarily on working visas, and this is recognised under the rubric of 'internationalisation' (*kokusaika*). These elite white-collar workers are acceptable in that they share many of the features of the elite white-collar Japanese worker, except for the feature [+Japanese blood].

So far, the Japanese Department of Immigration has failed to permit immigration for the purpose of engaging in unskilled labour. There are, however, several major loopholes. Students may engage in limited part-time work, some workers enter the country as 'trainees,' and others as 'entertainers.' As we have seen above, a special category for those of Japanese ancestry has brought immigrants from Japanese-descended communities in Latin America to Japan as workers, usually in 'non-skilled' positions.

It is seen as 'natural' that Japanese young people are increasingly reluctant to engage in manual work, and that these places may be taken by immigrant workers, even if illegally. The phrase 'difficult, dirty and dangerous' (*kitsui, kitanai, kiken*) used to describe these marginalised occupations aligns them with the abject (Mackie 1998; Creighton 1997). Because of the official prohibition on importing 'unskilled' labour, it is illegal to import labour for the purpose of domestic work, although anecdotal evidence suggests that some families are finding ways to employ overseas domestic workers. Japan is thus relatively distinctive in not importing large numbers of domestic workers. Diplomatic personnel may employ domestic workers or chauffeurs who speak English. This allows for them to employ overseas workers, often from the Philippines. While such workers have a legitimate visa status, they do not come under the purview of the Labour Standards Law. The Labour Standards Law is the legislation that regulates the working conditions of regular workers, but does not apply to domestic workers.

The male immigrant worker shares the stigma of engaging in physical labour, and may sometimes be racialised in similar ways to the female immigrant worker. However, for male immigrant workers, their

engagement in what is seen as productive labour means that there is a
space for discussion of their situation, and even space to consider
granting them a limited form of citizenship as 'guest workers.'

Sexual labour

A separate category of 'sexual labour' is necessary in addition to the
distinction between 'white-collar' work and 'non-white-collar' work. As
argued above, it is seen as 'natural' that most Japanese people will be
reluctant to engage in occupations that are 'difficult, dirty and dangerous'
(*kitsui, kitanai, kiken*). Women in the entertainment industry bear a
further stigma due to their engagement in sexualised work. Not only is
prostitution illegal, it is stigmatised due to its association with sexuality.
Prostitution is 'embodied labour' in a very particular sense.

Despite the illegality of prostitution, it is allowed to continue and is
given tacit recognition through zoning regulations, which regulate establishments such as 'soaplands,' massage parlours or hostess bars (Taylor
forthcoming). Such regulations allow heterosexual males to have access
to commodified sexual services provided by women who are stigmatised
by their engagement in such occupations. This sexual access is what I
refer to as the 'sexual subtext' of citizenship for heterosexual male Japanese
citizens.

Because prostitution is not recognised as work, prostitutes are denied
the protection afforded other kinds of workers, and do not have access to
the social prestige associated with engagement in socially recognised
occupations. From this we derive the category [+chaste labour] to describe
socially sanctioned occupations, and [−chaste labour] to describe the
marked category of sexual labour. In some countries arguments are being
made for the recognition of prostitution as work, and the decriminalisation of prostitution. Similar prostitutes' advocacy groups have recently
appeared in Japan. While the decriminalisation of prostitution has recently
been debated by feminists in Japan, this argument is seldom heard from
advocates working with immigrant workers, who recognise the coercive
conditions many of these women work under (Momocca 1999: 178–81;
Group Sisterhood 1999: 87–97; Ehara et al. 1997: 38–52). The crimi-
nalisation of prostitution dates from the Baishun Bōshi Hō (Prostitution
Prevention Law) of 1956. Until that time, a system of state-regulated
licensed prostitution existed in Japan. At various times, there were attempts
to set up unions for workers in cafes, bars and similar establishments: in
the labour federations prior to World War Two and in the immediate post-
war period (Fujime 1997).

Where the sex worker is an undocumented immigrant worker, her
marginality is all the more extreme. While economic rationalist arguments

may be made for the recognition of immigrant workers in manufacturing and construction, another group of workers remains beyond the pale of discourses of citizenship. These are the women who engage in entertainment, waitressing, and prostitution. Like their male counterparts, they are subject to voyeuristic attention, with an added element of sexualisation. While male workers' jobs are physically dirty, these women bear the stigma of sexualised labour. Like their male counterparts, they engage in work with long hours and difficult working conditions, with the added dangers of violence and sexually transmissible disease.

In popular culture in Japan, there is a consciousness of the physical characteristics attributed to Europeans, Africans, and those from other parts of Asia (Creighton 1997; Inagaki 1996; Pollack 1993; Mackie 1998). However, I would argue that, in addition to these perceived physical differences, it is embodied practices that reinforce inequalities. The embodied practices of work in the 'difficult, dirty and dangerous' occupations reinforce the connections between immigrant workers and physical labour. Embodied practices also reinforce gendered and racialised hierarchies. Immigrant workers in the bars and brothels of the urban centres of Japan offer a range of personalised and often embodied services. The daily repetition of encounters between Japanese white-collar workers and immigrant workers in the entertainment industries reinforces the opposition between Japanese and non-Japanese, mental labour and physical labour, sexualised labour and non-sexualised labour. As discussed above, hierarchies are also reinforced through the practice of using immigrant labour in jobs which are thought to be 'dirty, difficult and dangerous': jobs which are seen as increasingly undesirable by young Japanese people entering the workforce, but appropriate to be carried out by immigrant workers.

Trans-sexual citizenship?

As we have seen, the Eugenic Protection Law, and its successor, 'The Law for the Protection of the Maternal Body,' is concerned with the conditions for the control of reproduction. Until its amendment, the Eugenic Protection Law was interpreted so as to prevent sex change operations, according to the provisions that prevented medical procedures that affected healthy reproductive organs, except under specified conditions. In 1970 a medical practitioner who had carried out operations to remove the male sex organs of three men was prosecuted under this law. The modification of Article 3 in 1996 has apparently opened the way for the practice of sex change operations in Japan.[14]

The first officially sanctioned operation was carried out in Japan during 1998. Until this time, those who wished to undergo a sex change needed to go overseas.[15] This operation was carried out on a female in her 30s in October 1998 at Saitama University Hospital. She had been receiving counselling and had been administered male hormones, and had been living as a male. The doctors from the Saitama University Hospital had commenced application for ethics clearance for such an operation in 1995, and subsequently set up a clinic for the treatment of those wishing to undergo a sex change. The Japan Psychiatric and Neurological Association had issued guidelines for the treatment of gender dysphoria in 1997. Saitama University Hospital gave ethics clearance in May 1998. The first stage of the operation was carried out in October 1998, and a further operation carried out six months later (Takano, 1998; Newsplanet Staff, 1998). Saitama University Hospital has counselled over 200 patients with gender dysphoria, and the Japan Psychiatric and Neurological Association estimates between 2200 and 7000 such cases in Japan. Saitama University Hospital initially reported that a majority of consultations were about female-to-male reassignment, but at the time of writing it was not possible to ascertain the reliability or typicality of these figures.

For the purposes of the present discussion, let us consider the position of the trans-sexual with respect to the discourses and practices of national inclusion and exclusion. The laws that have until now prevented the practice of sex change operations are those that ensure state control over the reproductive bodies of citizens. Even the recent permission for the first legal sex change operation became possible after the amendment of the Eugenic Protection Law and its replacement with the Law for the Protection of the Maternal Body, which still affirms the jurisdiction of the Japanese state over the reproductive body. If there is any doubt that it is reproductive capacity that the state is interested in controlling, compare these operations with other ways in which individuals modify their bodies. There is no prohibition of tattooing, piercing, shaving, or cosmetic surgery.

Even before the recent legal changes and reinterpretation of the administration of the Law, some Japanese citizens were simply living as transvestites, were partaking of black market hormone treatments, had received sex change procedures illegally, or had undergone such procedures overseas. Mako Sennyo (1997) has written about the situation of such individuals.[16] Before the creation of the Saitama Clinic, individuals who experienced gender dysphoria were not able to access counselling about their situation. While the surgical part of the sex change process was illegal, it was not feasible to set up clinics to deal with other aspects of gender reassignment. So, those who wished to undergo such procedures would do so overseas, but without taking advantage of the counselling which would ascertain the desirability (or otherwise) of such surgery, and without the psychological back-up to help deal with the stresses of their situation.

Trans-sexuals find themselves unable to receive treatment for medical problems related to the sex change. For example, individuals identified as male on their national insurance cards would be unable to receive hormone treatments or treatment for complaints related to their trans-formed body. Male-to-female trans-sexuals suffering such complaints would need to pay for such treatments without the assistance of medical insurance, go through the (illegal) charade of borrowing a woman's medical insurance card, or find a sympathetic doctor who would treat them and disguise the true nature of their complaint. Hermaphrodites have similar problems in receiving treatment that does not match the sex they were assigned at birth: that is, the sex that is recorded on their *koseki* (family registration), medical insurance card, and other official documents (Mako 1997: 101).

Although driving licences do not show the sex of the holder, most other official documents do. It is often necessary to show an extract of the family register for the purposes of employment, so that someone whose name, gender and sex do not match this entry will be disadvantaged – at the very least they will have difficulty in verifying their identity. This means that trans-sexuals are often marginalised from fulltime, permanent, career positions, and will be more likely to find employment in casual and part-time work, particularly in the entertainment sector.

There have been cases of hermaphrodites who have applied to the Court to be recognised as having a different sex to that assigned at birth, but because the *koseki* records each child as being 'eldest son,' 'eldest daughter,' 'second son,' 'second daughter,' and so on, this has neces-sitated the modification of the entries for each sibling. Those who have undergone the most recent sex change operations have applied to the Court for official recognition of their new sexual identity, but so far this has been denied. As same-sex marriage is not recognised in Japan, a female-to-male trans-sexual who wishes to marry a woman, for example, will be unable to do so because of the sex recorded on the family register entry. Although common-law heterosexual couples in Japan are starting to be treated in the same way as married couples for the purposes of inheritance, this is not true of same-sex couples, or those couples with a trans-sexual partner where the state treats them as a same-sex partner-ship. The same is true of tax concessions, family allowances and welfare benefits (Mako 1997: 103–4).

The above analysis suggests two features that need to be added to the profile of the archetypal citizen. I will use the feature [+monosexual] to describe the expectation that individuals will have the same sex and gender for the whole of their life. The feature [–monosexual] describes the trans-sexual who belongs to the 'marked' category. A further feature can be derived from the analysis of the situation of trans-sexuals. Sex change operations are problematic because they alter the individual's reproductive capacity, seen to be a matter of state policy. We thus derive the feature [+fertile], which will receive further attention below.

The fertile citizen, the non-fertile citizen and the fertile non-citizen

The state's interest in promoting the production of healthy Japanese citizens and discouraging the modification of the reproductive capacity of healthy citizens has been canvassed in several sections above. Despite the pro-natalist policies of Japanese governments, and regular conservative panics about the ready availability of abortion, the birthrate has continued to drop until it is now at an all-time low. This suggests some resistance to official pro-natalist and pro-family policies. This does not yet mean a total rejection of the family system, as most Japanese still marry and live in heterosexual nuclear families, although the age of marriage is getting steadily older. The shape of those families, however, has been transformed in the latter half of the twentieth century. The government's Angel Plan, established in 1994, is an attempt to come to terms with this issue (Roberts, Chapter 3 this volume).

The feature [+fertile] becomes more interesting when considered in conjunction with the feature [+Japanese blood]. The people who are encouraged to reproduce are those who can pass on 'Japanese blood'. The problem with immigrant workers is not simply their residence in the host community, but that they may reproduce. They are thus subject to what Ghassan Hage has called 'the dialectic of inclusion and exclusion' (Hage 1998: 134–8). Immigrant workers are included to the extent that surplus value may be extracted from their labour, but excluded from full participation in local communities. Indeed, as Hage argues (with reference to a different national community), it is the very marginality of such workers that allows for their efficient exploitation. For most immigrant workers, then, their fertility is seen as undesirable, whether they are immigrant males who threaten the 'right' of Japanese males to pass on their bloodline, or immigrant women who are stigmatised through their engagement in sexualised work.

There is a special category of immigrants, however, whose fertility is not only desirable but also probably a necessary condition for their inclusion. These are the women who come from overseas as marriage partners for Japanese men. As long as their fertility is harnessed in the service of the patriarchal family unit, they may have a place in the family and the local community. In this case alone, the feature [+fertile] is more important than the feature [+Japanese blood]. Their children will be seen to possess Japanese blood through their father's line. The pattern of marriage between a Japanese man and a non-Japanese (Asian) woman is the most common form of international marriage in Japan today (Itō 1992: 300).[17] In these marriages, issues of ethnic difference are being worked out at the most intimate level, and the children of these marriages will be the embodiment of hybridity.[18]

By comparing the two extreme cases of the 'non-fertile citizen' (the Japanese trans-sexual who wilfully interferes with their reproductive capacity) and the 'fertile non-citizen' (the immigrant worker whose fertility is seen as undesirable), we can start to see that reproductive capacity is an important feature of the archetypal citizen.

The features of citizenship in contemporary Japan

We can summarise the above discussion by means of a matrix of features, which will allow us to identify the features which are seen to be 'natural' attributes of the Japanese citizen, and those which work to naturalise the exclusion of certain figures from discourses of citizenship. In opposition to the archetypal citzen, then, are various groups with diverse combinations of marked features: features in dynamic interaction with each other. As argued above, the archetypal citizen is the unmarked centre of all representations of Japaneseness. It is the white-collar, heterosexual, able-bodied, fertile, Japanese male, with a secure place in the sex–gender system, who occupies this central position (see Figure 9.1). Others will be marginal to the extent that they embody some of the marked features of gender, sexuality, bloodline and marked categories of labour. Even someone who has the feature of [+Japanese blood] will be marginalised if they display marked features in the other dimensions of citizenship.

The female Japanese citizen is socially disadvantaged to the extent that social policy is based on the assumption that the addressee of social

+Japanese blood
+male
+heterosexual
+monosexual
+fertile
+white collar
+chaste labour
+able-bodied

Figure 9.1   The archetypal citizen

policy is a male, heterosexual worker in a stable and permanent occupation. As long as she does not share other marked features, however, her position may be relatively central, compared to the marginal figures discussed below (See Figure 9.2).

As discussed above, the manual or casual worker is marginal compared with the archetypal white-collar worker. A male working-class worker may still share some patriarchal privilege with the male white-collar worker, but the female manual worker embodies two marginal features (Figure 9.3).

The male homosexual will be marginal to the extent that he does not participate in the heterosexual nuclear family system, but may still have some of the social privileges accruing to males, particularly if he is also engaged in a prestigious occupation (Figure 9.4).

The lesbian is seen as being more marginal than the male homosexual, because she has none of the privileges accruing to males. She may however, achieve some legitimacy from her occupation. She will be even more marginalised from the full privileges of citizenship if she has other marked features (Figure 9.5). The issue of sexual preference and the fact that many non-heterosexuals do have children and live in non-conventional families highlight the need for analytical precision in distinguishing between sexual behaviour, reproduction, sexual identity, and parenting.

Citizens who are not able-bodied will be marginalised to the extent that they cannot fully participate in the prestigious occupations that provide social legitimacy. If the disability further affects the ability to participate in the heterosexual nuclear family system, then this will lead to further marginalisation (Figure 9.6).

The prostitute will be marginalised because of participation in sexual labour. If the sex worker is female, she will be marginalised in the same ways as other women, with additional stigma attached to the sexualised occupation, and further marginalisation from the family system. The male homosexual prostitute will be marginalised due to his association with homosexuality (Figure 9.7). The act of sexual intercourse may thus, in different circumstances, be seen as recreation, as procreation, or as work. Indeed, the same act may be seen as recreation by the purchaser of sexual services, and as work by the provider of this service. The act will take on a different dimension where coerced labour is involved.

The trans-sexual is marginalised due to the lack of a stable place in the sex–gender system, and the renunciation of the expectation to reproduce healthy national subjects. The lack of a stable place in the sex–gender system and the difficulties in verifying identity make it difficult for the trans-sexual to have a stable place in the employment and family systems (Figure 9.8).

The descendant of Japanese emigrants who comes to work in Japan shares most of the features of the archetypal citizen, particularly the

```
+Japanese blood
−male
+heterosexual
+monosexual
+fertile
+white collar
+chaste labour
+able-bodied
```

Figure 9.2   The female citizen

```
+Japanese blood
±male
+heterosexual
+monosexual
+fertile
-white collar
+chaste labour
+able-bodied
```

Figure 9.3   The manual worker

```
+Japanese blood
+male
-heterosexual
+monosexual
+fertile
+white collar
+chaste labour
+able-bodied
```

Figure 9.4   The male homosexual

```
+Japanese blood
−male
−heterosexual
+monosexual
+fertile
+white collar
+chaste labour
+able-bodied
```

Figure 9.5   The lesbian

```
+Japanese blood
±male
+heterosexual
+monosexual
+fertile
+white collar
+chaste labour
−able-bodied
```

Figure 9.6   The person with a disability

```
+Japanese blood
±male
±heterosexual
+monosexual
+fertile
+white collar
-chaste labour
+able-bodied
```

Figure 9.7   The prostitute

feature of possessing a Japanese bloodline. The lack of cultural and linguistic competence, however, is likely to push the descendant of emigrant families into a non-white-collar occupation (Figure 9.9).

By contrast, international workers in prestigious occupations related to education, finance, information, media, science and technology are likely to share many of the features of the archetypal white-collar citizen, except for the feature of Japanese bloodline (Figure 9.10).

The male immigrant manual worker is marginalised through the lack of Japanese bloodline and through distance from the white-collar ideal. The fertility of the immigrant worker is seen as a threat (Figure 9.11).

The female immigrant worker in a manual occupation shares all of the marginal features of the male immigrant manual worker. If she is engaged in sexual labour, she possesses a further marginal feature. Her fertility is also seen as a threat (Figure 9.12).

The marriage migrant differs from other female immigrant workers in that her fertility is seen as desirable. Because her sexual labour, reproductive labour and domestic labour are harnessed for the needs of the patriarchal, heterosexual nuclear family system, her labour does not bear the stigma of other sex workers (Figure 9.13).

These figures may be contrasted with the second and third generation members of Korean and Taiwanese immigrant families (commonly abbreviated as '*Zainichi*' 'resident in Japan'). These residents lack only the feature of Japanese bloodline, and many have full cultural and linguistic competence. They will be further marginalised according to the number of marked features they possess (Figure 9.14).

It is tempting at this stage to posit an 'archetypal non-citizen' who embodies the greatest number of marked features. However, in the context of the present discussion, I will close by commenting that the spectrum of citizenship is multidimensional, and that the features posited here operate in a dynamic and interactive, rather than a simply summative, fashion.

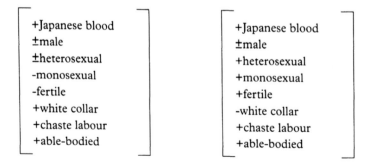

+Japanese blood	+Japanese blood
±male	±male
±heterosexual	+heterosexual
-monosexual	+monosexual
-fertile	+fertile
+white collar	-white collar
+chaste labour	+chaste labour
+able-bodied	+able-bodied

Figure 9.8 The trans-sexual   **Figure 9.9** The *Nisei*

```
┌                        ┐
│  -Japanese blood       │
│  ±male                 │
│  +heterosexual         │
│  +monosexual           │
│  +fertile              │
│  +white collar         │
│  +chaste labour        │
│  +able-bodied          │
└                        ┘
```

Figure 9.10   The 'international' worker

```
┌                        ┐
│  -Japanese blood       │
│  +male                 │
│  +heterosexual         │
│  +monosexual           │
│  +fertile              │
│  -white collar         │
│  +chaste labour        │
│  +able-bodied          │
└                        ┘
```

Figure 9.11   Male immigrant manual worker

```
┌                        ┐
│  -Japanese blood       │
│  -male                 │
│  +heterosexual         │
│  +monosexual           │
│  +fertile              │
│  -white collar         │
│  +chaste labour        │
│  +able-bodied          │
└                        ┘
```

Figure 9.12   Female immigrant manual worker

```
┌                        ┐
│  -Japanese blood       │
│  -male                 │
│  +heterosexual         │
│  +monosexual           │
│  +fertile              │
│  ±white collar         │
│  +chaste labour        │
│  +able-bodied          │
└                        ┘
```

Figure 9.13   The marriage migrant

```
┌                        ┐
│  -Japanese blood       │
│  ±male                 │
│  +heterosexual         │
│  +monosexual           │
│  +fertile              │
│  ±white collar         │
│  +chaste labour        │
│  +able-bodied          │
└                        ┘
```

Figure 9.14   *'Zainichi'* resident

NOTES

1 Research for this chapter was carried out as part of a series of linked projects on Citizenship in Modern Japan, funded by the Toyota Foundation and the Australian Research Council Small Grants Scheme. Papers related to this chapter have been presented at the JAWS Conference on the Anthropology of Social Policy in Japan, National Museum of Ethnography, Japan, April, 1999; the Conference of the New Zealand Asian Studies Association, University of Otago, November 1999; Conference of the Japanese Studies Association of Australia, Central Queensland University, December 1999. I am indebted to colleagues at those conferences for their comments, and to Roger Goodman, Tessa Morris-Suzuki and Alison Tokita for more detailed comments. Romit Dasgupta kindly assisted in locating newspaper reports on the first sex change operations, and Hideko Nakamura assisted in locating recent versions of the legislation mentioned in this chapter.

2 Fukuoka Yasunori (1993) and Ross Mouer and Yoshio Sugimoto (1995) have recently attempted classifications that can deal with the 'pure Japanese,' the '*Nisei*' immigrant and the resident Korean. My own framework is different in attempting to systematically analyse those groups which may belong to the formal category of 'Japanese citizen' but which may still be marginalised from full participation as citizens, and in focussing on the concept of 'embodiment.'

3 This was true until quite recently. The Constitution of Japan, for example, has explicit provisions prohibiting sexual discrimination, while the Constitution of the United States has not yet added an Equal Rights Amendment. The new Constitution of South Africa, however, includes provisions on such issues as sexual orientation which is found in few other legal instruments. On the South African Constitution, see Vandenberg (2000: 229).

4 Unlike Hage, I will retain the word 'citizenship' to refer to all of these modalities of national belonging.

5 The notation employed is adapted from the methods of describing distinctive features in phonological analysis (Hyman, 1975: 24–58). This notation works best with binary features. Where a binary classification has not been possible, as in the set [+ white collar work, + 'chaste' work], this has been dealt with in two steps. Where a feature has been shown as [±] in a particular matrix, this either means that the feature is not distinctive in this context, or that the feature works in a dynamic way with other features. The more features that are in the 'unmarked' category [+], the closer the type will be to the 'archetypal citizen;' the more features which are in the 'marked' category [–], the more marginal the figure will be.

6 Mouer and Sugimoto variously refer to this feature as 'biological pedigree', or having 'pure Japanese genes.' While the reference to genetics is more scientifically accurate, references to 'blood' or 'bloodline' are perhaps closer to popular understandings (1995: 237–69). Fukuoka (1993: 5) refers to this feature as *kettō* (bloodline).

7 I differ from Valentine's analysis in that I believe that he collapses several different kinds of marginality when he includes members of outcaste communities under this heading.

8 The protective attitude expressed in legislation specifically directed at women
   in discussed more fully in Mackie (1995: 95–113); Barbara Molony (1993:
   122–9) discusses the 'body-centred' emphasis of the Labour Standards Law.
9 Eugenic Protection Law, translation in Sakamoto (1987: 194–205). Between
   1940 and 1948, surgical abortion and sterilisation were regulated by the
   National Eugenics Law (Kokumin Yūsei Hō).
10 Botai Hogo Hō, Article 3, accessed at <http://myriel.ads.fukushima-u.ac.jp/
   data/law/botai.html>
11 This section has been informed by my reading of Ōno (1996), Ali (2000),
   Thomson (1997), Mitchell and Snyder (2000), Tabata et al. (1999).
12 Ototake's autobiography has appeared in several editions since 1998. I will be
   referring to the 2000 edition which was designed to appeal to children. The
   English translation appeared with the inspired title, *Nobody's Perfect*.
13 On working class cultures, see also Kondo (1990) and Roberts (1994).
14 The following terminology will be employed in this discussion: 'hermaphrodite' refers to someone whose sexual organs have the features of both biological
   sexes to a greater or lesser degree; 'transvestite' refers to someone who dresses
   in the clothes of the opposite gender; 'transgender' refers to someone who
   adopts the demeanour and behaviour of the opposite gender, and 'trans-
   sexual' refers to someone who undergoes surgery and hormone therapy in
   order to transform the sexual organs and secondary sexual characteristics into
   those of the other sex. 'Sex change operation' will be used to refer to an
   operation (or series of operations) to modify the primary and secondary
   sexual characteristics, but it should be understood that such operations are
   normally accompanied by the administering of hormones and by extensive
   counselling and training in the behaviour appropriate to the newly assumed
   gender. Thus, it is not always easy to analytically separate out the parts of the
   process where biological sex is at issue, and where societal gender norms are
   at issue. In popular reporting of the issue, these elements are rarely
   distinguished systematically, and this is true of the most recent Japanese case.
   Because scholarship on transgender issues is developing rapidly, the
   terminology is also subject to rapid transformation, often with little agreement between different commentators. See Stryker (1998), Mackie (2001).
15 My point in this discussion is not to evaluate the desirability of sex change
   operations as a way of dealing with gender dysphoria. Rather, I am interested
   in considering what the issue of sex changes reveals about state attitudes to
   citizens' control over their reproductive capacity.
16 Mako's article (revised and reprinted from an earlier article) was apparently
   completed before the revision of the Eugenic Protection Law, but in the
   context of the present discussion is most useful for its survey of the social
   situation of transvestite, transgender and transsexual individuals in contemporary Japan.
17 On social policy related to immigrant women as mothers, see Chapter 4 by
   Stevens and Lee in this volume. They conclude that the marginalisation of
   non-Japanese women, and their difficulty in accessing maternal and child
   health care due to linguistic and cultural barriers and lack of information,
   result in higher-risk pregnancies for foreign-born women.
18 Cf. Kathryn Robinson's (1996: 54) comments on the representation of
   marriages between Australian men and Filipino women in Australia: '... this

is not like other forms of immigration where the newcomers can be ghettoized. Here they are introduced into the most remote regions into Australian households, giving birth to Australian children.'

REFERENCES

Agora, No 28, 1983.

Ali, Suki. 2000. 'Who knows best? Politics and ethics in feminist research into "race",' in *Global Feminist Politics: Identities in a Changing World*, ed. Suki Ali, Kelly Coate and Wangi wa Goro. London: Routledge.

Allison, Anne. 1994. *Nightwork: Sexuality, Pleasure and Masculinity in a Tokyo Hostess Club.* Chicago: Chicago University Press.

——. 1996. *Permitted and Prohibited Desires: Mothers, Comics, and Censorship in Japan.* Boulder, Colorado: Westview Press.

Buckley, Sandra. 1988. 'Body politics,' in *Modernization and Beyond: The Japanese Trajectory*, ed. Gavan McCormack and Yoshio Sugimoto. Cambridge: Cambridge University Press.

Buckley, Sandra and Vera Mackie. 1986. 'Women in the new Japanese state,' in *Democracy in Contemporary Japan*, ed. Gavan McCormack and Yoshio Sugimoto. Sydney: Hale and Iremonger.

Chalmers, Sharon 1995. 'Inside/outside circles of silence: creating lesbian space in Japanese society,' pp. 88–97 in *Feminism and the State in Modern Japan*, ed. Vera Mackie. Melbourne: Japanese Studies Centre.

——. 1998. 'Inside/outside circles of silence: lesbian subjectivities in contemporary Japan.' PhD thesis. Griffith University.

——. Forthcoming. *Emerging Lesbian Voices in Japan*. London: Curzon Press.

Creighton, Millie. 1997. '*Soto* others and *uchi* others: imaging racial diversity, imagining homogeneous Japan,' in *Japan's Minorities: The Illusion of Homogeneity*, ed. Michael Weiner. London: Routledge.

Dasgupta, Romit. 2000. 'Crafting masculinities: the salaryman at work and play.' *Japanese Studies*, No 2, 2000. 189–200.

Ehara Yumiko, Nakajima Michiko, Matsui Yayori, and Yunomae Tomoko. 1997. 'The movement today: difficult but critical issues,' pp. 38–52 in *Voices from the Japanese Women's Movement*, ed. AMPO: Japan–Asia Quarterly Review. New York: M.E. Sharpe.

Fujime Yuki. 1997. *Sei no Rekishigaku* (The Historiography of Sex). Tokyo: Fuji Shuppan.

Fujita Kuniko. 1987. 'Gender, state and industrial policy in Japan.' *Women's Studies International Forum.* 10 (6).

Fukuoka Yasunori. 1993. *Zainichi Kankoku Chōsenjin* (*Korean Residents in Japan*). Tokyo: Chūkō Shinsho.

Gatens, Moira. 1998. 'Institutions, embodiment and sexual difference,' in *Gender and Institutions: Welfare, Work and Citizenship*, ed. Moira Gatens and Alison McKinnon. Cambridge: Cambridge University Press.

Grosz, Elizabeth. 1994. *Volatile Bodies: Toward a Corporeal Feminism*. Bloomington: Indiana University Press.

Group Sisterhood. 1999. 'Prostitution, stigma and the law in Japan: a feminist roundtable discussion,' pp. 87–97 in *Global Sex Workers: Rights, Resistance and Redefinition*. eds. Kamala Kempadoo and Jo Deozema. London: Routledge.

Hage, Ghassan. 1998. *White Nation: Fantasies of White Supremacy in a Multicultural Society*. Sydney: Pluto Press.

Hindess, Barry. 1992. 'Citizens and people.' *Australian Left Review* (June).

Hunter, Janet. ed. 1993. *Japanese Women Working*. London: Routledge.

Hyman, Larry M. 1975. *Phonology: Theory and Analysis*. New York: Holt, Rinehart and Winston.

Inagaki Kiyo. 1996. 'Nihonjin no Firipin-zō: Hisada Megumi "Firipina o Aishita Otokotachi" ni okeru Firipin to Nihon (Japanese images of Filipinos: on the Philippines and Japan as portrayed in Hisada Megumi's "Men who Love Filipinas"),' pp. 271–96 in *Ajia no Kōsaten: Zainichi Gaikokujin to Chiiki Shakai* (The Crossroads of Asia: Regional Society and Non-Japanese Residents), ed. Aizawa Isao. Tokyo: Shakai Hyōronsha.

Itō Ruri. 1992. '"Japayukisan" genshō saikō – 80nendai Nihon e no Ajia josei ryūnyū. (The "Japayuki" phenomenon reconsidered: the entry of Asian women into Japan in the 1980s)' in *Gaikokujin Rōdōsharon* (On Foreign Workers in Japan), ed. Iyotani Toshio and Kajita Takamichi. Tokyo: Kōbundō.

Iwai Tomoaki. 1993. '"The Madonna boom": women in the Japanese Diet.' *Journal of Japanese Studies*, 19 (1) pp. 103–120.

Kazama Takashi. 2000. '"Homo-gari" to dōseiaisha e no bōryoku ("Gay-hunting" and violence against homosexuals).' *Gendai Shisō*, 28(8).

Koike, Kazuo. 1996. *The Economics of Work in Japan*. Tokyo: LTCB International Library Foundation.

Kondo, Dorinne K. 1990. *Crafting Selves: Power, Gender and Discourses of Identity in a Japanese Workplace*. Chicago: University of Chicago Press.

——. 1997. *About Face: Performing Race in Fashion and Theatre*. New York: Routledge.

Linder, A. and D. Peters. 1995. 'The two traditions of institutional designing: dialogue versus decision?' in *Institutional Design*, ed. D. L. Weimer. Boston: Kluwer.

Mackie, Vera. 1995. 'Equal Opportunity and Gender Identity,' pp. 95–113 in *Japanese Encounters with Postmodernity*, ed. Johann Arnason and Yoshio Sugimoto. London: Kegan Paul International.

——. 1998. '"Japayuki Cinderella Girl": containing the immigrant other.' *Japanese Studies*. 18 (1) pp. 45–63.

——. 1999. 'The Worlds of Japanese Fashion', in *Tokyo Vogue*. eds. Craig Douglas and Bonnie English. Brisbane: Brisbane City Art Gallery.

——. 2000a. 'Sexual violence, silence and human rights discourse: the emergence of the military prostitution issue,' in *Human Rights and Gender Politics: Asia-Pacific Perspectives*, ed. Anne Marie Hilsdon, Martha Macintyre, Vera Mackie and Maila Stivens. London: Routledge.

——. 2000b. 'The dimensions of citizenship in modern Japan: gender, class, ethnicity and sexuality,' in *Democracy and Citizenship in a Global Era*, ed. Andrew Vandenberg. London: Macmillan.

——. 2001. 'The trans-sexual citizen: queering sameness and difference.' *Australian Feminist Studies*, (July) 185–92.

Mako Sennyo. 1997. 'Genzai Nihon de TG ga chokumen suru mondaiten (Issues facing TGs in contemporary Japan),' in *Queer Studies 1996: Queer Generation no Tanjō*, ed. Queer Studies Henshū Iinkai. Tokyo: Nanatsumori Shokan.

McLelland, Mark. 2000. *Male Homosexuality in Modern Japan: Cultural Myths and Social Realities*. London: Curzon.

Mitchell, David T. and Sharon L. Snyder. 2000. *Narrative Prosthesis: Disability and the Dependencies of Discourse* Ann Arbor: University of Michigan.

Mitsui, Mariko. 1994. *Seku Hara Hyakutōban (Sexual Harassment Hotline)*. Tokyo: Shūeisha.

Molony, Barbara. 1993. 'Equality versus difference: the Japanese debate over motherhood protection, 1915–1950,' pp. 122–9 in *Japanese Women Working*, ed. Janet Hunter. London: Routledge.

Momocca Momocco. 1999. 'Japanese sex workers: encourage, empower, trust and love yourselves!' pp.178–81 in *Global Sex Workers: Rights, Resistance and Redefinition*, ed. Kamala Kempadoo and Jo Deozema. London: Routledge.

Mouer, Ross and Yoshio Sugimoto. 1995. '*Nihonjinron* at the end of the twentieth century: a multicultural perspective,' in *Japanese Encounters with Postmodernity*, ed. Johann Arnason and Yoshio Sugimoto. London: Kegan Paul International.

Murata Minoru. 1994. *Kurumaisu kara mita Machi* (The City as Seen from a Wheelchair). Tokyo: Iwanami Junia Shinsho.

Newsplanet Staff. 1998. 'Japan's First Legal Sex Change.' accessed at <http://www.ifga.org/news/1998/june/nws6058d.htm>, 25 October 1998.

Ōno, Tomoya. 1996. *Shogaisha wa ima* (The Disabled Today). Tokyo: Iwanami.

Ototake Hirotada. 2000. *Gotai Fumanzoku* (Nobody's Perfect). Tokyo: Kōdansha.

Pollack, David. 1993. 'The revenge of the illegal Asians: aliens, gangsters, and myth in Ken Satoshi's world apartment horror.' *Positions: East Asia Cultures Critique*, 1 (3): 676–714.

Roberts, Glenda. 1994. *Staying on the Line: Blue Collar Women in Contemporary Japan*. Honolulu: University of Hawaii Press.

Robinson, Kathryn. 1996. 'Of mail-order brides and "Boys' Own" tales.' *Feminist Review*, 52: 53–68.

Sakamoto, Sachiko. 1987. 'Japanese feminists: their struggle against the revision of the Eugenic Protection Law.' M.A. thesis. University of Hawaii.

Standish, Isolde. 1998. '*Akira*, postmodernism and resistance,' in *The Worlds of Japanese Popular Culture: Gender, Shifting Boundaries and Global Cultures*, ed. D. P. Martinez. Cambridge: Cambridge University Press.

Stevens, Carolyn S. 1995. 'Day labourers, volunteers and the welfare system in contemporary Japan.' *Urban Anthropology and Studies of Cultural Systems and World Economic Development*, 24 (3–4): 229–53.

Stryker, Susan. 1998. 'The transgender issue: an introduction.' *GLQ*, 4 (2): 145–58.

Tabata, Hideomi et al. 1999. 'The bather: self-portraiture from a movable chair.' *Public Culture*, 11(3): 417–50.

Takano, Satoshi. 1998. '"*Seitenkan Shujutsu*" iryō kōi to shite hatsu 30dai josei hantoshi kakete kanryō (First sex change operation as medical procedure: 30-year old woman completes six-month treatment).' *Mainichi Shinbun* (16 October), accessed at <http://www.mainichi.co.jp/old-news/199810/16/1016e071-400.html>, 25 October 1998.

Tanaka, Hideo and Malcolm Smith, eds. 1976. *The Japanese Legal System.*Tokyo: University of Tokyo Press.

Taylor, Veronica. 1995. 'Gender, citizenship and cultural diversity in contemporary Japan,' pp. 110–29 in *Feminism and the State in Modern Japan*, ed.Vera Mackie. Melbourne: Japanese Studies Centre.

——. Forthcoming. 'The regulation of commercial sex in contemporary Japan.'

Thomson, Rosemarie Garland. 1997. *Extraordinary Bodies: Figuring Physical Disability in American Culture and Literature.* NewYork: Columbia University Press.

Valentine, James. 1990. 'On the borderlines: the significance of marginality in Japanese society,' in *Unwrapping Japan*, ed. Eyal Ben-Ari et al. Honolulu: University of Hawaii.

Vandenberg, Andrew, ed. 2000. *Citizenship and Democracy in a Global Era.* London: Macmillan.

West Australian. 2000. 'Same-sex unions to get civil status in Vermont.' (18 March): 27.

Index